OAKLAND COMMUNITY COLLEGE

Oakl C0-AJY-329
Orchard Ridge Campus Library
27055 Orchard Lake Road
Farmington Hills, MI 48334

3 2355 00270716 4

P 92 .I5 S46 2000
Sen, Krishna, 1954-
Media, culture and
politics in Indonesia /
32355002707164

DATE DUE			
10/23/08			

OAKLAND COMMUNITY COLLEGE
ORCHARD RIDGE LIBRARY
27055 ORCHARD LAKE ROAD
FARMINGTON HILLS, MI 48334-4579

DEMCO

Media, Culture, and Politics in
Indonesia

To Herb Feith
who taught us about Indonesia

And to Mita
who says we're taking a long time to learn

Media, Culture, and Politics in
Indonesia

Krishna Sen
David T. Hill

OXFORD
UNIVERSITY PRESS

OXFORD

UNIVERSITY PRESS

253 Normanby Road, South Melbourne, Victoria, Australia 3205
Oxford University Press is a department of the University of Oxford.
It furthers the University's objective of excellence in research, scholarship,
and education by publishing worldwide in

Oxford New York

Athens Auckland Bangkok Bogotá Buenos Aires Calcutta
Cape Town Chennai Dar es Salaam Delhi Florence Hong Kong Istanbul
Karachi Kuala Lumpur Madrid Melbourne Mexico City Mumbai Nairobi
Paris Port Moresby São Paulo Singapore Taipei Tokyo Toronto Warsaw

with associated companies in Berlin Ibadan

OXFORD is a registered trade mark of Oxford University Press
in the UK and certain other countries

© Krishna Sen and David T. Hill 2000
First published 2000

This book is copyright. Apart from any fair dealing for the purposes
of private study, research, criticism or review as permitted under the
Copyright Act, no part may be reproduced, stored in a retrieval system,
or transmitted, in any form or by any means, electronic, mechanical,
photocopying, recording or otherwise without prior written permission.
Enquiries to be made to Oxford University Press.

Copying for educational purposes
Where copies of part or the whole of the book are made under Part VB
of the Copyright Act, the law requires that prescribed procedures be
followed. For information, contact the Copyright Agency Limited.

National Library of Australia
Cataloguing-in-Publication data:

Sen Krishna, 1954– .
    Media, culture and politics in Indonesia

    Bibliography.
    ISBN 0 19 553703 3.

    1. Indonesia in mass media.
    2. Mass media—Political aspects—Indonesia.
    3. Mass media—Indonesia.
    I. Hill David T. II. Title.

302.2309598

Edited by Adrienne de Kretser
Text designed by Derrick I. Stone Design
Cover design by Modern Art Production Group
Typeset by Desktop Concepts Pty Ltd, Melbourne
Indexed by Russell Brooks Indexing Services
Printed by Kin Keong, Singapore

P 92 .I5 S46 2000
Sen, Krishna, 1954–
Media, culture and
politics in Indonesia /
32355002707164
ocor

CONTENTS

ACKNOWLEDGMENTS

This book was written from our six months fieldwork in Yogyakarta, made possible by an invitation from Professor Ichlasul Amal, then Director of Postgraduate Studies, currently Rector of Gadjah Mada University. The staff of Gadjah Mada were extremely helpful. We appreciated especially the technical assistance and advice of Tri Kuntoro Priyambodo, the Network Manager of GAMA-net, who patiently explained the intricacies of the Internet in Indonesia. His assistant Bagus Winarko spent dozens of hours helping us with our computers, trying to find viruses, configure modems and generally overcome our technological illiteracy, while sharing some of the insights of an undergraduate in Yogya.

Our gratitude also to Nellie van Doorn and Paul Harder, who kindly offered us their home while they were away on sabbatical, and to Bu Ije, Bu Tumirah, Pak Sunoto and Bu Stience, who helped in various ways during our time in Samirono Baru.

For personal and intellectual support in Indonesia, we would like to thank Harry and Melanie Bhaskara, Bwee Wisuda, Atmakusumah Astraatmaja, Daniel Dhakidae, Amir Effendi Siregar, Ashadi Siregar, Slamet Riyadi Sabrawi, Theodore KS, Made Tony, Lance Castles, Herb and Betty Feith, Retno Intani, Ishadi SK and several others who may prefer to remain unnamed. Of the dozens of other media practitioners whose expertise we drew upon, we particularly thank the staff of *Kompas* research section, TVRI and RRI Yogyakarta, Radio Unisi,

Bernas daily, *Tempo Interaktif* and the various radio stations around Indonesia which responded to our e-mail queries.

Friends who have taken the time to read and comment on drafts of parts of this book, for which we are extremely grateful, include Keith Foulcher, Paul Tickell, Barbara Hatley, John McGregor, Ariel Heryanto and Phillip Kitley. Thanks also to our research assistants Luita Aribowo, Wendy Sahanaya and Ruth Stone.

Our absences from teaching commitments would not have been possible without the support of our Executive Dean, Tim Wright, and our colleagues in the School of Asian Studies and the School of Media Culture and Communication at Murdoch University, who inevitably had to carry some of the duties we temporarily avoided while on research leave.

The research upon which this book is based was undertaken with the financial support of a Large Grant from the Australia Research Council. In the Asia Research Centre at Murdoch University, which also provided generous funding, we would like to thank particularly Richard Robison, Del Blakeway, Geoff Paton, Mandy Miller and the various researchers who made the Centre their base throughout our writing project. The Centre has played a major role in supporting our work—and that of dozens of others—over many years.

To all these individuals and organisations, plus others too numerous to name, we express our sincere appreciation.

Finally, while this book has been a major collaboration for us, it pales into insignificance compared to our main shared endeavour, Su-mita. She has lived with this book as long as we have, shared our fieldwork and our writing, and gained and lost much along the way. For her own valuable experience of 'fieldwork in Yogya', she would need to thank the staff and students of YIS, especially her teachers, John Stroud and Ibu Ratna, and Anne and the Hogarth family. She will now claim weekends and school holidays, without our laptops!

ABBREVIATIONS

ABRI	Armed Forces of the Republic of Indonesia
AJI	Alliance of Independent Journalists
APJII	Indonesian Internet Service Providers Association
ASIRI	Sound Recording Industry Association of Indonesia
BPPT	Agency for the Assessment and Application of Technology
BSF	Board of Film Censorship
Deparpostel	Department of Tourism, Post and Telecommunications
Deppen	Department of Information
Dewan Riset Nasional	National Research Council
DPR	People's Representative Council
FKKS	Surabaya Christian Communication Forum
GBHN	Broad Outlines of State Policy
Golkar	'Functional Groups', government political organisation
G30S	Thirtieth of September Movement
HANKAM	Department of Defence and Security
ICMI	Indonesian Muslim Intellectuals Association
IKAPI	Indonesian Book Publishers Association
ISAI	Institute for the Study of Information Flows

KADIN	Indonesian Chamber of Commerce
Komnas HAM	National Human Rights Commission
LAPAN	Indonesian Aeronautics and Space Institute
LIPI	Indonesian Institute of Scientific Research
LSF	Institute of Film Censorship
manga	Japanese-style comic
MPR	People's Consultative Assembly
NGO	non-government organisation
PAPPRI	Association of Indonesian Composers and Musical Arrangers
Pancasila	State ideology of Five Principles, namely: belief in the one and only God; just and civilised humanity; the unity of Indonesia; democracy guided by the inner wisdom of deliberations of representatives; and social justice for all the Indonesian people
PDI	Indonesian Democratic Party
pengamen	busker
PIJAR	Centre for Information and Action for Reformation
PKI	Indonesian Communist Party
PPP	United Development Party
PPPI	Indonesian Association of Advertising Agencies
PRD	Democratic People's Party
PRSSNI	Indonesian Private Commercial/National Radio Broadcasters Association
PWI	Indonesian Journalists Association
RRI	Radio of the Republic of Indonesia
SIUPP	Press Publication Enterprise Permit
SPS	Newspaper Publishers Association
TVRI	Television of the Republic of Indonesia
warnet	Internet kiosk
wartel	telecommunications (telephone) kiosk

A Note on Spelling

Generally we have used the spelling system adopted by Indonesia in 1972 (known as 'EYD'). Thus, Soeharto is referred to as 'Suharto'. We have made occasional exceptions to this where individuals have another firm preference for their personal name or are better known by their pre-1972 spelling (e.g. Pramoedya Ananta Toer).

INTRODUCTION: MEDIATING POLITICS AND CULTURE

This book is about the institutions and policies that determine what Indonesians write and read in their books and papers and on their computer screens, say and hear on their radios, tape-recorders and CD players, perform and watch on their films, videos and television screens. It is about understanding the texts of these media as records, on the one hand of a 'national' culture and political hegemony constructed by the New Order, and on the other, of contradictory, dissident, political and cultural aspirations and anxieties of Indonesian citizens in the last quarter of the twentieth century. The media, we argue, did not cause the demise of the Suharto regime. But in its pores one could see the impending end of an order.

That 'the conduct of democratic (or undemocratic) politics nationally and internationally depends more and more' on the media is widely acknowledged.[1] What is much more disputed is exactly how media, culture and politics are articulated, how one phenomenon shapes the other, and what else needs to be taken into account to answer these questions. Studies of media in authoritarian nations have most frequently adopted what might be called a command and response model, concentrating on propaganda, censorship and the fate of texts and authors who challenge these. It is not unusual for Australians, and Western observers of Indonesia more generally, to see in the media only a litany of repression—press-bans and censorship by the government.

In 1995 we started working on a research project to explore the patterns of state control of media texts and institutions at a time when middle-class discontent against the Suharto regime was rising and new technology and transnational media business were colluding to make all national boundaries culturally permeable. The project was transformed by our experience of fieldwork in the second half of 1996. Politics of that half-year was dominated by the conflict between supporters of Megawati Sukarnoputri and the Suharto government. The massive riots in Jakarta in July, followed by arrests, intimidation and a media blitz to sell the government's side of the story arguably marked the beginning of the end for the Suharto regime. In that context it became clear that what needed urgent explanation was not the ability of the regime to control culture and politics through ownership, bans and censorship in the media, but rather what lay outside or escaped these modes of state control. Those escape routes were not forged only by the self-conscious work of resistance or bureaucratic inefficiency (which existed, of course); they were to a large extent inherent in the ownership patterns, technologies and modes of consumption of media texts and institutions of New Order Indonesia.

The resignation of Suharto on 21 May 1998 shifted the parameters of research on Indonesia. This book is no exception to that rule. What was being written as an observation of the unfurling of a regime became in a sense an epitaph to it. How then should we understand the media in the long survival and slow collapse of the New Order? What legacy has the New Order left behind? The resulting book is more historical, less engaged in the day-to-day reading of events in and around the media that shaped our fieldwork. However, there is no attempt to achieve apolitical objectivity. All analyses of media are necessarily (though not always overtly) political. Ours is openly, though not uncritically, sympathetic to the middle-class, urban opposition that is being largely credited with the fall of one of Asia's longest-serving rulers.[2] In the rest of this Introduction we want to elaborate the political and analytical assumptions about the media and about Indonesia that underlie the questions we ask and try to answer in this book.

The New Order in Indonesia
The New Order was 'the authoritarian form of government through which Indonesia [was] ruled since 1966'.[3] It replaced

Sukarno's populist Guided Democracy, characterised by charismatic leadership of the President and intense ideological debates. In the name of restoring order and stability, the New Order effectively barred political activism and even political debates.

The New Order came into existence after 1 October, when General Suharto defeated the coup by young army officers led by Lt-Col. Untung. In less than twenty-four hours Suharto's forces gained control of Jakarta's central Merdeka Square, bounded on the north side by the Presidential Palace, on the east by Suharto's Kostrad (Army Strategic Reserve Command) headquarters, on the west by the Republic of Indonesia Radio (RRI) station, and on the south by the telecommunications centre. Soon after dawn on 2 October Suharto forces took control of Halim Air Force Base, and found the bodies of six generals murdered by Untung supporters. The 'Thirtieth of September movement' (as the Untung coup was dubbed) was quashed less than forty-eight hours after it had been launched.[4] Over the next thirty-two years, however, Indonesian public discourse was shaped by the production and reproduction of mythologies about the coup and Suharto's counter-coup.

The Commander-in-Chief of the Army, Achmad Yani, had been murdered at Halim, so Suharto was able to assume interim control of the Army and was appointed Commander-in-Chief by President Sukarno on 14 October.[5] Over subsequent months, he strengthened his support within the armed forces until, on 11 March 1966, the President gave Suharto all the power required to 'secure order'. This was, in effect, an authorisation for martial law. Suharto was formally installed by the provisional parliament as Acting President in March 1967 (when Sukarno was stripped of his office), and appointed full President a year later. The Army under Suharto was in control.

The New Order government asserted that the Indonesian Communist Party (PKI) had master-minded Untung's actions. This premise quickly solidified into incontestable 'fact' in the endorsed histories of the New Order.[6] It was used to justify the total elimination of the Communist Party and all organisations associated with it. In the months following Suharto's counter-coup, the Army, along with anti-Communist vigilante groups, slaughtered approximately half a million people in what a US CIA report described as 'one of the worst mass murders of the twentieth century...one of the most significant events of the twentieth century, far more significant than many other events that have received much greater publicity.'[7]

Another half-million people were imprisoned without trial, many for more than a decade. A small number were convicted in show trials; some of them were only released in 1999. Whether or not the PKI hierarchy was involved in Untung's coup, or indeed whether Suharto himself had prior knowledge of it, are not at issue here. There is no evidence that the PKI rank and file had any knowledge of it. And clearly Suharto had much to gain from an ill-conceived coup whose easy demise propelled him into the nation's top job. What is significant from our point of view is that the myth of a 'Communist coup' was the key to legitimising an authoritarian regime. Through the Suharto years anyone accused of left-wing sympathies was in danger of political persecution. Any text regarded as promoting 'Communism/Marxism/Leninism' was banned. To the very end of his rule, Suharto continued to rely upon the bogey of a 'latent danger' of a 'Communist threat' to justify repression of his opponents, widespread infringement of basic human rights and the suppression of all dissent. That this myth was repeated in the media is well-known. What is more interesting, from the point of view of understanding post-Suharto Indonesia, is that the story was not believed by large sections of the Indonesian population.

With the key policy doctrine of economic development, the New Order ushered in a period of remarkable economic growth, and of increasing (though not without ups and downs) links with the global economy. Reviewing the New Order's economy up to the early 1990s, Hal Hill (1994) identified 1971–81 as a period of 'rapid growth'. The rate of growth declined from 1982 to 1986 as a result of lower international oil prices. The economy recovered from 1987 and in the early 1990s, and was marked by increasing liberalisation of the market and consequent 'independence of the private sector'.[8]

Mackie and MacIntyre reviewing the New Order (in Hill 1994) cite a parallel political periodisation:[9] 1966–74, 1974–83 and 1983 to the early 1990s. Until 1974 the Army was dominant but was experiencing internal schisms, as rivals jockeyed for power and influence. In 1974, rivalries between two senior military officers and widespread disapproval of the senior military's increasingly cosy financial relationships with Chinese and Japanese financiers fuelled the first large-scale civil unrest since the anti-Communist pogroms of 1966. Anti-government student demonstrations coinciding with the visit of the Japanese Prime Minister on 15–16 January escalated into widespread looting and arson. These events are commonly referred to as Malari (15 January Disaster). Richard Robison has observed that, 'for the liberal intellectuals, 1974 was to be the beginning of the end. Since that time the New Order has successfully devoted its energies to controlling the bases of liberal influence: the universities, the press and the civil service'.[10] Malari signified a breach between the New Order leadership's alliance with students and intellectuals who had supported Suharto against Sukarno. But rapid economic growth strengthened Suharto's position as President. A second spate of student demonstrations in 1978 were stemmed with a battery of regulations to depoliticise campuses and implement widespread Pancasila indoctrination programs.

Falling oil prices in the early 1980s leading to a restructuring of the economy marked a third political phase. But by this time Suharto's personal hold on power was uncontestable, and remained so for the next decade. Oil revenues had fallen, but as mentioned earlier the economy recovered after 1986. It was now more diversified, and large domestic conglomerates created under the protection given to Suharto's family and friends played a greater role, in collaboration with foreign enterprises. Deregulation of the economy progressed, allowing greater freedom of market forces. In the late 1980s many saw signs of political liberalisation, and anticipated the emergence of a transparent, if not democratic, system as a result of Indonesia's links with global capitalism.

We must add the final phase of the New Order—a period of decline when neither the threat of Communism nor the promise of economic development legitimised Suharto's harsh control. From an economist's point of view, this decline clearly dates from the Asian financial collapse which reached Indonesia in 1997 and wiped out years of growth. The value of the rupiah plummeted against the US dollar (from about Rp. 2500 in August 1997 to Rp. 17 000 in January 1998). Few companies were able to service foreign debts, particularly on short-term loans.[11] The domestic financial system was unable to cope, and public confidence was undermined by the closure of sixteen banks on 1 November 1997. Suharto agreed to several bail-out packages with the IMF, then reneged.

In terms of overt political dissent, critical events marking the beginning of the end of the regime might be the riots of 27 July 1996, or the banning of three popular news magazines˙in June 1994. Certainly, the June 1994 crackdown ended the process of political liberalisation which had been widely referred to in the Indonesian media as *keterbukaan* (openness) or *glasnost*. The pro-hibition triggered a response unlike those prompted by the 1974 Malari riots and the 1978 student demonstrations. In 1994 there was a sustained, organised campaign of vocal criticism of the gov-ernment over the bans. In an unprecedented drawn-out legal battle, the editor of the most prestigious of the three proscribed publications, *Tempo*, won two well-publicised court cases chal-lenging the Minister of Information's authority to impose the ban. When the Supreme Court finally upheld the Minister's appeal it only reinforced the common view that, at the highest levels, the judicial system was corrupt and susceptible to political pressure. Arbitrary state power had been used to close not just mainstream, middle-class magazines, but profitable businesses. This book will return many times to the theme of the media's location at the cusp of culture, politics and economics. It is enough to note here that the media were not simply reporting or even reflecting political opposition to the New Order—they were also large business organisations overtly driving the dissent.

In 1996 the government intervened in the activities of one of two so-called opposition parties, the PDI (Partai Demokrasi Indonesia), ousting the elected leader Megawati Sukarnoputri and replacing her with a government appointee. On 27 July a group reportedly organised by the Army attacked PDI's Jakarta head-quarters to recover it from Megawati's supporters. The attack unleashed a public outpouring of anger and resentment at the New Order on a scale unseen since 1974. The resulting looting and havoc spilled down the main boulevards of the capital, and was graphically captured by domestic and international media.

In the midst of the worst economic crisis since his accession to power, and one to which he had no response, Suharto was re-elected President for a seventh term in March 1998, by the 'upper house' (MPR, People's Consultative Council). During the New Order the MPR had done little more than reanoint Suharto every five years. The 1998 Cabinet included his daughter, long-time cronies and his protégé B.J. Habibie as Vice President. The re-election and the new Cabinet were unacceptable to international markets and to Indonesian dissidents. Student protests increased in frequency and intensity. Popular support for them grew. That the mood for reform had spread to usually politically conservative professionals was dramatically demonstrated when hundreds of bankers, entrepreneurs and financial managers from the Jakarta Stock Exchange took to the streets on 19 May calling for the President, guilty of 'paralysing' the economy, to stand aside.[12] The professional middle class created by the New Order's economics was now openly opposed to its cronyism, arbitrariness and authoritarianism and, above all, its financial mismanagement.

This book attempts to tell the story of the media in an overall picture of the New Order. The question we address is twofold. How did the New Order shape the media both directly through policy and indirectly through providing a certain political, cultural and economic framework? What role did the media play in the establishment, securing and, finally, collapse of the New Order?

What Media?

The story of the media in Indonesia (as anywhere else in the world) has many strands. And any attempt to disentangle media, culture and politics, or one medium from another, requires some simplification. Even deciding where to stop and start when writing about the media is not clear. The Media Bill drafted under Habibie's Kabinet Reformasi (Reform Cabinet) will supersede the existing press laws, film laws and the highly controversial Broadcast Bill (discussed later in some detail). It covers press, television, radio, film and the Internet and related forms of digital communication. In Indonesia, legally and institutionally these were the media, and controlled by the Department of Information. We have added book publishing and musical recording. In the New Order's institutional divide, these industries were not defined as media. Much less restricted, they were controlled by the Department of Education and Culture.

That institutional demarcation disappeared in October 1999 when President Abdurrahman Wahid closed down the Department of Information. The department, established in 1945 by the nationalist government in Yogyakarta, had been central to the ideological drive of both the leftist Sukarno government and the developmentalist New Order under Suharto. But as we will find in the chapters that follow, through the last decade of Suharto's rule the legitimacy of censorship and propaganda—the key functions of the department—eroded. Indeed, in a mediascape that was increasingly diverse and global, it became impossible for the department to carry out those functions. In that sense, this book explores the re-definition of the media beyond the limits imposed upon it by the older (now out-dated) Indonesian political institutions. Textbook definitions of modern media most frequently depend on two common characteristics: first, the mechanical reproduction and multiplication of aural, written and visual texts and, second, the widespread and simultaneous distribution and consumption of them. In the second half of the twentieth century, a range of new technologies increasingly complicated the issue of simultaneity of consumption. Tape-recorders and videos, for example, allowed us to use films and radio broadcasts much the same way as we use books—in our own time and individually, but knowing that the same text is available to many others in many places. We based our demarcation of the media largely on the grounds that have become the common-sense of media studies textbooks: commercialised, mechanically reproduced and widely distributed texts.

Books are clearly the beginning of such culture industries. Even in an age when the audio-visual media are far more popular (in the sense that more people use them more often), books remain central to the transport of ideas. On a more empirical level, books intersect constantly with the other media: novels are filmed, popular television serials are published as comics, translated Japanese cartoons are sold as books and television programs. Much the same applies to the music industry, as music is sold largely through radio and television for simultaneous consumption by mass audiences. Including the music industry also allowed us to home in on the point when popular politics and popular culture elide.

Analysing Media and Culture

Culture is widely used in at least two senses: as art and as a way of life. The meanings have become almost inseparable in academic areas such as cultural studies and media studies, which increasingly analyse what is probably best described as popular culture—newspaper articles, fashions, advertising, television soaps, box-office hits. These are part of everyday work and leisure of ordinary citizens but, like art, they have an ideational aspect. In popular culture, capitalist industrial arrangements of mass production and marketing occur, alongside ideas and ideals about ourselves and our communities. Books, films, radio and CDs all contain ideas and distribute them to markets of varying sizes. Where these ideas come from and how they are interpreted is a central question in any study of the media or culture industries.[13]

At the risk of oversimplifying highly complex ideas, it is possible to see at one end of the debate an older tradition, which starts from the production/industrial/organisational[14] aspects of culture industries, and at the other end the audience studies of the 1970s onwards. As Hartley points out, in the older tradition the question of the power of the media is 'posed as their power over the populace and the power of the economic or political elites over them'.[15] On the other hand, the ethnographies of audiences focus on diverse and aberrant readings of media messages. There have been many attempts in recent cultural studies to swim between the two opposing currents.[16]

This anecdote might provide a starting-point to explain our attempt to both understand the ways in which texts are restricted and how they offer a range of alternative readings, which can be circulated in particular contexts. A student at the University of Gadjah Mada in Yogyakarta told us in 1996 that he and his friends had been devoted fans of the US series *MacGyver,* which was shown on RCTI (Rajawali Citra Televisi Indonesia, Indonesia's first private television station) some years earlier. Their devotion was because 'MacGyver always stood up for human rights'. The RCTI's programming decision had nothing to do with the content of the *MacGyver* stories, but everything to do with the series' bargain-basement price and the new station's need to fill broadcast hours. The programmers knew the series rated well but had no idea of the possible reason for its popularity. The profit-oriented television station read prices and ratings, the government censors (who would have vetted the series before it went on air) must have considered it not subversive, and some politically disenchanted students read into it a political message that the censors did not see. This example suggests contradictions between the market-oriented media managers, the security-conscious ideological apparatus of the government and politically disenchanted citizens in search of radical positions in their work and entertainment. These differences are central to our understanding of the media in Indonesia.

In looking at the audiences we have focused particularly on the mounting disenchantment with the New Order government, which opened gaps between the practices of state authorities (whether they were acting as censors, publicists or policy-makers) and the people who participated in the media as workers or audiences. Censorship does not work if the censors and programmers, the creators of cultural texts and their consumers interpret differently. The military's Internet webpage does not serve as propaganda if no one turns to it for information or opinion. This is not an argument about individuals interpreting texts as they please, but an acknowledgment of the agency of citizens as producers and consumers of cultural texts. This agency is both limited and made possible by structures, institutions and technologies.[17] The nature of the audience itself is determined by wider cultural and social practices and the immediate context of the reception.

In other words, different media enable different kinds of audience response, not only because of the nature of the technology but also because of particular institutional histories. As we will see later, in the particular context of the late New Order, radio talk-back, public support for banned magazines, political discussions among Internet users, and above all the outbreaks of riots at rock concerts (see Chapter 6), all suggest 'active audiences'[18] who were participating in, rather than simply consuming products of, the culture industry—and participating in ways that the economic and political captains of the industry could not fully apprehend or control. The media does not always work this way. Our argument is about how the media worked in the historically specific context of New Order Indonesia; any analysis of the media needs to be historically contingent.

Culture and Politics

In the common-sense of Western democratic societies, politics and culture are generally seen as quite separate phenomena: high culture is above politics and pop culture somewhere below. Cultural studies offers sophisticated theories to make explicit the immanent links between these phenomena. In Indonesia, however, culture and politics are overtly intertwined as much in academic studies of politics as in government policy documents. In the last years of his rule, Sukarno attempted to harness all cultural work to his radical nationalist politics. In that context, apolitical art and pop culture signified anti-Sukarnoism. In the early years of the New Order the notion of culture as apolitical retained intellectual currency, but all cultural production was bounded by political regulations, which emerged from governmental practices and were codified over the next three decades.

Explicitly in some instances (especially film and television) and implicitly in all, the New Order defined the media as vehicles for the creation of a 'national culture' that would allow uncontested implementation of its development policies and more generally its authoritarian rule. There were guidelines on what to say, what not to say and who could speak in which medium.

Anyone suspected of Communist sympathies was barred from what the government defined as 'the media'. Left-wing cultural institutions were destroyed, thus wiping out systems of institutional support for certain kinds of cultural expression. As with industry generally, the New Order government adopted a corporatist approach to the culture industry. For each group, the government authorised a single representative 'professional organisation'. These corporatist bodies, premised on the New Order principle of 'family values' (*asas kekeluargaan*), were responsible for implementing government prescriptions and proscriptions for the industry, weeding out undesirable participants and suppressing any conflict in industrial relations or in the texts produced.

All institutions had to adhere to the state ideology of the Pancasila (Five Principles), initially enunciated by Sukarno in a June 1945 speech. Somewhat revised by the New Order, these principles were: belief in the one and only God; just and civilised humanity; the unity of Indonesia; democracy guided by the inner wisdom of deliberations of representatives; and social justice for all Indonesian people.[19] Since 1978, courses on the Pancasila (known

11

as P-4) were compulsory at all levels of education, from primary school to university, and for all public servants, including those working in state radio and television. More specifically, there was a ban on any text that might inflame 'primordial' ethnic (*Suku*), religious (*Agama*), racial (*Ras*) or 'group' (*Antar-golongan*, a euphemism for class) tensions. This restriction, referred to as 'SARA', was used to limit news reporting of ethno-religious tensions and control the public interpretation of all socio-political conflicts, to exclude (as in the case of Chinese) and to restrict languages used in the media in various ways (see particularly Chapters 4 and 5, on television and film).

For most of the New Order, the media appeared to be under the command of the government, controlled through layers of formal and informal censorship processes and, increasingly, through ownership. Overt political dissidence—expressed as textual or institutional practices—occupied only a very small space in the culture industries. At times of political disturbance such as Malari, the political sympathies of journalists or film-makers surfaced briefly and led to a few bans. Clearly, too, as indicated earlier, the government had only limited control over the ways in which citizens might participate in cultural activities. In the last decade of the New Order, however, the state was losing control of media products in a more general sense, due to changes in media technologies and economies. How the walls of state regulation and control were breached differed from one medium to another. In the case of the Internet the nature of Internet technology had not been anticipated in the mechanisms of state control. In the case of the audio-visual media, the sheer volume of visual material defeated government attempts to censor it. The music industry, which was central to the expression of generational dissent, had never been controlled, because music was defined as apolitical. What is common across the culture industries, though, is the way what might be called 'media ecology' worked against the express policies of the New Order: where the policies wanted a single voice of national culture, the ecology produced diverse and hybrid forms involving national, global and local codes.

Although academic writing involves categorisation, it is impossible to see where culture stops and political economy begins. When a rock concert is sponsored by an Army unit and appears on a commercial television channel in Indonesia, where does politics stop and popular culture begin? Perhaps our position is best summarised in the 'media–culture–politics' continuum of the book's title, the media mediating in the translation of culture into politics and politics into culture.

Global Media in Local Practices

It has never been possible to draw a line around nations and devise a perfect way to shape a 'national' culture that is free of prenational local practices or cross-border cultural transfers. Terms such as media ecology or media-scapes emerge from attempts to understand the overall contexts in which media operate. National governments' media policies are part of these ecologies, but so are many other factors within and beyond the control of governments and indeed nations.

Globalisation

As we will see, over half the television programs on Indonesia's domestic channels are imported from the USA, Japan, Hong Kong and India; half the music played on many radio stations is Western music; books and magazines draw heavily on originals in other languages; and the traffic on the Internet defies any attempt to pin down a terrestrial location. Huge parabola antennae, perched on roofs even in small towns and *kampung*, announce the hunger for messages from afar. It is impossible to draw a picture of the Indonesian media without reflecting on the world beyond national borders, and on theories about globalisation which attempt to understand the increasing interconnections between nations and the media.[20]

'The core of the idea [of globalisation] is that the world is undergoing a process of ever-intensifying interconnectedness and interdependence so that it is becoming less relevant to speak of separate national economies, or separate national jurisdictions founded upon principles like the sovereignty of the territorial nation-state.'[21] There are serious arguments about when the process started and whether it is inexorably leading to the death of the sovereign nation-state. We do not discuss questions of world historical processes. Our starting-point is the relatively well-established, empirically based argument that in the last two decades of the twentieth century, satellite and digital technologies, and the related financial integration of the world, have made it infinitely more difficult to keep foreign cultural products outside national media borders. This is not a simple quantitative change—that more films or books now enter the country . The change is multi-dimensional—more media products cross national borders, from more directions and enter a nation at many more ports and terminals (in the new double sense of those words). Nor do these lines of change move in a single direction. The same technologies of digitisation, satellites and miniaturisation that deliver more foreign media messages into more points in Indonesia, also carried further into the nation the centrally controlled national broadcasts and made possible highly parochial connections at the same time. This book tries to document this complex transformation, to describe from within Indonesia these boundary-spanning and boundary-dissolving faculties of communication technology and media.

Globalisation underlies a paradigm shift from the modernisation theory and dependency theory that dominated analysis of media in the non-Western world since the 1960s. Most scholars reviewing the rise of globalisation as a dominant theme in media and cultural studies have tried to locate its inheritance and its differences from ideas of media/cultural dependency or imperialism.[22] There are two consistent themes in discussions about globalisation that seem to mark its conceptual difference from imperialism. First, globalisation implies that 'interconnections and interdependency of all global areas...happen in a far less purposeful way' than any view of imperialism would permit.[23] Second, globalisation implies that messages and images come from diverse sources and not just from the former colonial masters in Europe and the neo-colonial USA. Many globalisation theories see the world as simultaneously more unified and more fragmented. As Buell puts it, the 'single system has come to be perceived as more and more complex, increasingly centreless, and featuring a multiplication of interacting parts that are increasingly fragmented and unstable'.[24] At a more empirical level, Tracy shows in his discussion of television that the flow of programming is 'not a one-way street: rather there are a number of main thoroughfares, with a series of not unimportant smaller roads'.[25] Recent work on global televison has identified India, Hong

Kong, Japan, Mexico, Brazil and others as among the increasingly busy thoroughfares. We observe such cross-roads and by-ways in the culture industries of Indonesia as a whole.

In media policy discourses of the New Order government (and South-East Asian governments generally), globalisation often appears as yet another and more pernicious phase of media imperialism, marked by more Western messages beaming down from the sky and creeping up modem wires. But in practice the New Order presided over Indonesia's increasing openness to outside media. Some of this it probably could not have stopped, other openings it colluded in and even initiated. Significantly, after the 1970s the critics of the New Order have not been particularly concerned about foreign interventions or influences. In the closing months of Suharto's rule, the murmuring about foreign media remained peripheral. To the mainstream opposition, the global media appeared as an ally against an ageing ruler. Students and other critics saw their own images on CNN, heard their own voices on the BBC, e-mailed up-to-the-minute information on demonstrations to Japan, Malaysia and Australia. Understanding globalisation as something other than Americans meddling in national affairs was part of activists' political and cultural map in Indonesia through most of the 1990s. Many texts of Indonesia's domestic culture industries, particularly those deployed against the New Order, were made possible by global media.

'Local' questions

If the New Order presided over the increasing integration of Indonesian citizens into global cultural and economic markets, it also tried relentlessly to make Jakarta the centre of domestic industry and culture. The appearance of Jakarta as not only the political capital but also the economic and cultural epicentre was due to the New Order. Hildred Geertz, summarising the available data on 'Indonesian Cultures and Communities' in 1963 (in the last phase of Sukarno's government), wrote 'One of the more interesting characteristics of Indonesian urban development, in contrast to that in other South-East Asian countries, is that it is not dominated by a primate city which funnels all national affairs. Although Jakarta is popularly termed the *pusat* ("centre") it is pre-eminent only in the fields of government, politics, finance and commerce and to some extent education'.[26] To scholars who have known Indonesia only since the middle years of the New Order, this observation comes as a surprise. The collective academic wisdom of the 1980s seemed to suggest that a Javanese culture mediated through Jakarta's political power was the driving force in all national affairs.

We went to Yogyakarta for fieldwork in 1996 partly to understand the Javanese moorings of 'national culture' on the media. Administratively, 'Yogya' (as it is known) is a 'special region' located in the middle of the province of Central Java.[27] With a population of about half a million, it is a small town, but in many senses it is the cultural capital of Indonesia's ethnic majority, the Javanese. The town was founded in 1755 by Sultan Hamengku Buwono, and remains proud of its reputation as epitomising Javanese courtly culture. During the war of independence, the Republican government was based in Yogyakarta (1946–49) at the invitation of Sultan Hamengku Buwono IX, who played a key role in the independence movement. During this period the Sultan turned over part of his palace to become the Republic's first university, Gadjah Mada.

Our assumptions about the centrality of Java in Indonesian culture industries changed, however, as we spoke to media workers and audience. Neither saw their 'locale' reflected in the nation's media. There may be more Javanese making media policies and working in the media, but they were not writing in their language or putting Javanese art-forms on the national screen. We do not comment on whether Javanese culture is inherent in New Order politics. Our argument is much more limited: that, with the exception of radio, all regional cultures (even that of the pre-eminent ethnic group) effectively had only minority status in the national culture industries.

Regional language and culture are only part of what we understand by 'local' in this book. There have always been sub-national communities formed by particular cultural texts and practices. Media technologies have facilitated the construction of many kinds of parochial communities, some with a particular terrestrial location, some without. We view the media in the New Order as a site of constant struggle between the homogenising tendencies of national cultural policy and the various parochial, regional, localised interests, histories and identities.

This book goes to press in the midst of a turmoil as Indonesian national identity negotiates a new relationship to both the 'local' and the 'global'. In anticipating reshaping of the very ways of being Indonesian, this book speaks very much in the present tense, even though much of the data are from a time that conventional political periodisation may consider closed. And in discussing changes and transformations, the book necessarily leaves questions open and provides only partial answers.

Notes

1   See, for instance, one of the standard textbooks in media and communication studies: Denis McQuail, *Mass Communication Theory: An Introduction*, 3rd edn, Sage, London, 1994. The quotation is taken from p. 1.

2   See, for example, Edward Aspinall, Herb Feith & Gerry van Klinken (eds), *The Last Days of President Suharto*, Monash Asia Institute, Clayton, 1999.

3   R. William Liddle, *Leadership and Culture in Indonesian Politics*, Allen & Unwin, Sydney, 1996, p. 3.

4   The actions of the 'Thirtieth of September movement' were almost entirely based in Jakarta. Harold Crouch, *The Army and Politics in Indonesia*, Cornell University Press, Ithaca, 1978, pp. 100–1, notes various incidents in support of the Thirtieth of September movement in Central Java, but there was little if any support elsewhere in the country.

5   Suharto was promoted from major-general to lieutenant-general four months after the 'coup' and to full general in July 1966: Jamie Mackie & Andrew MacIntyre, 'Politics' (pp. 1–53) in Hal Hill (ed.), *Indonesia's New Order: The Dynamics of Socio-economic Transformation*, Allen & Unwin, Sydney, 1994, p. 48, fn 1.

6   Nugroho Notosusanto & Ismail Saleh, *The Coup Attempt of the 'September 30th Movement' in Indonesia*, Pembimbing Masa, Jakarta, 1968, is usually regarded as the officially endorsed history of the incident.

7   Central Intelligence Agency, Directorate of Intelligence, 'Intelligence Report: Indonesia—1965, the coup that backfired', Central

Intelligence Agency, Washington DC, 1968, p. 71, quoted in Robert Cribb, 'Problems in the historiography of the killings in Indonesia', in Robert Cribb (ed.), *The Indonesian Killings, 1965–1966: Studies from Java and Bali*, Monash Centre of Southeast Asian Studies, Melbourne, 1990, p. 41.

8   Hal Hill, 'The economy' (pp. 54–122) in Hill, *Indonesia's New Order*. See especially pp. 62–3.

9   Mackie & MacIntyre, 'Politics'. The phases are schematised on Table 1.2, p. 9.

10   Richard Robison, *Indonesia: The Rise of Capital*, Allen & Unwin, Sydney, 1986, p. 165.

11   See Hal Hill, 'The Indonesian economy: The strange and sudden death of a tiger' (pp. 93–103) in Geoff Forrester & R.J. May (eds), *The Fall of Soeharto*, Crawford House, Bathurst, 1998.

12   'Broker BEJ pun Berdemo', *Jawa Pos Online*, 20 May 1998, http://202.149.241. 231/jplalu/mei98/20mei/de20mi4.htm (sighted 30 January 1999).

13   The term 'culture industry' comes from the work of the Frankfurt School, a group of leftist European scholars who radically rethought the liberal framework of US media studies in the 1940s. Almost every survey of media or cultural theory includes a reference to the Frankfurt School.

14   Here we can think of either the conventional pluralist democratic studies of mass media which assumed that media can deliberately create modernist meanings everywhere, or we can think of the Frankfurt School who viewed the capitalist media owners controlling the cultural products and offering the same ideological message (legitimisation of capitalism) whatever the textual form. For a discussion of the contending theories of media and society see McQuail, *Mass Communication Theory*, Chs 2–4. For a more recent and dense account, see Toby Miller & Alec McHoul, *Popular Culture and Everyday Life*, Sage, London, 1998, Ch. 1.

15   John Hartley, *The Politics of Pictures*, Routledge, London, 1992, p. 84.

16   See, for example, Hartley, *Politics of Pictures*, Ch. 4; Ien Ang, *Living Room Wars: Rethinking Media Audiences for a Postmodern World*, Routledge, London, 1996 (especially the Introduction); and Alec McHoul & Tom O'Regan, 'Towards a paralogics of textual technologies', *Southern Review*, 25:1, 1992, pp. 5–26.

17 It is not this purpose of this book to enter the theoretical debate over structural/economic/technological determinism vs human agency in the analysis of social change. We do not equate political and cultural agency with individualism or authorial autonomy. We understand agency within the limits of structural and technological constraints. One useful way to think about this is via Giddens' argument about the constraining and enabling aspects of institutions, which has been taken to understand the relation between creativity and institutions and technologies. See, for instance, Janet Wolff, *The Social Production of Art*, Macmillan, London, 1981, Ch. 1, for a discussion of the institutions and the production of art.

18 For an excellent critical review of studies of media audiences, see Ang, *Living Room Wars*, especially Part I, 'Rethinking Audiences'.

19 Paraphrased slightly from Department of Information, *Indonesia 1992: An Official Handbook*, Indonesian Department of Information, Jakarta, 1992, p. 38. For a partial translation of Sukarno's initial formulation, 'The birth of the Pancasila', see Herbert Feith & Lance Castles (eds), *Indonesian Political Thinking 1945–1965*, Cornell University Press, Ithaca, 1970, pp. 40–9. For a discussion of the 'New Order' reinterpretation, see Michael Morfit, 'Pancasila: The Indonesian state ideology according to the New Order government', *Asian Survey*, XXI:8, August 1981, pp. 838–51. Douglas E. Ramage, *Politics in Indonesia: Democracy, Islam and the Ideology of Tolerance*, Routledge, London and New York, 1995, presents the most comprehensive study of the Pancasila as New Order political ideology.

20 The number of books on the subject of media globalisation is huge. For a review of various theories, see Barrie Axford, *The Global System: Economics, Politics and Culture,* Polity Press, Cambridge, 1995.

21 Axford, *The Global System*, p. 27.

22 For a brief and excellent discussion see Frederick Buell, *National Culture and the New Global System*, Johns Hopkins University Press, Baltimore and London, 1994, pp. 1–39.

23 John Tomlinson, *Cultural Imperialism*, Johns Hopkins University Press, Baltimore and London, 1991, p. 175.

24 Buell, *National Culture*, p. 10.

25 Michael Tracy, 'Popular culture and the economics of global television', *Intermedia,* 16:2, 1988, pp. 9–25.

26 Hildred Geertz, 'Indonesian cultures and communities' (pp. 24–96) in Ruth T. McVey (ed.), *Indonesia*, Southeast Asia Studies, Yale University and HRAF Press, New Haven, 1963, p. 38.

27 Indonesia's only other 'special regions' are the national capital, Jakarta, and Aceh, in north Sumatra. Information on Yogyakarta is drawn from *Kamus Besar Bahasa Indonesia*, 2nd edn, Departemen Pendidikan dan Kebudayaan RI, Balai Pustaka, Jakarta, 1989, p. 1070. Central Bureau of Statistics population figures for Yogyakarta are found on the website http://www.bps.go.id/profile/diy.shtml, sighted on 3 February 1999.

1

BOOKS: TRANSLATIONS AND TRANSGRESSIONS

Indonesian literature, generally in translation, is often the first point of entry for foreign students into Indonesian culture. Indonesian literary figures like Pramoedya and Rendra are far better known in Australia, for instance, than any Indonesian film star or musician, even though in Indonesia film stars and musicians are far more marketable in their own country. This chapter, however, is not about literature as an aestheticised sphere of individual creative work, but about the publishing industry which brings 'literary' works, and many other kinds of writing, into the market.

Looking at the structure of the industry and a small number of individual authors, we argue that the book publishing scene has been a significant locus of globalisation of Indonesian cultural life during the New Order. This argument is elaborated around three themes. We start by looking at the rise of a Jakarta-based national commercial publishing industry which, both in business style and in products, becomes increasingly international (and cross-media) through the New Order period. In the second half of the chapter, we look at published 'literature'—the popular novels sold by mainstream publishing houses, and semi-underground but culturally and politically significant literature. We argue that both the mainstream popular and underground politicised literatures of the New Order were, in different and complex ways, embedded in globalised cultural and political economies.

Our discussion is complicated by the constant tensions over what constitutes literature, who defined it and how, in New

Order Indonesia. Even what constitutes a 'book' is not always obvious. Many published manuscripts in Indonesia, some by respected intellectuals and sold in book shops, contain no ISBN (International Standard Book Number), which in the context of the international publishing industry is a formal requirement for all books.[1] Some name no Indonesian publisher or printer.[2] How, moreover, should we demarcate 'Indonesian' publications, when Indonesian-language manuscripts are published abroad by emigrant groups?

We focus on Indonesian-language books, for reasons related to our definition of the national media discussed in the Introduction, but more particularly because regional-language publications are a tiny minority. Despite the numerical dominance of the Javanese in the population,[3] very few books are published in that language, let alone the languages of smaller ethnic minorities.[4] Indeed, as our discussion on types of publications shows, even Indonesian works (texts originally composed and conceived in the Indonesian language) are a minority in the mainstream book market. On the other hand, a significant amount of what might be called 'original' Indonesian writing—literary, popular and political—has circulated through small, local, sometimes semi-underground ventures.

Early History, Persistent Issues

Almost since the beginning of book publishing in Indonesia, there seem to have been attempts to lay down state-sponsored literary ethics, aesthetics and politics as well as resistance to those codes. Publisher Balai Pustaka (Hall of Books) was established by the Dutch colonial government in 1908 'to create a new and modern Malay language and an equally new and modern literature'.[5] Maier argues that the state-owned publishing house was part of the Dutch colonial state's project to define the Indonesian (more correctly, in the colonial historical context, Malay) language by separating it from the 'heteroglossia' (a mixture of various local and European languages) that was the spoken language of the Indies. At the same time, Balai Pustaka purged nationalist themes[6] by constructing an Indonesian literature suitable for the emerging indigenous elite. The project was successful in the sense that the canons of early Indonesian literature, through at least the first half of the twentieth century, were defined almost exclusively by authors such as Marah Rusli, Nur Sutan Iskandar, Sutan Takdir Alisjahbana and others published by Balai Pustaka. But both before and after the establishment of Balai Pustaka, an unregulated publishing industry churned out *bacaan liar* ('wild' reading materials), texts deemed inappropriate by, and beyond the control of, the Dutch colonial authorities.[7]

Balai Pustaka became, after independence, the government publishing house of the new republic. To survive the financial lassitude of the 1960s, it was forced to endlessly reprint well-known novels used as school texts. Its capacity to solicit new manuscripts was hampered by the polarised 'left/right' politics of the time and the strained economic circumstances. Like many literary and cultural institutions, Balai Pustaka was purged of leftists after Suharto gained control of the government. It was largely unable to recapture its command of the publishing industry and was soon overtaken by national commercial publishers, more attuned to the economic opportunities of the 1970s and beyond. By 1995, struck by the declining market for what it considered 'literature' (which had been Balai Pustaka's stock-in-trade) and hampered by poor distribution and promotion, the government-owned operation faced an uncertain future. As part of the gradual privatisation of state-owned enterprises, in 1996 Balai Pustaka was partially privatised. In the New Order, the large commercial publishers and their foil, the small, local and semi-underground publishers, became far more important in the book industry financially, as well as in determining and defying political and aesthetic canons, than the state's publishing house.

Writing about New Order literature, Ariel Heryanto notes the continuing though often unsustainable attempt, partly by the state, partly through historically established aesthetic codes of Indonesia's cultural institutions, to define Indonesian literature by distinguishing it from what it is not.[8] Heryanto argues that literature is defined by distinctions between four categories of publication:

1 those accepted as 'high' literature by literary journals like *Horison* and cultural institutions approved by the New Order state;
2 those banned by the government on the basis of their political content, though not rejected on literary merit, such as some of Rendra's works and works by Pramoedya Ananta Toer (discussed later in this chapter);
3 those pilloried by the guardians of literary aesthetics, including the most popular forms of fiction in Indonesia, pop novels and comics;
4 those separated from Indonesian literature as either non-Indonesian (any literature in the regional languages) or as non-literature.

Following partly from Heryanto's questioning of these categories, we suggest here that the politics of the late New Order and the political economy of publishing increasingly eroded the boundaries through which Indonesian literature had been historically defined: the boundaries between Indonesian and foreign, literature and non-literature, between the New Order's 'authorised reading' and 'reading on the wild side' (*bacaan liar*). Ironically, in the final decade of the New Order some of the most acclaimed 'high literature' (such as works by Pramoedya) were also simultaneously *bacaan liar*, in the sense that they remained outside the mainstream publishing industry and transgressed the state's regulation of content and circulation of books.

The Industry in the New Order

The book publishing industry in Indonesia is small by regional standards. Through the 1980s Indonesia published 4000–5000 titles per year.[9] In 1992, this figure went up to over 6000, but Indonesia still produced fewer books per head of population than most of its neighbours and even in absolute terms remained lower than South Korea and Thailand, which have much smaller populations.[10] Indonesia's Central Bureau of Statistics (henceforth BPS) does not even include book-reading in its 'socio-cultural' data, which measures the usage of all other media (radio, television, newspapers and magazines) as well as sports and community participation.[11]

Categorised as 'culture' and thus under the aegis of the Department of Education and Culture, book publishing was less regulated by the New Order than film, television or the press, which were under the Department of Information. No special permits were required to publish books, other than normal requirements for registering the company or foundation with the Departments of Trade and Industry. Even the bar on former political prisoners owning, operating or performing on television, radio and film, did not apply to book publishing—Pramoedya's publisher, Hasta Mitra, was openly owned and run by former political prisoners. Nor was there any attempt to control the industry by forcing membership of a single government-controlled professional association. Membership of the Indonesian Publishers Association (Ikatan Penerbit Indonesia, henceforth IKAPI) was never made compulsory—neither Tutut's Citra Lamtoro Gung Persada nor Hasta Mitra, the most frequently banned publisher, were members. The organisation remained politically weak, capable neither of acting as the state's agent in the industry nor intervening on behalf of its members.

Also unlike the press and television, book publishing as an industry was generally ignored by the crony capitalists. The only notable exception was PT Citra Lamtoro Gung Persada, established by Suharto's daughter Siti Hardiyanti Rukmana (known as 'Tutut') to publish autobiographical works by her father.

The lack of restriction allowed a proliferation of publishing ventures. Large publishers such as Gramedia subdivided amoeba-like, to form an ever-increasing number of cells, each with its own specialisation and focus, competing to increase its market share. Small regional publishers came and went and political opposition groups were able to publish surreptitiously a wide variety of material. The pirating of publications remained rampant despite the copyright legislation of 1982 (UUD Hak Cipta No.6 Tahun 1982, revised in UU Hak Cipta No.7 Tahun 1987), introduced under international pressure.[12]

In the early 1990s, according to IKAPI's figures, half of Indonesia's publishers were in Jakarta, another 42 per cent elsewhere in Java, less than 6 per cent in Sumatra, 0.5 per cent were in Bali, and less than 1 per cent in the remainder of eastern Indonesia (from Kalimantan to Irian Jaya).[13] Although such figures do not account for every publishing house, they indicate a general pattern of concentration in the capital. The only publisher in eastern Indonesia with any national profile is Nusa Indah, on Flores, which specialises in Christian and educational materials. There is virtually no commercial publication in any regional language, except for school textbooks and a small number of religious books. Very few books produced outside Java and Sumatra flow to the capital or to other metropolitan centres. It would be rare to find a book on sale in a Jakarta or Yogyakarta store which was published in Irian Jaya, for instance.

Local bookshop: Yogyakarta

A few hundred metres north of the intersection where the university campuses of IKIP Yogyakarta, Sanata Dharma and Atma Jaya meet at Gejayan Street, is a small Yogya publishing house and bookshop, the Social Agency bookshop, with its open shopfront, walls stacked ceiling-high with books, piles of discount stock on the floor, and the musty atmosphere of an antiquarian bookseller. It stocks an impressively comprehensive range of books from the ubiquitous government-published school texts, to highly ornate quality imprints on Indonesian arts, all packed into a crowded shallow shopfront. The well-thumbed appearance of the stock is due more to the constant stream of customers poring through the collection, than to the age of the books. In a novel twist to bargaining (a practice still common in Yogya's markets and street-stalls but not acceptable in the new shopping complexes) the Social Agency automatically discounts every book by about 10 per cent, before anyone asks and without advertising the practice. It has a telephone, located at the back of the shop, behind a swinging bookshelf/wall, but no fax, no e-mail, no credit cards, no promotional materials. We never saw advertisements for the shop in our six months in Yogya.

Social Agency's proprietor also owns a small publishing company, Pustaka Pelajar, which produces attractive volumes of works, notably by local Yogya (or Central Java) intellectuals and academics.[14] While these are distributed in Jakarta and other Javanese cities, the reach of the enterprise is limited and its market small. Pustaka Pelajar is just one of twenty-seven publishers in

Yogya that are members of IKAPI. But Pustaka Pelajar does not participate in IKAPI's annual promotional Book Fair, nor does it list its publications in the association's yearly booklist (*Daftar Buku*).[15] It is typical of the hundreds of small regional publishers around Indonesia which struggle but survive.

A kilometre or two to the south-west of Social Agency stands the multi-storeyed Yogya branch of the national publishing-house, Gramedia, alongside large banks and office buildings, dominating the intersection of Jenderal Sudirman and Cik Ditiro. From the basement carpark, customers walk up the broad front steps into the expansive foyer, filled with gleaming glass counters and displays of stationery, cassettes, sporting goods and office equipment. A central stairway sweeps up to the next floor, with its travel goods, array of English-language novels, travel guides and art books, linking books to Gramedia's many other business interests. A special promotional board on the stairway featuring newly published local texts is the only hint at the store's geographical location. The rest, with rows of books, computer games, CD-ROMs and magazines, differs little from Gramedia shops in Jakarta, Surabaya or any other city.

National publisher: Gramedia

Yogya's Gramedia bookshop is one in a nationwide chain of more than thirty bookstores, the first of which was established in Jakarta in 1970. By the 1980s the Kompas–Gramedia Group (Kelompok Kompas-Gramedia, KKG) was the country's largest publishing house. In 1995 KKG was estimated to be Indonesia's fifty-eighth largest conglomerate, with more than forty sub-sidiary companies.[16]

As an adjunct to publishing *Kompas* daily newspaper, in 1973 Gramedia ventured into book publishing with Marga T's *Karmila*, which had been serialised in *Kompas*. The first of a raft of new-style popular (and lucrative) novels, *Karmila* outstripped all competition, demonstrated the potential market for such books and began a generation of popular authors.[17] In 1980 a general publishing unit, PT Gramedia Pustaka Utama (GPU), was established, which by 1995 had an annual output of about 250 new titles.[18]

To diversify and strengthen its control over new markets, the conglomerate established a division of Book Publishing and Educational Infrastructure (Kelompok Penerbitan Buku dan Sarana Pendidikan, KPBSP Gramedia), incorporating GPU and two other book publishing units. One, PT Gramedia Widiasarana Indonesia (known as Grasindo), founded in 1990, specialised in educational and school books. It sold more than ten million copies in its first four years and by 1995 was publishing about twenty new titles each month. But the commercial achievements of both GPU and Grasindo were outstripped by Gramedia's third book publishing unit, PT Elex Media Komputindo (EMK), founded in 1985 and specialising in computer technology and electronics materials (including CD-ROMs), business and management manuals and children's comics.[19] It increased its titles from 231 in 1991 to 567 in 1994. By 1996 it had its own merchandising division to promote spin-off products, mainly from its highly profitable comics, and a growing software and multimedia division. EMK also hosted the Internet homepage for Gramedia Pustaka Utama, one of four Internet sites established by Indonesian publishers (as of April 1997). In late 1996 EMK established its own commercial Internet Service Provider (ISP), UniInternet. Promotional materials on recent publications were regularly updated on a special link on the Gramedia website. By the end of 1998 the Gramedia Online Bookstore (KPG Bosol) was offering online credit purchases of its books.[20] The conglomerate's book publishing ventures, like its newspaper and magazine concerns, were supported by PT Gramedia Printing, opened in 1972. From its headquarters in Jakarta, Gramedia produced about 20 per cent of the nation's new books. In a December 1995 list of top-selling titles, Gramedia companies published all the listed fiction titles and two out of seven non-fiction.

On the Yogya landscape the local Gramedia store remains a retail outpost for a national conglomerate. Unlike Pustaka Pelajar and Social Agency, it is neither dependent on nor committed to publishing local works. Despite its initial successes with Marga T and other aspiring authors in the same genre (like Yogya's Ashadi Siregar), by the mid 1990s KKG's most successful books were translations of foreign manuscripts, either US business manuals or

Japanese cartoon comics, negotiated through its agreements with over sixty international literary agents and publishers.

The Books

IKAPI's 1996 *Book List* of 8299 titles, albeit a flawed guide (since the list is neither comprehensive nor the categories consistent from year to year), provides some indication of the genres of books produced and bought. The largest single category in the list was *fiksi* ('fiction', including 'fiction for schoolchildren'), with 868 titles. Only thirty-two titles were categorised as 'literary novels', sixty-nine were 'popular novels', eighteen were 'poetry' (*puisi*), but 239 were classified as comics or picture stories. If all of these are accepted within a broad definition of 'literature' it amounts to 1226, 15 per cent of the total listing. Novels unequivocally declared *sastra* (Literature with capital L) constituted less than 0.5 per cent of books published.

The second-largest category of titles was 'Islam'. As in many other nations, religious texts were among the first books printed in the Dutch Indies and have constituted a substantial proportion of books published in Indonesia.[21] In the 1990s approximately 10 per cent of publishers (who were members of IKAPI)[22] nominated 'Islamic books' as their principal products. Most of them, however, were small publishers, located outside Jakarta, and some were selling books for as little as Rp. 600 (national daily newspapers sold for Rp. 700). Many of the titles in the 'Islam' category of IKAPI's list were translations of Arabic texts.

In many of the categories of publication—particularly science and technology and social sciences, designed primarily as school and university textbooks—it is almost impossible to separate translations from originals. Indeed, in IKAPI's 1996 list, neither Bhagavat Gita (the Hindu religious text) nor a book titled in English, *Total Quality Management,* appear as translations! Based on late 1970s data, Kimman estimated that excluding 'unauthorised translation and adaptation...only about 30–35 per cent [of books published in Indonesian] is original'.[23] The concept of 'originality' is, of course, fraught, and separating adaptation from original a matter of judgment. But in the 1990s acknowledged translations were very prominent in many of the fast-growing market sectors—comics, popular fiction and books on computers.

For Indonesia's largest commercial publisher Gramedia, the best investment and the fastest-selling products seem to be practical self-improvement and business management guides, cookbooks and translations of foreign popular romance and mystery novels, by authors whose names are as familiar in Gramedia's bookshops in Jakarta as they are in airport lounges in New York or London: Sidney Sheldon, Agatha Christie, Danielle Steel, Jackie Collins and so on.

Even before the establishment of Balai Pustaka, works from other languages found their way, via translations and other transmutations, into Indonesia. In purely commercial terms, it is often cheaper to translate a proven international bestseller than to pay reasonable royalties (on early 1990s figures, between one and two million rupiah for a first edition of about three thousand copies) for an original Indonesian manuscript. Gramedia often manages to publish its translations of foreign books within months of the original, thereby 'piggy-backing' on international publicity about the work or its author. Increasingly marketed with the original English-language cover with an Indonesian translation in small print, the strategy seems to be to identify the translated book as closely as possible with the English language. In IKAPI's December 1995 list of the top seven fiction titles, all were translations of comics by Gramedia companies: two were Japanese, the other five were American.

Translated comics

American comics remain dominant, but sources of translated comics have diversified since the early 1980s. First the French *Asterix* and then the Mexican *Minim,* both published first in the evening paper *Sinar Harapan* then serialised by its book-publishing arm Pustaka Sinar Harapan, took Jakarta by storm.[24] Japanese comics began to appear in Indonesia in the early 1990s, on the lists of publishers which had previously published mainly American comics.[25] The most prolific publisher of these is Elex Media Komputindo. Of the 1500 titles published by EMK between 1985 and 1994, 606 were children's comics, about 90 per cent of them from Japan. Popular flagships, like the serials *Dragon Ball* (first edition 1992), *Doraemon* (1992) and *Sailor Moon* (February 1994), had sold forty, fifty and sixty-five thousand copies respectively by 1995.[26] Their popularity is not peculiar to Indonesia. In Malaysia and Hong Kong half the comic titles sold on newsstands are translations from Japanese; in Korea, where the importation of Japanese cartoons is prohibited, pirated copies thrive.[27] The animated cartoon series of *Sailor Moon* is screened in eighteen countries, including Indonesia, with characters' images appearing on stationery, stickers, toiletries, cosmetics, confectionery, linen, clothes, schoolbags, CDs, electronic notebooks, videos and more.[28] A cursory search of the Internet shows about 200 fan-sites devoted to *Sailor Moon* alone, including one located on Indonesia's RADnet server, and countless other sites devoted to other *manga* (the Japanese word for 'comic', now understood in many parts of the world) heroes.

Sailor Moon and EMK's other Japanese comics can be bought individually, in boxed sets or in book-and-audiotape packs. Armed with full Indonesian rights to the comic characters, the firm negotiated agreements with four of Indonesia's five private television stations, which screened associated cartoon series in children's prime-time. The marketing of *manga* is both global and multi-media.

The levels of violence and sex in some *manga* series have caused problems for South-East Asian distributors. One Malaysian distributor reported, 'We are very selective…Most Japanese comics have too much violence'.[29] In Indonesia, where teledramas and indigenous comics often include martial arts scenes of gory beheadings, violence has not been a major concern. But nudity or sexual images are excised. Our comparison between the Japanese original and the Indonesian version of the first volume of *Dragon Ball* highlights the nature and extent of the censorship.[30] Female breasts, genitals and even underwear which appear in the original are either redrawn or blacked out. Male genitals are erased only sometimes! Occasionally whole pages are deleted to sanitise the Indonesian version of the sexualised images and sadism in the Japanese originals.

Such adjustments for national tastes and state regulations are not unique to Indonesia. In the USA *Sailor Moon* dolls were restyled to give them slightly more Caucasian features. But the product generally travels well across borders. 'Our greatest rival is Disney', asserts a director of the international department of the Japanese company which produces *Sailor Moon* and *Dragon Ball Z* (a sequel to *Dragon Ball*).[31] The *manga* appear more self-consciously global than provincial cartoon characters like Archie Andrews and even the somewhat better-travelled Donald Duck and relatives, which the USA has exported since the 1950s. The author of the *manga* (whose name is shown only on the spine, not on the cover) may be 'foreign' but the text is international, adaptable and available. Indeed, origins are glossed over in marketing. EMK's Japanese comics frequently appear with English titles: *Little New York, Miss Modern, Take the 'A' Train, Secret Five, Seven Magic, Apple Dream, Black Dance, Saint Roommate, Silent Scream, Sweet Love, Dark City* and more. In its 'Serial Cerita Dunia' ('Stories from the World' Series) the English classic *Little Women* by Louisa May Alcott appears as *Young Girls,* authored by 'Olcott' and Yoko Kitajima, having travelled to Indonesia via a Japanese comic version of the novel![32]

Some have argued that the market for indigenous comics, commonly age-old folktales and epics, too overtly didactic for their ostensible youth market, is declining in the face of foreign competition.[33] However, anecdotal accounts suggest readerships of foreign translated comics and locally created ones are quite distinct.[34] Indonesian comics have always been produced by small, backstreet operators, and distributed through kiosks and hawkers. Japanese comics, on the other hand, like their American counterparts, are the preserve of large publishers and big bookshops. There have been attempts to reformat local comics into the style of upmarket publishing houses inhabited by foreign comics. Popular novelist Motinggo Busye published several comics with Grafiti (one of the large publishers, discussed in the next chapter). In 1992 EMK published a single series of the local comic-strip *Panji Koming* (likened by one commentator to the French comic *Asterix,* also popular in Indonesia), serialised in *Kompas*. In 1996 EMK launched a *Panji Tengkorak* series (based on a traditional Javanese tale and title of a television series screening that year). Independently of the major publishers, in the mid 1990s a group of Bandung art students launched a monthly 24-page black-and-white comic *Kapten Bandung*, as an Indonesian superhero. None has achieved success comparable to the translated comics.

The failure to fit 'Indonesian' content into an international format of comic-strips is partly explained in Tim Lindsay's analysis of the Indonesian comic versions of the Javanese epic *Ramayana* (published in 1980). Lindsey argues that the sophistication and intricacy of the epic and its *wayang* (traditional theatre) retellings are lost in the attempt to fit it into the model of Captain Marvel and Batman: 'The *Ramayana* comic book's only role is to entertain, and in an increasingly transient and changing society, it becomes of decreasing significance even as entertainment'.[35] In a market that is insensitive to origin, originality and cultural specificity, how 'local' can comics, or indeed other genres seeking commercial success, afford to be?

National fiction

In 1995–96, GPU, Gramedia's most diverse book-publishing unit, published forty-six books in the category 'fiction for adolescents (*remaja*) and children'.[36] Only ten were authored by Indonesians, four were from the 'Lupus' series. The young and somewhat delinquent protagonist Lupus, created by Hilman Hariwijaya, was originally popularised in Kompas-Gramedia's weekly youth magazine *HAI*. Lupus books first appeared in 1986. It would be impossible to enjoy Lupus without some knowledge of English and the signs and symbols of a global popular culture: 'Read my stories and you'll *ngocol* forever' declares the banner across the Lupus book entitled *Interview with the Nyamuk*. 'National bestseller, sold over 1.421.000 [sic] copies'[37] shouts a line at the bottom of the cover. On the back is a photo of the author and a bleach-blond musician with the caption: 'Hilman with Nick Rhodes (Duran Duran)'. Apart from the publisher's address there are only two 'Indonesian' words on the cover: *ngocol* (youth slang for 'brag' or 'boast') and *nyamuk* (mosquito). The punctuation in the sales figure of '1.421.000' follows the Indonesian practice of separating with full stops rather than commas, and the inside cover is followed by a 'bookografi'! The language of the fiction is the racy slang (*prokem*) of Jakarta's urban youth, peppered with English terms (fashionable, catwalk, impossible, top-scorer), and prestige markers of 'international' consumer culture (sepatu Airwalk, fettucini, pizza, black forrest [sic], Toblerone, walkman, skateboard, grunge). Some of its linguistic humour is completely dependent on wordplay between English and Indonesian: 'Ayam *sorry*, Ayam *sorry*, Mom! Gout lagi *busy* sekalle!' (p. 120). 'Ayam', which sounds like the English 'I am', means 'chicken' in Indonesian. The nuances of this humour eludes translation into any single language, strictly defined.

Lupus stories are not unique in Indonesian fiction in the way they work between languages. Some of the most celebrated works of post–1965 literature are replete with Javanese expression. Linus Suryadi's *Pengakuan Pariyem* (1981) included a forty-page glossary of Javanese terms. Even the use of English within the genre of ABG (Anak Baru Gede, adolescent)[38] literature is not new. Yudhistira Ardi Nugraha's critically acclaimed *Arjuna Mencari Cinta* (1977) based its humour on classical Javanese names and *prokem* Indonesian, peppered with double meaning from English–Indonesian puns. What is new in the Lupus series is the almost exclusive use of English in the title and the cover, as well as the dedication 'for forever friends…thanks buat kontribusinya' ('thanks for your contribution') and the English-language chapter titles, which makes these books visually indistinguishable from the translated fictions with which they compete. Second, most uses of English terms and global signifiers, from fettucini to grunge, do not imply a self-conscious strategy. Rather, these words are unavoidable (how does one translate grunge?) because they are part of the milieu of the fiction and its readers. The English in the Lupus series is part of its Indonesian.

Lupus, like his creator Hilman, works for *Hai*, a popular magazine for teenagers. His mother sells cakes and his sister Lulu dates 'Bule' (whitey). It is not entirely clear if Bule is indeed a 'bule' (a white foreigner), though in the black-and-white sketches Bule's hair is white. He is rich, is (like almost every other character) defrauded by the *nyamuk* (mosquito), a nickname for the 'bloodsucker' Lupus. 'In Lupus' room are rows of translations of works by John Grisham through to Donald Duck…Lupus likes best the detective stories of Sherlock Holmes' (p. 79). In another reference to books, Lupus demonstrates his knowledge of 'books by Roald Dahl, Jules Feiffer, Katherine Paterson' and so on, through translations by his academic aunt who lives by translating because 'her own stories don't get any circulation' (p. 152): a telling comment on the state of the publishing industry, in which Lupus circulates!

It is not unlikely that the foreign signs and symbols in Lupus are encouraged by the publisher's marketing ploy to make the Indonesian 'product' look like the more popular international merchandise. After all, his favourite books are those published by Gramedia, which publishes all of Hilman's fictional work. But the language and the narrative of Lupus stories seems to erode the lines between 'inside' and 'outside', 'Indonesian' and 'foreign'. Lupus travels as easily to Hong Kong as his sister goes 'picnic' to Yogya in another story. In the second-last story Lupus goes to his 'dreamland' USA. The story starts with what might seem an almost conventional nationalist critique:

> All his life Lupus had wanted to see for himself the country he had seen so much in films which monopolise the theatres in Indonesia. So much so that they have pushed out local films. This commodity exporter is the country of Clinton, because beside importing [read 'exporting'] films, America also automatically imports [read 'exports'] the American life-style to teenagers here. Rap music, metal, Levi's, Coca-Cola, Marlboro, not to mention all the other clothes and accessories that are typically American. Which have become the life of the teenagers in Indonesia (p. 150).

But the awareness of the 'foreign' dissolves in the rest of the story and indeed the rest of the book where those 'American' objects are naturalised as part of Jakarta teenagers' life. That statement, learnt from the nationalist discourses of other generations, irrelevant to Lupus' life, appears more a statement of fact than any questioning of the American presence in the life of Jakarta's young. At the end of his American story Lupus learns about life from his American friend Bill, that here too 'Only those who are very successful are rich, those like me are just ordinary. I don't even have a car' (p. 168). Lupus returns from a trip to the mountains with Bill and finds a long letter from friends in Jakarta, about their trip to Yogya, the last story in the *Nyamuk* collection.

Across generic difference, we can read Lupus in line with Ben Anderson's reading of the political cartoons of Johnny Hidajat in the early New Order. Comparing cartoons of Sibarani (pre-1965, left-wing) and Johnny Hidajat (1970s, populist), Anderson argues that the 'jousting with foreign signs and symbols shows Sibarani precisely as a "nationalist"—a man who sees the nation as an *enterprise*...defining what is national is a complex project of juxtapositions and separations between the "foreign" and the "indigenous"'.[39] Hidajat's Djon Domino cartoons contain no foreign words and no foreign characters. 'How is one to explain the absence of foreigners in Hidajat's cartoons, when Hidajat's Jakarta is so conspicuously filled with their dominating presence?' (p. 192). Anderson's answer to his own questions may apply now to our understanding of Lupus: that 'at bottom the foreigners make no difference. Including them in the world of cartoons would not change its character, but merely extend it farther into space...In Hidajat's work American...can be counterposed to nothing: They would merely be further ramifications of an indefinitely extended "family"' (p. 192).

The Jakarta of Lupus and his fans is even more full of words, objects, people and symbols which have come from outside Indonesia. We could see the deluge of foreign elements into Indonesia as part of the globalisation of cultures and economies, eroding national borders. But even in the early New Order, the lack of foreigners in Djon Domino cartoons may have suggested, as Anderson's reading indicates, an erosion of the line between Indonesian and foreign. Lupus has inherited Domino's world, not Sibarani's, where the difference between 'us' and 'them', between Indonesian and Western languages and symbols, was important. The use of foreign words and images in Lupus is no different from their non-use in the Domino cartoons: 'at bottom they make absolutely no difference'. Bule is part of Lupus' extended family, as are his American friend Bill and 'Bapak and Ibu Green', academic 'green' friends of his aunt. Despite his comment about the 'Indonesian films', Lupus shows no familiarity with any Indonesian books, films or popular music. He is both a commentary on 1990s globalised Jakarta, and a sign of the naturalisation of this culture.

Regulations and Restrictions

Active political interventions by the New Order state, economic transformations and the transnational trend towards globalisation all contributed to Lupus' radical separation from the ideals of pre-

1965 left-wing nationalism of the kind represented by Sibarani. We now look at direct interventions by the New Order state to excise certain kinds of discourses, and suggest that leftist literary traditions may have survived the massacres of 1965–66 and subsequent censorship practices and been recovered by a new generation as part of their rejection of the New Order.

As discussed in the Introduction, the New Order destroyed leftist political and cultural institutions. Censorship regulations were mobilised to keep out of publication any direct criticism of the New Order, especially any discourse that can be identified as leftist either by its content or its author's political associations. Government censorship of books, however, was more erratic than its censorship of other media.

In 1996 it was estimated that two thousand books had been banned since 1965.[40] On 30 November 1965 (two months after the coup of 1 October which brought Major-General Suharto to power), seventy titles were banned from educational institutions nationally by Colonel K. Setiadi Kartohadikusumo, from the Department of Basic Education and Culture. This was followed by bans on all works by eighty-seven authors linked to the Indonesian Communist Party (PKI). For the next few years, various government institutions continued to ban and destroy publications by suspected leftist authors and institutions. The 'Team for the Implementation/Supervision of the Bans on the Teachings of Communism/Marxism-Leninism and Marxism-Mao Tse Tungism' forbade the ownership, circulation or sale within the Jakarta City region of 174 books and magazines, in March 1967. Books continued to be banned throughout the New Order, but in smaller numbers. By one calculation, in the 1980s on average fourteen books were banned per year.

In principle, any publication could be banned if it was 'disturbing to public order', the definition of which was broad and elastic.[41] Books have been banned for being pornographic—not only adult magazines, but at times even sex education books intended for children. However, politics was the single most frequent reason for bans. There were never specific guidelines detailing unacceptable topics. However, experience suggests that anything could be banned if it was deemed contrary to the state ideology of Pancasila (Five Principles), the 1945 Constitution or the Broad Outlines of State Policy (GBHN) set down by the joint sitting of the parliament (MPR) every five years; if it propagated the demonised triumvirate of Marxism-Leninism-Communism; if it threatened national stability and unity; if it undermined society's faith in its national leadership; if it promoted obscenity or pornography; if it was anti-religious or could give offence to any religion officially acknowledged in Indonesia; if it impeded the implementation of national 'development'; or if it might exacerbate tensions between ethnic groups, religions, races or social groups. Any perspective on the PKI, even slightly divergent from the official New Order interpretation, was likely to be banned. Works of all left-wing writers from the pre-1965 period, including those of Indonesia's most celebrated novelist Pramoedya Ananta Toer, remained banned at the close of the New Order. So too a number of foreign academic studies of the New Order published abroad.[42]

The authority to ban publications rested with the Attorney-General (Kejaksaan Agung). By law (depending on 1963 legislation), publishers were required to submit to the Attorney-General copies of each publication, but this was never systematically enforced. As with the print news medium (see Chapter 2) there were no mechanisms to vet a text prior to publication, nor were publisher or author notified that a text was under scrutiny or given any opportunity to argue their case either before or after a ban.

Scrutiny usually only commenced if attention was drawn to a publication by the news media. The Mass Media Security Sub-Directorate of the Attorney-General's Political Directorate (under the Junior Attorney-General for Intelligence) investigated titles drawn to its attention and presented a report to a nine-member 'clearing-house'.[43] If banned, the text had to be withdrawn from the market: stock was recalled, and could be confiscated and destroyed by the police. In practice, stock was rarely seized or destroyed since rumours of an impending ban guarantee a run on booksellers, a quick sell-out, and a booming underground market in photocopies.

Even after the 27 July 1996 affair, which increased repressive measures by a regime on its last legs, bans on books remained erratic. For example, a small book by the septuagenarian former Socialist leader, Soebadio Sastrosatomo, was banned in March 1997. But a similar manuscript, including a controversial speech by the deposed leader of the Opposition PDI, Megawati Sukarnoputri, and a report by the National Commission on Human Rights concerning the 27 July incident, was peddled unhampered on the Jakarta–Bogor train even while Megawati was being interrogated.

If a publication was officially banned, action (though rare) was occasionally taken against those who circulate it. In 1989 three Yogya activists were charged under the Anti-Subversion Law for selling one of Pramoedya's banned novels; they received sentences of up to eight years in prison.[44] Pramoedya's publisher, Hasta Mitra, with perhaps the longest list of banned titles to its credit, was not closed, but was brought to its knees by the financial burden of publishing books under the shadow of confiscation. A ban was of dubious value in restricting distribution, given the active underground trade in books. Works such as Pramoedya's had wide regional circulations. Pramoedya's novels were even available through mail and e-mail order from an alternative publisher in Malaysia, where his novels are set texts in university literature courses.

Much more importantly, however, as we suggest in the next section, the New Order's cultural policy failed in a more general sense. The definition of what constituted 'good' Indonesian literature could not be contained in official cultural policy. Nor did the destruction and censorship erase from history and memory all left-wing literary practices.

Literature

As stated earlier, literature, as defined in Indonesian intellectual discourse, is unimportant in the political economy of publishing in Indonesia. That, however, is not to deny that in Indonesia, as in any modern nation, literature is central to the definition of a national culture, as a repository of ideas and intellectual histories transferred through generations. We discuss briefly the careers of two Indonesian authors, as symptoms of cultural practices which defied the political and economic parameters set by the New Order state.

Pramoedya Ananta Toer

No course on Indonesian literature since the 1960s is complete without reference to Pramoedya. Translated into more than twenty languages, Pramoedya's novels and short stories are for many non-Indonesians the point of entry into Indonesian literature, and indeed, into Indonesia. Imprisoned by every political regime in which he has lived—the colonial Dutch, the nationalist government of Sukarno and the New Order—Pramoedya is the icon of literary transgressions against government limits. In the discourse surrounding him in the 1990s, we can observe political debates about literature inherited from the pre-1965 period as well as new trends that make those tensions seem dated.[45]

Born in Central Java in 1925, Pramoedya was a leading member of the group of authors who became prominent during the physical struggle for independence (1945–49) and who were dubbed the 'Generation of 1945'. His early works were smuggled out of Jakarta's Bukit Duri prison, where he was detained by the Dutch for participating in the anti-colonial struggle. He later spent a year in detention during Sukarno's presidency (over a book he wrote sympathetic to Indonesian Chinese).[46] Because he was an office-bearer in a left-wing cultural organisation, the Institute for People's Culture (Lekra), banned by the New Order government as a Communist front, he was swept up in mass arrests in October 1965 and held without trial for the next fourteen years, including a decade on the infamous penal island of Buru. After his release in December 1979 he published a string of historical novels composed during detention.

His four-volume epic, *This Earth of Mankind*, *Child of All Nations*, *Footsteps* and *House of Glass*, explored the emergence of Indonesian nationalism in the early decades of the twentieth century. The tale was narrated to fellow inmates on Buru before prisoners were permitted writing materials. After international protest at his treatment, Pramoedya was eventually allowed to compose on a typewriter discarded by the garrison, as long as carbon copies were given to prison authorities. Published by Hasta Mitra, these books have been translated into many foreign languages but banned in Indonesia, purportedly for transgressing the prohibition against Marxist-Leninist ideas. A brisk underground trade in his banned works persisted despite the draconian sentences given to three Yogya activists for selling these.

Pramoedya won the 'Freedom to Write' Award in 1988 from PEN's American Center, and a string of other international honours. Rumours about nomination for the Nobel Prize for literature added to his reputation at home. In August 1996 UNESCO's Executive Council awarded Pramoedya the Madanjeet Singh Prize for his services to the cause of non-violence and tolerance.[47] Pramoedya is the only Indonesian writer to have had the majority of his fictional works published in translation by large international commercial publishers. Around the world, his unjust treatment by the Suharto government stimulated interest and sympathy.

At his seventieth birthday party, on 6 February 1995, attended by the foreign press and a veritable Who's Who of the Jakarta literati, Pramoedya launched the most damning of his works to date, a prison diary entitled *Nyanyi Sunyi Seorang Bisu* (*The Silent Song of a Mute*, Lentera, Jakarta, 1995). No publishing company was prepared to produce it so he published it himself, using the name 'Lentera', the title of a literary supplement in the leftist *Bintang Timur* newspaper in the 1960s. The mainstream media would not report the event or the publication and one commercial television station was instructed to remove a report from its evening news bulletin minutes before scheduled transmission. The semi-underground magazine, *Independen* (Independent), likened the book to Solzhenitsyn's *Gulag Archipelago*.

The announcement in Manila on 19 July 1995 that Pramoedya Ananta Toer was to receive the 1995 Ramon Magsaysay Award for Journalism, Literature and Creative Communication Arts, one of Asia's most prestigious literary accolades, triggered a passionate and vitriolic two-month debate among Jakarta's intelligentsia. 'Not since the 1960s has there been a reaction of this intensity to a literary event...Up till the beginning of September [1995], there were no less than seventy articles, news items, radio interview transcripts, or declarations in circulation.'[48]

The Magsaysay Award brought to the surface the smouldering tensions of the mid 1960s, when Indonesia's writers and other cultural workers were increasingly divided between the pro-

Communist cultural organisation Lekra and the various right-wing oppositions to it. Twenty-six writers and intellectuals, all over fifty years old, signed a statement opposing Pramoedya's award. A previous Magsaysay Award winner, author and journalist Mochtar Lubis, declared he would return his award in protest. On 9 September a day-long seminar, 'Cultural Reflections', was organised at the Jakarta Arts Centre Taman Ismail Marzuki by the Jakarta Arts Institute, the Cultural Work Network (Jaringan Kerja Budaya, JKB) and the cultural journal *Kalam*.[49] The rekindled anti-left passions of the older generation were matched by a spirited defence of Pramoedya by younger intellectuals, some from outside Jakarta. A young *Kompas* columnist commented that 'those who had been born since 1965 were amazed by the statement of some intellectuals' against Pramoedya being awarded the Magsaysay Prize (14 August 1995).

Since the publication of *Bumi Manusia* in 1980, Pramoedya had attracted the admiration of a generation of students and intellectuals who had grown up after 1965. But with the Magsaysay Award this support became more public and visible and indicated a clear generational schism between those who read Pramoedya in the light of an old ideological Cold War, and those who took pride in him as Indonesia's world-famous novelist. One hundred and fifty-four Indonesians including students (thirty-one, the largest single group), researchers and academics, journalists, artists and others signed and circulated a statement of support for Pramoedya, which concluded thus: 'WE COMPLETELY SUPPORT the granting of the award to Pramoedya, an award for a writer, his literature, *and his society*. The papers presented at the Cultural Reflections seminar were published by an Open Dialogue Committee, which organised to have the material printed and distributed, characteristically bypassing commercial publishers.

Wiji Thukul

There are other, younger and much less famous writers, who, like Pramoedya, worked against constraints of the New Order, outside the large commercial national publishing houses and with varying degrees of integration into global cultural economies. One of the better known of these is poet and political activist Wiji Thukul, a signatory of the pro-Pramoedya statement cited above. Born in

Solo in 1963, the son of a trishaw (*becak*) driver, Wiji Thukul started as a busker (*pengamen*). He established the People's Art Work Network (Jaringan Kerja Kesenian Rakyat, known as 'Jaker') aligned with the unauthorised, and (after 27 July 1996) banned, Democratic People's Party (PRD). He has been arrested, tortured and spent long periods in hiding, evading arrest.

Wiji Thukul has published poetry in various regional newspapers but never achieved his early ambition of being accepted in *Horison*, Indonesia's premier post-1966 literary magazine.[50] His first two anthologies were published by Taman Budaya Surakarta, one of the state-funded cultural centres established in provincial towns and cities in the 1970s. The third anthology, *Mencari tanah lapang* (*Looking for Open Ground*), was published in Holland in 1994 by Manus Amici, established by emigrant leftists to publish Pramoedya's writings. In 1991 Wiji received the Wertheim Encouragement Award (named after the leading radical Dutch scholar W.F. Wertheim) and in 1994, shortly after the publication of *Mencari,* toured various Australian cities, performing poetry readings at several universities.

In the aftermath of the 27 July affair the Indonesian government propagated the notion that PRD and connected organisations like Jaker were modelled on the PKI and its mass organisations such as Lekra. Such continuities are probably much less conspiratorial than the government suggested and should be seen in the context of both literature and politics. When Wiji Thukul started writing poetry in the 1980s, he turned to Sutardji Calzoum Bachri, then the doyen of New Order poets, as a model, but later rejected Sutardji's poetry as too esoteric.[51]

Where then did Wiji and his politicised contemporaries turn for poetic models? Are their poetic styles, rhythms, structures, words and images (not just the political content) recovered from traditions suppressed since 1965? That research is yet to be done. But there is little doubt that classic works by leftist Indonesian writers were back in the public domain by the late 1980s, after thirty years of suppression, and may well have provided an alternative to the largely depoliticised literature of the New Order.[52]

A year before the fall of Suharto, a radical bulletin on the Internet (3 April 1997) started with lines from the most celebrated poem *Matinya Seorang Petani* (The Death of a Peasant, 1955) by Agam Wispi, the most famous leftist poet in pre-1965 Indonesia:[53]

Mereka yang berkuasa
tapi menindas rakyat
harus turun dari tahta . . .
Sebelum dipaksa!
(Those who are in power
but plunder their people
must leave their throne
before they are forced)

It seems symptomatic of the literary connections between radical literature of the 1960s and the 1990s that Wiji Thukul's most frequently cited lines, the poetic battle-cry of the PRD, seem to follow from that much older work: [54]

Apabila usul ditolak tanpa ditimbang
suara dibungkam kritik dilarang tanpa alasan
dituduh subversif dan mengganggu keamanan
maka hanya ada satu kata: lawan!
(And if suggestions are rejected without consideration
voices silenced, criticisms banned without reason
accused of subversion and disturbing security
then there is only one word: resist!)

The connections between Wiji and Pramoedya, between Lekra and Jaker, may well be central to our understanding of Indonesian literature since the 1980s. But those connections cannot be explained by any simplistic conspiracy theory, nor are they limited to the similarities in Wiji and Pramoedya's institutional location in the politics and economics of publication in Indonesia and abroad. They must be seen in relation to a tradition of modern Indonesian literature, politically suppressed for over a quarter of a century, recovered in the 1990s by a new generation not content with either the politics or the poetics of the New Order.

Postscript

We have treated Lupus and Wiji Thukul as instances of two kinds of literature spawned by the New Order. Lupus is the commercially popular (saleable) genre produced by commercial publishing houses, embedded in the economic transformations achieved in the New Order. Wiji is popular too, in the different sense of emerging from the grassroots political opposition provoked by the repressions of the New Order. Both, however, are made possible by the articulation of Indonesian cultural life in globalised discourses. The Lupus text, as we have suggested, cannot be conceived without a host of global icons. We will come across many similar texts in other Indonesian media, which have appropriated global signifiers to negotiate discourses that are locally and temporally specific to New Order Indonesia. Wiji's work is doubtless rooted in local struggles. At the same time, his ability, and that of many others who challenged the New Order, to continue to struggle depended on various international networks of support.

The self-conscious critical politics of Wiji's work is superficially a foil to the apolitical entertainment of Lupus and his ilk. But, as we will explain further in later chapters, it is possible to see many commercial texts as transgressing the national political and cultural parameters that the New Order state sought to establish. In the late New Order the commercially viable did not necessarily equate with the politically compliant.

In the post-Suharto disorder another measure by which we have distinguished the 'oppositional underground' and 'commercial popular' publication may also be disappearing. The 'new books' display at the Gramedia bookshop in Yogyakarta seemed transformed three months after the resignation of Suharto. Alongside the most recent glossy translations published by Gramedia, and smartly produced works of Indonesian writers by Pustaka Pelajar and others, were various slim volumes in cheap newsprint, sporting titles like *Suharto Family Wealth* and *Scandal in the Suharto Household*. At the point of distribution, the line between underground and commercial is eroding.

Notes

1   For instance, B. Bujono, P. Setia & T. Hadad (eds), *Mengapa Kami Menggugat*, Yayasan Alumni TEMPO, Jakarta, 1995, introduced by Goenawan Mohamad and including essays by writer Ashadi Siregar and prominent lawyer Mulya Lubis.

2   For example, the 100-page report into the 27 July incident, *The Pro-Democracy Movement Clobbered*, names the two US-based co-sponsors, the Robert F. Kennedy Memorial Center for Human Rights and Human Rights Watch/Asia, but no Indonesian publisher.

3   George Quinn estimates that there are at least 500000 readers of modern Javanese literature: 'The case of the invisible literature: Power, scholarship and contemporary Javanese writing', *Indonesia*, 35, April 1983, pp. 1–36.

4   Regional-language publications are mainly school language-learning texts, reprints or academic studies of classical texts or documents, and religious (notably Christian) tracts and Bible translations. In the IKAPI listing of books in circulation for 1995, for example, the only regional-language books which appeared were about a dozen books in Sundanese.

5   H.M.J. Maier, 'From heteroglossia to polyglossia: The creation of Malay and Dutch in the Indies', *Indonesia*, 56, October 1993, p. 57.

6   On Balai Pustaka (and an historical survey of Indonesian literature more generally) see A. Teeuw, *Modern Indonesian Literature*, Vols 1 and 2, Martinus Nijhoff, The Hague, 1967 and 1979. Paul Tickell, 'Good books, bad books, banned books: Literature, politics and the pre-war Indonesian novel', unpublished MA thesis, Monash University, 1982, examines and compares Balai Pustaka novels with those published by non-government commercial publishers.

7   For an historical overview to the 1970s, see Eduard J.J.M. Kimman, *Indonesian Publishing: Economic Organizations in a Langganan Society*, Hollandia Baarn, 1981.

8   Ariel Heryanto, 'Masihkah Politik Jadi Panglima? Politik Kesusasteraan Indonesia Mutakhir', *Prisma*, 8, 1988, pp. 3–16.

9   George Miller, 'Current issues facing the Indonesian book publishing industry', *Southeast Asian Research Materials Group Newsletter*, 36, June 1989, p. 12.

10   Indonesia produced only 6303 titles in 1992, which compared unfavourably to the Republic of Korea's 27889 in 1992 and Thailand's 7626, though in absolute terms it was ahead of Malaysia's 3748 (1991), Sri Lanka's 2535 (1991), Bangladesh's 1209 (1988) and the Philippines' 825 (1991), all with much smaller populations. *Statistical Yearbook 1993*, UN, New York, 1995.

11   For example, Biro Pusat Statistik, *Statistik Sosial Budaya Hasil Susenas 1991*, BPS, Jakarta, 1992, pp. 25–30.

12 Insan Budi Maulana, Director of the Foundation of Intellectual Property Study Indonesia (FIPSI), expressed dismay at the relatively small proportion of copyright breaches which proceeded to court, compared with the substantial number of suspected contraventions. See 'Pembajakan Hak Cipta Diselesaikan di Pengadilan', *Kompas*, 13 November 1996, p. 10.

13 Publisher statistics are based on the table of 510 IKAPI members and eighty-seven non-members: 'Perkembangan Jumlah Penerbit Anggota IKAPI dan non-anggota IKAPI Tahun 1995', typescript document obtained from Pusat Informasi Kompas, dated 17 May 1996.

14 For example, Rachmat Djoko Pradopo, *Beberapa Teori Sastra, Metode Kritik, Dan Penerapannya*, 1995; Faruk, *Pengantar Sosiologi Sastra: Dari Strukturalisme Genetik Sampai Post-Modernisme*, 1994, and *Perlawanan Tak Kunjung Usai: Sastra Politik Dekonstruksi*, 1995. Both authors teach at Gadjah Mada University, Yogyakarta.

15 For example, Syamsul Rijal Hamid & Estu Rahayu (eds), *Daftar Buku 1996*, Ikatan Penerbit Indonesia (IKAPI), Jakarta, 1996.

16 'Peringkat 200 Konglomerat berdasarkan Volume Penjualan pada 1995', *Warta Ekonomi*, 27:VIII, 25 November 1996, pp. 36–7. On the Kompas-Gramedia empire, see David T. Hill, *The Press in New Order Indonesia*, University of Western Australia Press, Perth, 1994, pp. 83–6.

17 In 1975 the novel was made into a successful feature film. By August 1995 it was in its fourteenth reprint and Marga had sold more than 780 000 copies of about forty novels.

18 Teddy Surianto et al. (comps), *Kompas Gramedia Group Indonesia* (64-page promotional booklet produced for the Hanover Fair, 1995), Kompas Gramedia Group, Jakarta, 1995, pp. 3, 17.

19 By February 1995, Elex Media Komputindo had published 1995 titles, including 760 children's stories and comics and 447 about computers.

20 See http://bermuda.pacific.net.id/~gramedia (sighted 7 January 1999).

21 Kimman, *Indonesian Publishing*, pp. 39–45.

22 Ten of the 102 publishers recorded in the 1996 IKAPI *Book List*.

23 Kimman, *Indonesian Publishing*, p. 44.

24 Anon., 'Laporan Khusus: Banjir Bacaan Untung Siapa?', *Prisma*, May 1987, pp. 82-96, see p. 95.

25   For a study on the internationalisation of Japanese comics, with particular reference to Indonesia, see Saya S. Shiraishi, 'Japan's soft power: Doraemon goes overseas' (pp. 234–72) in Peter J. Katzenstein & Takashi Shiraishi (eds), *Network Power: Japan and Asia*, Cornell University Press, Ithaca and London, 1997.

26   Sujatmaka, Ishak Rafick & Hartono, 'Masa Keemasan Buku Praktis, Manajemen, Agama dan Anak-anak', *SWA Online*, August 1995, <http://www.swa. co.id/95/08/SIGI02.AGS.html>.

27   'A comical situation', *Asiaweek*, 5 January 1996, on <http://pathfinder.com/@@mjlASQYA★ZOGNy7s/Asiaweek/96/0105/feat2.html>.

28   Much of the general information on Japanese comics is drawn from Jose Manuel Tesoro, 'Asia says Japan is top of the pops', *Asiaweek*, 5 January 1996, on <http://pathfinder.com/@@mjlA SQYA★ZOGNy7s/Asiaweek/96/0105/ feat1.html> and Cesar Bacani & Murakami Mutsuko, 'A Japanese toymaker invades cyberspace', *Asiaweek*, 19 April 1996, on <http://pathfinder.com/@@mjlASQYA★ZOGNy7s/Asiaweek/96/0419/biz1.html>.

29   Quoted in Tesoro, 'Asia says Japan is top of the pops'.

30   The comparison is between Akira Toriyama, *Dragon Ball*, Book 1, Indonesian version (EMK, Jakarta, 5th imprint, July 1996) and the original Japanese (Bird Studio, Tokyo, 1985).

31   Quoted in Tesoro, 'Asia says Japan is top of the pops'.

32   See EMK's *Katalog Komik 1995–1996*, EMK, Jakarta, 1996.

33   Noor Cholis, 'Tentang Komik: Yang Menggemaskan, Yang Cerdas', *Kalam*, 7, 1996, pp. 41–51.

34   We draw our impression partly on the basis of a long interview (1981 in Jakarta) with Ganes TH, the doyen of the 1970s Indonesian comic creators. The author was involved in almost every stage of the production and distribution of these comics. Despite enormous success, including several films based on his comics, the economics of the market segment meant only very small financial returns from the kind of commercial publication discussed.

35   Tim Lindsey, 'Captain Marvel meets Prince Rama: 'Pop' and the Ramayana in Javanese culture', *Prisma*, 43, March 1987, pp. 38–52, esp. p. 51.

36   Data from Syamsul Rijal Hamid & Estu Rahayu (eds), *Daftar Buku*, pp. 160–3.

37 Hilman, *Lupus: Interview with the Nyamuk!*, Gramedia Pustaka Utama, Jakarta 1996, 3rd imprint (initially published in 1995). The sales figure of 1 421 000 refers to the total sales of Hilman's Lupus series, not this individual title.

38 *Anak Baru Gede* literally means 'a child just grown up'. However, ABG is applied almost exclusively to urban middle- and upper-class adolescents. *Gede* also means 'big' or 'important', as in *orang gede*, an important person (as opposed to *orang kecil*, a 'little' or 'unimportant person').

39 Benedict R. O'G. Anderson, *Language and Power: Exploring Political Cultures in Indonesia,* Cornell University Press, Ithaca and London, 1990, pp. 166, 192.

40 Stanley, 'Orde Baru 31 Tahun, 2000 Judul Buku Dibredel', paper presented at the seminar on Expression and Freedom, convened by the Lontar Foundation, 2–4 September 1996, Ciloto, West Java, listed on http://www.tempo.co.id/mingguan/29/n_kolom3.htm, edisi 29/01, and posted on indonesia-l@igc.apc.org mailing list, 15 September 1996. Much of the information in the following paragraphs is drawn from this detailed study.

41 Useful background information is found in Tri Agung Kristanto, 'Di Seputar Masalah Pelarangan Buku', *Kompas*, 18 September 1996, p. 26, from which much of the information in the following paragraph is drawn.

42 For example, Richard Robison, *Indonesia: The Rise of Capital*, Allen & Unwin, Sydney, 1986; Harold Crouch, *The Army and Politics in Indonesia*, Cornell University Press, Ithaca, 1978 (Indonesian translation: Pustaka Sinar Harapan, 1988); Yoshihara Kunio, *The Rise of Ersatz Capitalism in Southeast Asia*, OUP, Singapore, 1988; or Soe Hok Gie's University of Indonesia History Masters thesis, 'Di Bawah Lentera Merah', about the early political organisation Sarekat Islam in Semarang. 'Buku-buku Terlarang Tahun 1991–1995', *Kompas Online*, 16 January 1996, posted on <apakabar@access.digex.net> mailing list provided a good overview of bans to that time.

43 The composition of the clearing-house is outlined in SK Jaksa Agung Nomor Kep-114/JA/10/1989, dated 28 October 1989 (cited in Tri Agung Kristanto, 'Di Seputar Masalah Pelarangan Buku', p. 26).

44 For a detailed analysis of these cases, see Ariel Heryanto, 'Discourse and state-terrorism: A case study of political trials in New Order Indonesia 1989–1990', unpublished PhD thesis, Monash University, Melbourne, 1993.

45 A full listing of Pramoedya's work and a vast amount of detail about his life can be found on the Pramoedya Internet site http://www. access.digex.net/~bardsley/prampage.html.

46 The book, *Hoakiau di Indonesia*, was republished (by Garba Budaya, Jakarta) three months after the fall of Suharto.

47 'Sastrawan Indonesia Peroleh Penghargaan', *Kompas*, 11 November 1996, p. 10.

48 Daniel Dhakidae, 'Kesusastraan, Kekuasaan, dan Kebudayaan Suatu Bangsa', *Kalam*, 6, 1995, pp. 74–102 (quotation from p. 74).

49 The papers and commentaries at this seminar, plus subsequent newspaper coverage, have been collected in *Refleksi Kebudayaan*, Panitia Dialog Terbuka Refleksi Kebudayaan, Jakarta, 1996.

50 For details see David T. Hill, 'The two leading institutions: Taman Ismail Marzuki and *Horison*' (pp. 245–62) in Virginia Matheson Hooker (ed.), *Culture and Society in New Order Indonesia*, OUP, Kuala Lumpur, 1993.

51 Arief Budiman, 'Wiji Thukul: Penyair Kampung' (pp. vii–xvi) in Wiji Thukul, *mencari tanah lapang*, Manus Amici, Amsterdam, 1994, see p. ix.

52 David T. Hill, *Who's Left? Indonesian Literature in the Early 1980s*, Working Paper No. 33, Centre of South-East Asian Studies, Monash University, Melbourne, 1984.

53 Full translation in Keith Foulcher, *Social Commitment in Literature and the Arts: The Indonesian 'Institute of People's Culture' 1950–1965*, Monash Papers on South-East Asia, No. 15, Centre of Southeast Asian Studies, Monash University, Melbourne, 1986, pp. 68–9.

54 Wiji Thukul, 'Warning', in ASIET, *The Struggle for Democracy in Indonesia*, Action in Solidarity with Indonesia and East Timor, Sydney, 1996, pp. 22–3 (translated by James Balowski, Helen Jarvis, Max Lane & Vanessa Tanaja). The Indonesian original, 'peringatan', is in Wiji Thukul, *mencari tanah lapang*, Manus Amici, Amsterdam, 1994, p. 3.

2

THE PRESS: INDUSTRY
AND IDEOLOGY

For many, the newspaper and magazine industry—collectively referred to as 'the press'—is the media.[1] Its long and influential history[2] (compared with other media considered in this book) and the requirement that its consumers be literate have enabled this medium to 'set the political agenda' more than any other in Indonesia. It employs more journalists and concentrates more on news-gathering and dissemination than any other medium, particularly in Indonesia, where radio and TV news-gathering has been primarily the job of the government networks, RRI and TVRI. Despite reaching a much smaller readership than the electronic media's audience,[3] it is still the press which largely determines what is news, in Indonesia as elsewhere in the world. Not all of 'the press' (embracing all periodical printed materials including non-commercial publications, such as student newsletters)[4] wields such influence. This chapter focuses on the major national daily newspapers and weekly news-magazines which are the most important news medium in Indonesia.

As Dhakidae has demonstrated, the press in Indonesia was transformed in the New Order from a medium of political discourse to a commercially significant industry.[5] We look briefly at the development of a politically pliable and commercially viable press in the middle years (1970s–1980s) of the New Order, through censorship, corporatisation and investment. We suggest, however, that in the 1990s the press was being repoliticised, largely in response to rising middle-class dissent against the New Order government. But unlike the political press of the Sukarno era, the new politics

of the press was not dependent on the support of particular political interest groups; it was made possible by cashed-up and
technologically sophisticated, internationally connected media
conglomerates, spawned by the New Order, but no longer
entirely dependent on it for survival. The banning of three highly
successful weeklies in 1994 indicated that the state still had power
to send large press holdings reeling at ministerial whim. But
those bannings, and the challenges to the corporate structure of
the press that followed, were themselves signs that the press was
becoming a significant site of political struggle. What it can and
should be in the post-Suharto era is up for renegotiation.

The South-East Asia currency crisis in mid 1997, particularly
the free-fall of the rupiah against the US dollar from July, threatened the economic stability of the press. But the attendant political crisis also loosened the government's control over news
content. Here we try to understand the long-term trends in the
industry, that have not only survived the New Order but which
contributed to its demise.

A Partisan Press

The notion of a non-partisan Fourth Estate has never held
complete sway in Indonesia. At the turn of the century, with
the emergence of nationalism, papers critical of the colonial
Dutch quickly became the *pers perjuangan* ('press of political
struggle'), a collective with a partisan commitment to independence. During the early years of independence the press
was dubbed by President Sukarno a 'tool of the Revolution',
responsible for energising and mobilising public opinion.
Political parties became sponsors of the medium. By the early
1960s most papers were linked with political parties, an
arrangement formalised by a Decision of the Information
Minister in March 1965 which instructed all newspapers to
affiliate formally with a political party, a 'functional group' or
mass organisation.[6]

With the political transition after the coup of 1 October 1965,
the New Order government dropped the revolutionary rhetoric.
In keeping with the New Order's early obsession with order and
security, the press was charged with safeguarding national security against internal and external threats. It was to be the guardian

of the state ideology, the 'Pancasila' (Five Principles): belief in the one and only God; just and civilised humanity; the unity of Indonesia; democracy guided by the inner wisdom of deliberations of representatives; and social justice for all the Indonesian people.[7] As the guardian of the Pancasila, the press was to be 'free but responsible' in contrast to the 'liberal' Western press, seen as libertine and 'irresponsible'. The forced amalgamation of all political parties into two, the Indonesian Democratic Party (PDI) and the United Development Party (PPP), in 1973 effectively removed party-political influence from the press, although the government's electoral organisation Golkar retained its *Suara Karya* daily. Instead of representing party interests, the government urged the press to be its 'partner' in accelerating development, which meant, in effect, either supporting the government or eschewing political debates. To a large extent editors complied. The few who did not, risked being banned.

A system of press permits and controls had been inherited by the New Order from the closing years of Sukarno's Guided Democracy (1957–65).[8] These were extended after 1965 to ensure the government had, at all times, the authority to remove publications deemed a threat to security and order. Forty-three of the country's 163 newspapers were banned in the wake of the 1965 coup.[9] In 1974, after the 15 January riots known as Malari, twelve publications were banned and several journalists were arrested. Dozens of journalists were 'blacklisted' by the government (barred from subsequent employment in the industry). Similarly, in 1978, after an increasingly truculent press gave sympathetic coverage to student-led protests against the New Order, seven Jakarta dailies and seven student publications were banned as part of a crackdown on students and intellectuals.[10]

In comparison to the two previous decades, there were very few bans or withdrawals of publishing permits (known as SIUPP, *Surat Izin Usaha Penerbitan Pers*) in the 1980s. Devoid of a political party-based readership, papers had moved away from political journalism aimed at a particular readership to increasing their audiences across the political spectrum. Mass readerships, needed to get substantial advertisements, turned the press from a message-based medium into an audience-based one.[11] The persona of the 'crusading journalist', the journalist as activist, spawned by nationalism and bred in the open political conflicts of the 1950s and

1960s, receded in the New Order. In any case, partisan politics, except of the distinctly pro-government variety, had been delegitimised during the 1970s through a series of restrictions on political parties and students.[12]

The relative absence of media bans contributed to a growing assumption by the beginning of the 1990s that the government was fostering a new political openness (*keterbukaan*), which analysts compared with the Soviet *glasnost*. But in June 1994 three prominent news periodicals were dramatically closed. Intimidation continued throughout the preparations for the 1997 general election campaign, and in December 1997 the new Minister of Information, Hartono, took 'anticipative steps' (*langkah-langkah antisipatif*) by issuing 'stern warnings' to fifteen publications in the lead-up to the March 1998 General Session of Parliament (MPR) which would elect the President for the next five-year term.[13]

The bans, sackings and other government intimidation operated in conjunction with a myriad of formal regulation and New Order institutions which monitored and administered the daily functioning of the industry. Collectively these institutions minimised dissidence both in content and in the organisation of the workforce.

Corporate Institutions

In his doctoral research done in the 1980s, Daniel Dhakidae concluded that the Department of Information (Deppen) was one of the most powerful of the New Order's 'state apparati...because of its double role as an *information apparatus* and an economic apparatus'.[14] Some of that power was beginning to wane even in the 1980s as the department lost its control over newsprint supplies (see details pp. 61–2) and later its stranglehold over the professional organisation of journalists.

Though most of the New Order, however, the department was crucial to the economics of the press since it controlled the permits required for the production and distribution of printed materials. Until the mid 1980s, it also regulated the supply of newsprint. The Minister oversaw the Department's various official functions, including 'building the Pancasila national spirit', 'making a success of National Development through the Five-Year Development Plans', laying a base of national security and stability, and ensuring the success of the five-yearly general elections.[15]

The Journalism Directorate arranged various professional training and education programs and seminars, journalist accreditation (for national and foreign correspondents) and monitored overseas press reports about Indonesia. The Graphics Directorate was concerned primarily with technical and print industry skills development. The Publications Directorate functioned like a state publisher, coordinating the production and distribution of official speeches, legislation, state documents and public education and information materials.

Under a 1969 Department of Information ministerial Decree, Indonesian journalists were 'obliged to become members of an Indonesian Journalists Organisation which is authorised [*disahkan*] by the government'.[16] Until June 1998 only one organisation, the Indonesian Journalists Association (*Persatuan Wartawan Indonesia*, PWI), was so recognised. It was tightly regulated by the government, its leadership often comprising serving or retired military officers or Golkar functionaries, and senior members of the profession who enjoyed cordial working relations with the government.[17] The PWI Board's allegiance to its membership is questionable. It has repeatedly failed to support journalists' actions against ministerial intervention, particularly arbitrary withdrawals of publication permits. As a result, despite government provisions which required all practising journalists to be members of the PWI, the Department of Information's own statistics from 1995 indicated that only about two-thirds actually were.[18]

Like the PWI, the Newspaper Publishers Association (*Serikat Penerbit Suratkabar*, SPS), has been since 1975 the only body authorised to represent newspaper companies. While the SPS was an employer confederation and the PWI ostensibly represented wage-earning journalists employed by the companies, the membership of the two organisations' national boards partially overlapped.[19]

The shock banning of three weekly news publications in June 1994 triggered the establishment of the Alliance of Independent Journalists (*Aliansi Jurnalis Independen*, AJI) as a radical alternative to the PWI. In its founding Declaration, AJI members stated 'we reject all kinds of interference, intimidation, censorship and media bans which deny freedom of speech and open access to information' since 'freedom of speech, access to information and freedom of association...[are] the basic right of all citizens'.[20] AJI faced constant intimidation from the government, and four of its members received jail sentences in three separate trials in 1995 and 1997.[21] However AJI, not PWI, represented Indonesia in the International Federation of Journalists (IFJ) and its members received awards from the IFJ, the US-based Committee to Protect Journalists and the International Press Institute.

Commercial Press

The press companies which survived the mass anti-left bans of 1965–66 or which appeared in the next few years were small enterprises subsisting hand-to-mouth. The press lacked the capital to upgrade and seemed an unattractive investment, given the likelihood of falling victim to broader political volatility. Bannings, economic crisis and political turmoil generally halved the sale of newspapers and magazines between 1965 and 1967.[22] Those papers which survived by explicitly promoting the New Order regime, sought to translate their support into capital. They lobbied the government to include the press in the Domestic Capital Investment Law of July 1968, which provided tax and import-duty concessions and government loans.[23] The press was being formally reconstructed from an ideological tool for political groups to an industry producing goods for the market. As the domestic economy grew some newspaper companies gained substantial government bank loans. In 1972 the major morning daily paper, *Kompas*, for example, borrowed 75 per cent of the capital required to establish a new printery which enabled the paper to shave hours off its production times.

By the mid 1970s circulation figures had returned to pre-1965 levels and continued to rise (with small variations) into the 1990s. The tendency towards commercialisation intensified in papers which survived the bans of 1974 and 1978. They adopted a new pragmatism, accumulating capital and strategically reinvesting it, diversifying to guard against potential losses and bans in vulnerable areas. Professional managers and business strategists became as important as editors in calling the shots

From the mid 1970s, and even more clearly after the mid 1980s, although circulation figures climbed steadily, the number of publications declined in real and, much more dramatically, in proportional terms. In other words, there were fewer publications, concentrated in fewer hands but with larger readerships. By the mid 1990s a handful of groups—somewhere between thirteen and sixteen—owned two-thirds of the industry.[24] The common profile of these publishing empires was a strong flagship daily newspaper with a string of smaller regional papers, a family of magazines and a mix of non-press companies. The scale of this empire-building—exemplified by the two largest press conglomerates—demonstrates the growing economic power of press enterprises, and the changing nature of the press' relations with the New Order.

Kompas

The morning newspaper *Kompas* is Indonesia's most prestigious and largest-selling daily (more than half a million copies sold daily in 1995) and the largest 'quality' newspaper in South-East Asia. It was established in 1965 by Chinese and Javanese journalists at the initiative of the Catholic Party, but party connections had ceased by 1971 in the lead-up to the 1973 restructuring of political parties.[25] From its modest initial circulation of 5000, sales rose consistently as *Kompas* earned a reputation for analytical depth and polished style. Characterising its style as 'determined boringness', Ben Anderson described *Kompas* as 'the New Order newspaper par excellence'.[26]

By virtue of its cautious self-censorship on sensitive political issues, *Kompas* weathered the mass bans of the 1970s, albeit with heightened awareness of its vulnerability. It responded to that vulnerability with a strategy of massive diversification and reinvestment through the 1980s. By the beginning of the 1990s *Kompas* had an empire of around thirty-eight subsidiaries, known collectively as the Kompas-Gramedia Group. It included not only Gramedia book publishers and a printery (see Chapter 1), but also a radio station, offshoots in the travel agency, hotel, heavy machinery, supermarket, insurance, banking and advertising industries, and more.[27] Through books, magazines and newspapers, Kompas-Gramedia dominates the publishing industry.[28] *Kompas* newspaper regularly earns the largest share (more than a quarter) of the nation's newspaper advertising revenues.[29] Since 1989, under its special 'Regional Newspaper' (*Persda*) Division, Kompas-Gramedia has drawn in regional papers, from Aceh to Irian Jaya, via capital injection, editorial and managerial collaboration. In 1997 it included nine newspapers, five tabloids and fourteen magazines, in addition to substantial non-press investment.[30] Kompas-Gramedia demonstrated its willingness to operate within the constraints on news content imposed by the New Order government, while taking full advantage of its policies supporting big business since the mid 1970s. Its economic strength, spawned in the New Order, is set to survive that political regime.

Jawa Pos

The country's second-largest press empire, centred on the Surabaya daily, the *Jawa Pos* (*Java Post*), was established as a family concern in 1949. In April 1982, PT Grafitipers, which owned the country's leading weekly news-magazine *Tempo*, diversified by taking over the lacklustre *Jawa Pos*, which then had a declining circulation of under 7000. Dahlan Iskan, then head of *Tempo*'s Surabaya bureau, was selected to revamp the paper and within a decade had converted the dying provincial newspaper into one of the top 200 businesses in Indonesia.[31] In 1987 Iskan began acquiring majority shares in small regional papers outside Java, and revitalising them. By 1992 the *Jawa Pos* was the third-largest newspaper in Indonesia, with an estimated circulation of about 350000, with its own regionally based press empire. By 1997, the Jawa Pos Group spanned the archipelago with its twenty daily newspapers, five weekly tabloids and four magazines in addition to eleven printeries, one paper factory and nine non-publishing companies in fields as diverse as banking, hotels, Internet services and real estate. *Jawa Pos* is the first, and to date the only, paper outside the capital to grow into a major press conglomerate by concentrating almost exclusively on provincial markets. Having secured its provincial base, the company started to acquire Jakarta-based publications. By 1998 it had two Jakarta publications, one of the nation's oldest nationalist dailies, *Merdeka,* and a news-magazine, *Prospek*.

Both the Kompas-Gramedia and Jawa Pos Groups have demonstrated the capacity of large city papers to survive and expand into national commercial enterprises. Dhakidae has suggested that concentration of newspaper ownership began with the newsprint crisis in the early 1970s and was boosted by currency devaluation in the late 1970s, as smaller participants went under. That logic would suggest that media empires such as Kompas-Gramedia and Jawa Pos (particularly given their relative political autonomy) were least vulnerable to the political and economic crisis of the last days of the New Order, and best placed to move into the post-Suharto era.

A Palace Press?

Of the sixteen major press groups identified by Haryanto,[32] nine were closely connected to the palace or the ruling Golkar organisation. Most grew to significance in the 1980s, as a controlling interest in a media conglomerate came to be seen as a source of political and economic influence. Golkar had had its own newspaper, *Suara Karya,* since 1971 but its 'official' status stigmatised it and sales were dismal. Several Golkar-aligned entrepreneurs had accumulated significant press-holdings by the early 1990s. Most notable were Surya Paloh and Harmoko, with a considerable degree of conflict between them. Surya Paloh's friendship with President Suharto's son, Bambang Trihatmodjo, did not protect his paper, *Prioritas* daily, from a ministerial ban in 1987. He then acquired the *Media Indonesia* daily in Jakarta, to which he added eleven regional newspapers by 1990 (though by 1997 only four of these remained). Harmoko, Minister of Information from 1983 to 1997, not only had the *Pos Kota* Group (established prior to his ministerial ascension) but reportedly acquired financial interests (frequently covert) in more than thirty media ventures.[33]

In some cases, important government figures obtained fast-tracked licences SIUPP, such as did B.J. Habibie (then Minister for Research and Technology) for *Republika*[34] in 1993. Takeover bids were facilitated by political leverage. Grafiti Pers, for instance, publishers of the leading news weekly *Tempo* (banned in 1994), had been part-owners, together with a foundation involving senior figures in the Attorney-General's Office, of the successful news fortnightly *Forum Keadilan*, which assumed something of the mantle of the banned market-leader, *Tempo*. In 1997 Grafiti was forced to relinquish its share of *Forum* to PT Larsa, owned by Rahmat Ismail, a businessman from the Bukaka Group, considered close to Hartono (appointed Minister of Information in June 1997) and Habibie.[35]

Even small-circulation English-language papers became takeover targets for government functionaries and their cronies. In 1995 the three English-language dailies in Jakarta claimed circulation of about 90000 copies in total.[36] With an affluent, educated, English-literate readership of foreign and domestic business leaders, political opinion-makers and the diplomatic community, they had a prized (though numerically small) readership. The *Jakarta Post* had been unrivalled as a reliable, professionally produced and relatively independent English paper.

In September 1996 the *Indonesian Observer* came under the control of Peter Gontha, a leading businessman associated with Bambang Trihatmojo's Bimantara, one of the country's most powerful conglomerates. The new owner reinvigorated the paper, adding a glossy 112-page monthly lifestyle magazine *Unwind* as a supplement, which incorporated a program guide to the pay-TV network, Indovision, owned by the same conglomerate. Two months after Bimantara's entry into the *Indonesian Observer*, Habibie's *Republika* daily (founded as a vehicle for his Indonesian Muslim Intellectuals Association, ICMI) invested in the moribund pro-government *Indonesia Times*.[37]

Between the July 1994 bans and May 1998, publication permits (SIUPP) for national news-magazines went only to individuals or companies with close connections to the political establishment. In the wake of earlier bans, such as in 1974 and 1978, the government had allowed some of the penalised publishing companies to launch new, more compliant publications. In 1994 none of the three banned publications regained their publication permits. They were replaced by *Tiras* (*Circulation*), part-owned by then Minister for Labour Abdul Latief (who also had interests in a financial daily, *Neraca*); *Gatra* (*Phrase*), bankrolled by Suharto confidant and timber magnate Muhammad (Bob) Hassan (who had earlier investments in the political tabloid *Paron* and *Sportif* magazine)[38]; and *Target,* owned by senior Golkar office-bearer Agung Laksono (with interests in the AN-TeVe private television station). This openly politically motivated allocation of publication permits put the press on par with television, where all five licences had gone to Suharto's family and friends (see Chapter 4).

The threat of ministerial bans, wielded so decisively in 1994, remained. Other arbitrary measures were also employed to excise unflattering press coverage not only of the government but of the rich and powerful generally. In January 1996 the regional government of Indonesia's most populous province, East Java, apparently purchased the entire stock of the provincial magazine *Liberty* to suppress its feature story about the 'kept women' of the governor (who had been plagued by such rumours). In October 1996, when the fortnightly *Forum Keadilan* produced a cover story on a high-profile banker, the entire print-run was apparently purchased before it reached the newsstands. But a second printing capitalised on heightened public curiosity about the edition. In May 1997 30 000 copies (the entire print-run) of the reputable fortnightly business magazine *SWA*, carrying a similar corruption story, was reportedly purchased prior to distribution for around $US100 000, but the controversial story was already on *SWA*'s website.

Both for political and technological reasons some of the older modes of controlling news content in the press had become ineffectual in the 1990s. The embarrassing and drawn-out court battle between *Tempo* and the Minister of Information (won eventually by the latter) in the aftermath of the 1994 bans showed that even the malleability of the court system could no longer be guaranteed.

Open Markets

The 1966 Basic Press Law (No. 11, Article 13) states 'The capital of press companies has to be entirely national capital, and all founders and managers have to be Indonesian citizens' and 'Press companies are prohibited from giving or receiving services, help or contributions to or from foreign interests, except with the agreement of the government after hearing the opinion of the Press Council'. Nationalist rhetoric has been a common rationale for forbidding foreign investment in the media, while not restricting foreign-sourced content in publications. Since the mid 1980s, however, the New Order embraced the rhetoric of deregulation and market openness for the Indonesian economy as a whole.

Economic difficulties in 1986, triggered by an oil price tumble and devaluation of the rupiah, exposed a schism between the Department of Information's long-established practice of regulating the press for ideological reasons, and economic ministries such as the Department of Industry and Trade which increasingly recognised the press as a domestic industry. One key illustration of this tussle was over the management of newsprint. As noted above, newsprint was regulated by the Department of Information's Press Guidance Directorate, and rules were implemented in consultation with the Newspaper Publishers Association (SPS). Until 1985 this responsibility primarily meant overseeing newsprint imports, since Indonesia had no significant domestic production. Newsprint distribution was handled exclusively by PT Inpers, a commercial arm of the SPS, under an agreement between the Departments of Industry and Trade, and Information. However, when the Minister for Industry supported domestic newsprint production and joint-venture Korean firm Aspex Paper[39] commenced production in 1985, the Department of Information lost some of its stranglehold over the press. Newsprint—the most vital raw material for the press—losing its government subsidies and monopoly distribution, fell increasingly within the purview of the Department of Industry. Thus ideological control, in the hands of the Department of Information, was being separated from the economics of the industry under a different ministry.

The policy gap between financial expansion and ideological control of the media became wider in the early 1990s, as the free-market argument was pitched against the foreign investment prohibitions in the Basic Press Law. Entrepreneurs, who invested heavily in the press in the early 1990s, required capitalisation, deregulation and technological sophistication to meet market challenges.[40] Crucially, to prepare the industry for international competition, investors called for relaxation of the SIUPP restrictions to allow the market, not the Department of Information, to determine the viability of their publications.

On 2 June 1994, Government Regulation No. 20, initiated by the key economic ministries, opened various restricted sectors of the economy—including the media—to foreign investment and majority foreign ownership. The Information Minister (then Harmoko), having been excluded from negotiations which affected his portfolio, dissociated himself from the new Regulation, asserting that it contradicted superior Indonesian legislation (notably the 1966 Basic Press Law) which explicitly prohibited foreign investment or intervention in the press. For several days, the press reported extensively on the split and inconsistencies between the various Acts and Regulations concerning foreign investment in the media,[41] until Harmoko received presidential support to exclude the media from the new policy. The Department of Information and content-control won, for the moment, over economic ministries and open markets.

However, in attempting to cordon off the domestic media, the Department of Information faced a more fluid national and international mediascape in the 1990s than it did in the 1960s. National frontiers were blurring, as media content and capital moved throughout the world. Powerful financial interests, particularly members and associates of the Suharto family with investments in television networks and associated satellite technology, managed to evade restrictions on foreign investment in the media through transfers between media and non-media branches within their conglomerates. In 1997 Hearst Magazines International, part of the giant US-based Hearst Corporation and publisher of the international women's magazine *Cosmopolitan*, started an Indonesian-language edition, *Kosmopolitan*. The new glossy magazine piggy-backed on the publication permit of a languishing health magazine, *Higina*. In formal adherence to the 1966 Basic Press Law, there were reportedly no foreign shares in the publishing company, PT Higina Alhadin, half of which is held by *Suara Pembaruan* (Indonesia's largest evening paper) and the other half by Hard Rock Cafe franchise-owners in Indonesia. Instead, PT Higina Alhadin pays Hearst an (undisclosed) 'copyright' fee. *Cosmopolitan*'s English edition had long been on sale in Jakarta (for

Rp. 21000 in early 1998), where an estimated 250000 copies of foreign magazines sold each week,[42] but the Indonesian edition (at Rp. 7500) meant the world's best-known women's magazine, published in thirty-two countries and seventeen languages,[43] had broken financial and language barriers to another populous market.

The openness does not mean a one-way move of Western investment and media content into Indonesia. New regional markets are emerging. In 1996 the Jawa Pos Group's *Manado Post* began publishing a bilingual English and Indonesian weekly insert, *Polygon News*, targeted at the East ASEAN Growth Area encompassing Brunei, Indonesia, Malaysia and the Philippines.[44] In 1998 the *Peak*, a Singapore-based English-language bimonthly magazine, regularly targeted the Indonesian business community, both as readers and sources for advertising revenue. It included Indonesian-language advertising and widespread coverage of Indonesian business and political figures.[45] The emergence throughout South-East Asia of such economic subregions provided a more varied market for newspapers catering for linguistic and geopolitical border zones at the fringes of nation-states.

Technologies of Change

Technological advances speeding up communications have been generally interpreted as beneficial for the newspaper industry. Modern journalism worldwide was made possible partly by the invention of telegraph in the mid nineteenth century. In Indonesia, the introduction of the telegraph and telephone and the expansion of railways in the 1880s dramatically reduced the time-lag in news–gathering and distribution of papers.[46] It was almost a century before the Indonesian print media (and its counterparts elsewhere) experienced the beginning of another dramatic communications revolution.

There had been incremental changes over the hundred years. Since 1965, phenomenal growth in air transport had increased the reach of capital-city papers into distant areas. The introduction of web-offset printing technology in the late 1960s had transformed the industry. It had changed the way the papers looked, and greatly disadvantaged—and perhaps killed —many papers that could not afford the new technology. But digital technologies, portable computers and direct-access telecommunications (enabling the encoding and decoding of information either 'point-to-point' or by broadcast), which are transforming media around the world, ushered in a new era for the print media in Indonesia in the 1990s.

The most immediate result of digital technology is a change in relations between Jakarta-based (and therefore 'national' dailies) and provincial newspapers. Historically, local papers have had two major marketing advantages over national papers. First, they contain the local news which is of particular interest to local readers, but without national importance. Second, they beat the big national papers to the local newsstand. Even transported by air, Jakarta-printed papers cannot reach outlying regional distributors until late morning or even afternoon; local papers are available at dawn. New digital technology and telecommunications threaten to wipe out both advantages, as Jakarta dailies can now print localised editions and remove the time-lag of transporting printed pages from the centre to the nation's peripheries.

By the early 1990s, the large media companies were keen to adopt the 'long-distance printing system' (*Sistem Cetak Jarak Jauh*, SCJJ)—a combination of technologies that would permit newspapers to be largely composed in one place and printed, with localised inflections, in any number of distant provinces. In 1996 the government relaxed its initial prohibition against long-distance printing, ostensibly to permit the press to utilise innovative technologies in order to compete against the booming electronic media. The Information Minister emphasised that there would be 'continual surveillance of the application of "long-distance printing" to ensure that no party was disadvantaged'.[47] *Kompas* initiated long-distance printing on 1 September 1997 through a collaborative arrangement with the Semarang-based regional daily *Suara Merdeka*. The Semarang edition of *Kompas* could be on sale as early as any local competitors, not only in the provincial capital, Semarang, but throughout Central Java and Yogyakarta. But beyond advantages to specific papers, the new process promised to bring far-flung areas of the Indonesian archipelago within more immediate reach of the newspaper industry as a whole, and capital-city publications in particular.

The same digital technologies also further opened the nation to international possibilities. Technologically, the *New York Times* could publish a simultaneous Jakarta edition or *Kompas* could print a New York edition. The *Kosmopolitan* precedent demonstrated one strategy of evading government prohibitions on foreign involvement in the print media. Dramatic progress in the development of computerised 'machine translation' promised to break down language barriers. Already several major Indonesian dailies and weeklies provide English translations of key articles on their homepages, for international readers.[48]

It is too early to predict how the digital revolution will change the Indonesian press. Circulation numbers suggest an increased domination of the market by national papers located in Jakarta. In 1991 Jakarta, with only 6 per cent of the national population, had 67.2 per cent of the country's print circulation of 13 042 000 copies and 47 per cent of the 270 titles. By 1996 it accounted for 71.6 per cent of Indonesia's circulation, and 49 per cent of titles.[49] There was 3.78 per cent annual growth in the circulation of newspapers, magazines and other periodicals nationally in 1996. Circulation in Jakarta increased by over 6.5 per cent (600 000 copies), while circulation throughout the remainder of the country actually fell by 105 000 between 1995 and 1996, and by more than 430 300 between 1991 and 1996. Of the eight newspapers which officially ceased publication in 1996, seven were regional publications.

On the other hand, Dahlan Iskan, the founder of the Jawa Pos Group, one of the country's most successful press empires, declared that there had been a 'resurgence of regional newspapers'[50] in the 1990s as local papers joined large entities, while maintaining their individual identities. In August 1996, the *Surabaya Post* and four more of the country's oldest and strongest regional daily papers, together with the Jakarta-based *Republika*, formed the Indomedia Network. The aim was to syndicate columns, market advertising space collectively, run joint staff-development programs and share pre-printing technologies. Strong provincial papers, like the *Surabaya Post,* maintain about 70 per cent local content, emphasising their 'home-town' advertising and news-gathering edge,[51] thus maintaining their culturally and geographically specific markets through local perspectives and local news. By 1996 it had become relatively common for even small provincial papers (particularly those on Java)[52] to use low-level computerisation such as wordprocessing and modems. This significantly enhanced the capacity of correspondents who cover small-town local news, often working far from the newspaper's base in the provincial capital, to supply timely materials by phone, in a form ready for subediting. Yogyakarta's *Bernas* received about 80 per cent of its copy via modem from its bureaus in Semarang, Surabaya, Solo and elsewhere.

The decline of independent local papers and their replacement by large national and international conglomerates is a global trend, neither specific to Indonesia nor explicable by new communication technologies alone. Historically, Jakarta has had a disproportionately large number of newspapers compared to other Indonesian cities. At the turn of the century, of the twenty Indies newspapers, four were published in Jakarta (then Batavia).[53] By 1991, even before extensive use of new computer technologies, almost half of the nation's press was in Jakarta. However, digital and satellite technologies are bringing wholesale redefinition of the role of the print media as the primary source of news, particularly news from the provinces, as more and more people turn to the Internet (the implications of which are discussed in Chapter 7).

Martyrs for a Free Press

We suggested earlier that in Indonesia the ideology of a critical but non-partisan press never had the kind of hegemonic power that it does in Western democracies. We have argued that the erosion of political parties in the early years of the New Order weakened the basis of the partisan press with its crusading journalists, who before 1965 had been willing and able to criticise governments in the name of nationalism, socialism, Islam or some other creed. We have indicated that the increasingly commercialised press left little place for politically engaged journalism.

In the closing years of the Suharto regime, however, the prevailing structures of commercialisation and legal and extra-legal coercion were no longer able to guarantee a compliant press. The banning of three mainstream commercial magazines in 1994 demonstrated continuing use of arbitrary ministerial authority.

But the long court battle that followed, the establishment of AJI and the emergence of a virtual press on the Internet, all indicated fraying in the government's control over the quantity and nature of news circulation. Finally, the suspected murders of three investigative provincial journalists in separate incidents between August 1996 and July 1997 suggested that the issue of freedom of the press had become a political battle-ground. These murders/accidents (which at the time of writing had been inconclusively investigated by the police or were being actively covered up), shared some common features. In all cases the victims were investigative reporters in provincial towns who exposed corruption in the regional bureaucracy. More importantly, the killings were a first in the history of Indonesian journalism: never before had journalists been killed only because they followed their professional ideology of freedom to investigate and report.[54]

The first and most dramatic murder was that of *Bernas* journalist, Fuad Muhammad Syafruddin, better known as Udin. Udin's bold exposure in 1996 of various dubious and corrupt practices in the district administration in Bantul, near Yogyakarta, earned him the ire of the Bantul regent, Colonel Sri Roso Sudarmo. Udin reported the regent had demanded village heads ensure a '200 per cent' Golkar victory in their areas in the 1997 general elections, and argued that such exhortations by government officials constituted misuse of their office. He also alleged corruption and bribery for political favours from regent Sri Roso. Udin was subjected to a range of old strategies to silence him. He was offered bribes to stop writing, and threatened with physical violence if he did not. Anonymous telephone threats were made to the *Bernas* office and, a week before his death, three government officials threatened legal action against Udin and his paper.[55]

Udin was brutally bashed by unidentified assailants on 13 August 1996. He died three days later from his injuries. The murder immediately became a national *cause célèbre*, covered extensively by the Jakarta papers and followed by a stream of publications by and about Udin. Although Suharto's family was implicated, which made action politically dangerous, both PWI and AJI set up 'fact-finding teams' and published books on Udin. That these rival organisations both adopted Udin as a hero demonstrates the non-partisan nature of his work and the symbolic implication of his death to the profession as a whole.

The PWI was, for all practical purposes, an agent of government control of the press. The AJI had been established in opposition to the PWI and promoted an expressly democratic agenda for the press and the Indonesian polity as a whole. Udin's murder was interpreted differently by the two groups—the PWI was much more circumspect about pointing the finger at any member of government. But the interpretation of Udin's work was remarkably similar in the tributes published by AJI and the one authorised by the PWI. Introducing the latter, the Secretary-General of PWI wrote: 'The message that Udin was sending through his writing...was pretty ordinary really. Something quite normal and indeed that is how a journalist such as the late Udin would be expected to work!'[56] Radical intellectual Arief Budiman said much the same in his introduction to the AJI tribute: 'Udin often wrote critical articles on economic and political issues concerning Bantul...He was not an NGO activist, nor was he involved in the student movement. He was just an ordinary journalist who did an average job for a regional newspaper'.[57] Udin had worked for the Yogyakarta paper for almost a decade—an undistinguished, ordinary, politically non-aligned journalist. Udin was not championing a cause. In Udin the creed of journalistic freedom and truth had its first post-1965 martyr.

Two more suspected murders of journalists followed. The deaths marked a breach in the tacit accommodation between the Suharto government and journalists on the limits of acceptable criticism and the predictable consequences of journalistic work.

The More Things Change . . .

The downfall of Suharto in May 1998 triggered a flurry of policy changes towards the print media. Incoming President B.J. Habibie appointed Lieutenant-General Muhammad Yunus Yosfiah, then Armed Forces Chief of Socio-Political Affairs (Kassospol ABRI), to the position of Information Minister. Yunus Yosfiah was internationally notorious as the commander of Indonesia's clandestine Kopassandha (special forces) troops who allegedly killed five Australian-based journalists in Balibo when invading East Timor in October 1975.[58] But the new Minister quickly won over much of the profession with a series of popular actions.

He ended the PWI's status as the sole organisation for journalists and recognised AJI's right to exist, actively courting AJI by handing out the annual 'Udin Awards' (for services to independent journalism, named after the murdered journalist) at its fourth anniversary celebrations. Within a fortnight of his appointment he promised a review of press regulations and legislation, and rescinded an unpopular 1984 ministerial Regulation (Permenpen 01/1984) under which the Minister could revoke a publication's permit (SIUPP), as was done so dramatically in the July 1994 bans. Instead, Yunus Yosfiah's Regulation (Permenpen 01/1998) ruled that publishers would be taken to court for breaching permit conditions. He announced his intention to streamline the complex procedures for obtaining a SIUPP, to eliminate opportunities for corruption. Within his first six months of office, nearly 500 new permits had been issued, opening the industry to an unprecedented level of competition.[59] Among the new permit-holders were *DeTak*, produced by the staff behind the banned tabloid *DeTik*, and a new avatar of *Tempo* news-magazine. But many of the new publications died as quickly as they were started.

In late July the *International Herald Tribune* and the *Asian Wall Street Journal* flagged their intention to print editions in Indonesia, a move which would threaten the market of the domestic English-language press. The following month the Minister foreshadowed a new Media Law which would permit up to 25 per cent foreign ownership of Indonesian media companies. The unprecedented financial crisis which bankrupted the country is proving to be the Habibie government's biggest challenge. The domestic press industry is struggling to survive, often downsizing because of the high cost of newsprint. Some regional papers have shrunk to a quarter of their pre-crisis length. Foreign capital may offer hope for some press companies caught in the crisis.

Some of the changes, however, are superficial. Under his 1998 ministerial Regulation the Minister retains the power to 'suspend' the SIUPP 'for a certain [unspecified] period of time'. It was described by one senior editor as 'potentially more dangerous' than the regulation it superseded.[60] Journalists are still obliged to be members of a professional organisation, though not necessarily the PWI. When President Habibie suggested in July that journalists be 'licensed' (like doctors) annually, many interpreted this as intimating even tighter controls over the profession than had existed under Suharto. The strategy of using the legal system to curb critical press coverage is increasingly used by public figures, government officials and, in a new development, the military. In September 1998, the Jakarta Military Command (Kodam Jaya) threatened legal proceedings to seek massive damages from the fortnightly magazine *Tajuk* over adverse reports concerning factional splits within the military over the May unrest.[61]

The reformist agenda that spread through the Indonesian educated middle classes in the years leading up to the resignation of Suharto in May 1998 clearly included the demand for greater press freedom. The journalists, part of the professional middleclass, shared those aspirations. But more than that, in the competitive news market, papers had to remain relevant to their increasingly anti-government middle-class readerships. In a decade when commercial television was the biggest form of entertainment and the Internet seemed to be a bastion of free exchange of information, the press needed at least the appearance of freedom from the increasingly unpopular government in order to maintain its status as the primary news seller. The discourse of press freedom is embedded in the political economy of the late New Order. Having severed the party connections of the press, and enabled the rise of press conglomerates, having opened the nation to satellite and digital communication, the New Order may, unwittingly, have left behind a far more strongly anchored ideology of a free Fourth Estate and the first Indonesian martyrs for press freedom.

Notes

1   Linguistically, the Indonesian term *pers* (press) is sometimes used for both the print and electronic media. For example, at the December 1997 National Working Congress (*Konkernas*) of the Indonesian Journalists Association (PWI) in Pontianak, President Suharto's daughter, Siti Hardiyanti Rukmana, delivered an opening address

entitled 'The national strategy for increasing the human resources quality of national press staff (print media and electronic media)' (*insan pers nasional (media cetak dan media elektronik)*) (quoted in Rosihan Anwar, 'Apa yang Kau Cari, Wartawan?', *Kompas Online*, 10 December 1997, posted on <indonesia-p@indopubs.com>).

2   For histories of the Indonesian press, see Ahmat B. Adam, *The Vernacular Press and the Emergence of Modern Indonesian Consciousness (1855–1913)*, South-East Asia Program, Cornell University, Ithaca, 1995; Edward C. Smith, 'A history of newspaper suppression in Indonesia 1949–1965', PhD dissertation, University of Iowa, 1969; Oey Hong Lee, *Indonesian Government and Press During Guided Democracy*, Centre for South-East Asian Studies, University of Hull/Inter Documentation Co, Zug, 1971; David T. Hill, *The Press in New Order Indonesia*, University of Western Australia Press/ARCOSPEC, Perth, 1994; Yasuo Hanazaki, *Pers Terjebak*, Institut Studi Arus Informasi, Jakarta, 1998 (Indonesian translation by Danang Kukuh Wardoyo & Tim Cipinang of 'The Indonesian press in the era of Keterbukaan: A force for democratisation', PhD dissertation, Monash University, Melbourne, 1996).

3   In 1996, there were 283 newspapers and magazines of all kinds in Indonesia, with a total circulation per edition of about 13.5 million copies, of which the 165 daily and weekly newspapers amounted to about 8.5 million copies. This compares poorly with an estimated 40 million radio sets and 20 million televisions, the latter reaching an estimated audience of 100 million (Baty Subakti & Ernst Katoppo (eds), *Media Scene 1995–1996 Indonesia: The Official Guide to Advertising Media in Indonesia*, PPPI, Jakarta, 1996, pp. 27–9). One recent Minister of Information appeared to believe the discrepancy was even greater, having stated in early 1997 that radio reaches 95 per cent of the population and 'electronic media' (presumably television) reaches 75–80 per cent ('Deppen Kembangkan "Community Newspaper"', *Kompas Online*, 28 January 1997, posted KdP Net <kdpnet@usa.net>).

4   We are excluding non-commercial in-house company publications (such as public relations circulars), academic or other specialist journals or newsletters. Sometimes the definitional difference between a book or a periodical is hazy. For example, after the weekly news-magazine *Tempo* was banned in June 1994, some staff suggested circumventing the cancellation of their magazine publi-

cation permit by publishing in the guise of a 'book' with a different title each week! As indicated in Chapter 1, the procedure for publishing books is less stringent than that for newspapers and magazines.

5   This argument is developed by Daniel Dhakidae in his PhD thesis, 'The state, the rise of capital and the fall of political journalism: Political economy of Indonesian news industry', Cornell University, Ithaca, 1991.

6   The Ministerial Decision No. 29/SK/M/65 determined the 'Basic Norms for Press Enterprises within the Context of the Promotion of the Indonesian Press'.

7   Paraphrased slightly from the Department of Information, *Indonesia 1992: An Official Handbook*, Indonesian Department of Information, Jakarta, 1992, p. 38. For a partial translation of Sukarno's initial formulation, 'The Birth of the Pancasila', see Herbert Feith & Lance Castles (eds), *Indonesian Political Thinking 1945–1965,* Cornell University Press, Ithaca, 1970, pp. 40–9. For a discussion of the 'New Order' reinterpretation, see Michael Morfit, 'Pancasila: The Indonesian state ideology according to the New Order government', *Asian Survey*, XXI:8, August 1981, pp. 838–51.

8   Under its powers after the martial law declaration of 14 March 1957, the Supreme War Command (Peperti) issued Regulation No. 10 (*Peraturan Peperti No. 10/1960*) in 1960 specifying the obligations of press publications. These were reinforced in a 1963 presidential Directive (*Penpres No. 6/1963*) which required papers and magazines to hold a publication permit. This Directive was withdrawn with the passing of the 1966 Basic Press Law (UU No. 11) which stated (in Article 20) that 'for a transitional period' publishers required a publication permit (*Surat Izin Terbit*, SIT), obtainable from the Department of Information. In 1982 legislation was passed to replace the SIT with a press publication enterprise permit (*Surat Izin Usaha Penerbitan Pers*, SIUPP); this change was implemented two years later. From 1965 to 1977 an additional printing permit (*Surat Izin Cetak*, SIC) had to be obtained from the military security authority, Kopkamtib.

9   Atmakusumah, *Kebebasan Pers dan Arus Informasi di Indonesia*, Lembaga Studi Pembangunan, Jakarta, 1981, p. 169, fn 3.

10 For further details, see Hill, *The Press in New Order Indonesia*.

11 Dhakidae, 'The state, the rise of capital', p. 74.

12 See Robert Cribb & Colin Brown, *Modern Indonesia: A History since 1945*, Longman, London and New York, 1995, Ch. 9.

13 'Hartono: 15 Media Kena Peringatan', *Jawa Pos,* 21 December 1997 Internet edition, posted on <indonesia-p@indopubs.com> on 20 December 1997 from <http://www.jawapos.co.id/21 desember/dep21d1.htm>. Of the 1000 MPR members, 625 were selected by the President. See also Article 19, *Indonesia: Freedom of Expression and the 1997 Elections*, Article 19/Forum-Asia, London, 1997, particularly pp. 11–16.

14 Dhakidae, 'The state, the rise of capital', p. 432, italics in original. Dhakidae provides an incisive study of the political economy and ideological functions of the Department of Information (Chs 11, 12).

15 The two relevant decrees were *Keputusan Presiden No. 44 dan 45 tahun 1974* (see Kurniawan Junaedhie, *Ensiklopedi Pers Indonesia*, Gramedia Pustaka Utama, Jakarta, 1991, p. 48) and Departemen Penerangan RI, *Pedoman Pembinaan Pers, Grafika dan Penerbitan Pemerintah*, Deppen, Jakarta, 1982, p. 7.

16 No.02/PER/MENPEN/1969, Ch. 1, Article 3.

17 For further details see Hill, *The Press in New Order Indonesia*, pp. 67–73.

18 According to *Data Kewartawanan IPPPN Tahun 1995* (Proyek Pembinaan Pers, Departemen Penerangan, Jakarta, 1995/1996, pp. v–vii) there were a total of 6307 journalists (5533 males, 774 female) of whom 4135 (65.5 per cent) are members of the PWI. This is a notable increase since 1991, when 59 per cent were PWI members, and may be due to pressure on journalists to demonstrate their non-membership of a rival organisation, the AJI, established in 1994. It only became compulsory for journalists in the electronic media to join the PWI after the passing of the 1997 Broadcasting Act.

19 Five of the twelve members of the 1988–93 PWI Executive and Advisory Boards also figure among the twenty-six members of the 1989–94 SPS Executive Board, Advisory Council or Council of Honour (details from US Information Service, 'A brief guide to the Indonesian media', 2 vols, unpublished document produced by USIS, Jakarta, 1992, specifically Vol. 2, pp. 94, 97).

20 'Journalists' union set up in Indonesia', *West Australian*, 8 August 1994, p. 22; and Internet listing about AJI on apakabar@clark.net,

which included the full text in English and Indonesian of the Declaration made at Sirna Galih, near Puncak, West Java.

21 In 1995 AJI office-bearers Ahmad Taufik and Eko Maryadi were found guilty of 'spreading hatred against the Indonesian government through the bulletin *Independen*'. Their initial sentence of two years eight months was extended to three years by the Jakarta High Court after appeal by the prosecution. They joined Tri Agus Siswomihardjo, editor of the alternative magazine *Kabar dari PIJAR PIJAR News*, who had received two years jail for insulting the President. In an earlier trial, teenager Danang Kukuh Wardoyo, who cleaned AJI's office, received a twenty-month sentence as 'accessory' to the (then unproven) 'crimes' of Taufik and Maryadi. In 1997 Andi Syahputra was sentenced to thirty months jail for printing *Suara Independen* (the successor to *Independen*), declared a prohibited publication.

22 Figures cited in Dhakidae, 'The state, the rise of capital', p. 551.

23 See Richard Robison, *Indonesia: The Rise of Capital*, ASAA/Allen & Unwin, Sydney, 1986, pp. 138–9; Dhakidae, 'The state, the rise of capital', p. 249.

24 Christianto Wibisono, 'From fighting press to money-controlled media today', *Jakarta Post*, 13 July 1997, p. 9, lists thirteen 'networks': Jawa Pos, Kompas-Gramedia, Suara Pembaruan, Indomedia Network, Pos Kota, Femina, Suara Merdeka, Surya Persindo, Hasmuda Internusa Perdana, Republika, Gatra/Era Media, Grafiti Pers and Subentra Citra Media. Ignatius Haryanto ('Demografi Pers Indonesia Hari Ini', *Kompas Online*, 23 August 1997, on Indonesia-p, 22 August 1997), lists sixteen 'groups': Kompas Gramedia, Grafiti, Media Indonesia, Jawa Pos, Femina, Sinar Kasih, Bakrie, Cipta Lamtoro Gung, Bimantara, A Latief Corporation, Agung Laksono, Gatra, Subentra, Suara Merdeka, Pos Kota and Republika. The specific holdings of these groups are elaborated in Ignatius Haryanto (ed) *Laporan Akhir Tahun: Pers Indonesia Terus di-Pres*, Aliansi Jurnalis Independen/Lembaga Studi Pers dan Pembangunan, Jakarta, 1997, pp. 73–8.

25 On *Kompas*, see Dhakidae, 'The state, the rise of capital', pp. 230–54, on the paper's relationship with the Catholic Party see pp. 237–44.

26 Benedict Anderson, 'Rewinding "back to the future": The left and constitutional democracy' (pp. 128–42) in David Bourchier & John Legge (eds), *Democracy in Indonesia: 1950s and 1990s*, Centre of

South-East Asian Studies, Monash University, Melbourne, 1994, p. 140. A useful study of *Kompas* (concentrating on selected editorials and the coverage of particular political and social issues) is Tjipta Lesmana, *20 Tahun Kompas: Profil Pers Indonesia Dewasa Ini*, Erwin-Rika Press, Jakarta, 1985.

27 The figure of thirty-eight companies is given in Michael Vatikiotis, 'Masses of media', *Far Eastern Economic Review*, 26 July 1990, pp. 46–7.

28 The *Kompas* parent company, PT Kompas Media Nusantara, was listed as the thirty-second largest taxpayer in 1990 (see 'Seperempat Abad Oom Pasikom', *Tempo*, 30 June 1990, pp. 80–1). It fell to forty-sixth place in 1991, with the book-publishing wing, PT Gramedia, ranking 151 ('Daftar Perusahaan dan Perorangan Penerima Piagam Pembayar Pajak', *Editor*, 26 January 1991, pp. 80–1). In 1993, *Kompas'* publishing company alone, PT Kompas Media Nusantara, was estimated to generate Rp. 240 billion annually, with a clear profit of Rp. 30–35 billion ('Tonggak Dunia Bisnis Nasional', *SWA Online*, August 1995 special edition, on http://www.swa.co.id/95/08a/SAJ04.AKH.html).

29 See Subakti & Katoppo, *Media Scene 1995–1996*, p. 62, Table 7.8, 'Advertising Expenditures: Leading Earners, Print 1992–1996', which gives *Kompas'* projected earnings for 1996 as 28.5 per cent of total newspaper advertising revenue.

30 Since the Regional Press Division was established by the Kompas-Gramedia Group in 1988, management of its regional press interests has been handled by the company PT Indopersda Primamedia within the conglomerate (see Susanti Kusumasari, 'Pola Bantuan Manajemen KKG kepada Pers Daerah', unpublished *Sarjana* thesis, Jurusan Ilmu Komunikasi, Fakultas Ilmu Sosial dan Ilmu Politik, Universitas Gadjah Mada, Yogyakarta, 1994, pp. 72–80).

31 'Daftar Perusahaan dan Perorangan Penerima Piagam Pembayar Pajak', *Editor*, 26 January 1991, pp. 80–1.

32 Haryanto, 'Demografi Pers Indonesia Hari Ini'.

33 Anon., 'Jadi Menpen tiga periode: Ambil saham tigapuluh media', *Independen*, 10, 10 January 1995.

34 On *Republika* and the Islamic press, see Robert W. Hefner, 'Print Islam: Mass media and ideological rivalries among Indonesian Muslims', *Indonesia*, 64, October 1997, pp. 77–103.

35 Haryanto, *Laporan Akhir Tahun*, p. 33. Not all such overtures suc-
    ceed. Unconfirmed Internet reports in mid 1997 suggested
    Suharto's second daughter, Siti Hediati Haryadi 'Titiek' Prabowo,
    attempted to intimidate *Kompas* into giving her shares, but was
    resisted by the newspaper (see SiaR, 'Titiek Prabowo Minta 30
    Persen Saham KOMPAS', posted on kdpnet@usa.net on 9 June
    1997).

36 The *Indonesian Observer* claimed 16010, *Indonesia Times* claimed
    35 000 and the *Jakarta Post* listed 40 272 (*Data Tiras Peredaran
    IPPPN Tahun 1995*, p. 10). Only the *Jakarta Post* figure is credible.
    The others are likely to be three to four times actual circulation.

37 In November 1997, *Republika* withdrew its management services
    from *Indonesia Times*, apparently over financial differences with the
    original owners. On *Indonesia Times*, see USIS, 'A brief guide to the
    Indonesian media', Vol. 1, p. 13.

38 On Bob Hasan, see 'Berapa Besar Kekayaan Bob?', *SWA Online*,
    edition 02/1997, at http://www.swa.co.id/97/002/SAJ03.002.
    html. Hasan owns about 160 companies and has personal wealth in
    excess of $US1 billion.

39 When Aspex Paper was established, 20 per cent of the shares were
    held by PT Aspek, with the remainder held by Tecwin Trading,
    Hong Kong (Dhakidae, 'The state, the rise of capital', p. 509, fn
    145, citing Tambahan Berita Negara RI, 25-10-1985, No. 86).
    Industry observers believe that Yoga Soegama, former head of the
    military intelligence body BAKIN, was originally the figure
    behind the Indonesian shareholding, but that timber magnate and
    Suharto confidant, Bob Hasan, subsequently obtained the Indone-
    sian interest (confidential interview, 13 January 1998).

40 Soetrisno Bachir, 'Bisnis Pers di Tengah Arus Globalisasi', *Kompas*,
    10 February 1992. On Soetrisno Bachir's media interests, see Hill,
    The Press in New Order Indonesia, pp. 97–8.

41 On government Regulation No. 20 and the media coverage, see,
    for example, *DeTIK*, 8–14 June 1994, pp. 4–12; *Tempo*, 11 June
    1994, pp. 28–30; *Kompas*, various articles, 3–4 June 1994.

42 Foreign magazine sales estimate by Leo Batubara, Secretary-General
    of the Indonesian Publishers Association (SPS), cited in Riant
    Nugroho Dwidowijoto, 'Pers Indonesia 2020', *Kompas Online*, 23
    April 1997 (posted on indonesia-p@indopubs.com, 22 April 1997).

43 See 'Advertising: Cosmopolitan girl dresses up for summer debut in Indonesia', *Wall Street Interactive Edition*, 9 April 1997, posted on 'soc.culture.indonesia' and 'alt.culture.indonesia' newsgroups on 9 April 1997; 'Cosmopolitan: Gaya Helen Brown di Higina', *Gatra*, 41:III, 30 August 1997, on http://www.gatra.com/III/41/med-41.html, posted on Indonesia-p, 31 August 1997; 'Ada kemungkinan artikel Indonesia terbit di luar negeri', *Antara*, 6 August 1997, posted on Indonesia-p on 6 August 1997.

44 Haryanto, *Laporan Akhir Tahun*, p. 54.

45 'Iklan di "The Peak" Berbahasa Indonesia', *Media Indonesia Minggu*, 'Special Komunikasi & Bisnis' supplement, 18 August 1996, p. 23.

46 See Adam, *The Vernacular Press*, p. 42.

47 Dody Kuskridho, 'Koran Daerah Menjelang Era Cetak Jarak Jauh', *Kompas*, 9 February 1996, pp. 4, 5.

48 In addition, since December 1997, the Internet news-magazine *Tempo Interaktif* has included daily English-language news items from the *Jakarta Post* (http://www.tempo.co.id/min/41/sdr.htm, on 17 December 1997).

49 Figures in this paragraph are from Ignatius Haryanto, 'Demografi Pers Indonesia Hari Ini', *Kompas Online*, 23 August 1997 (on Indonesia-p, 22 August 1997), which cites Department of Information (IPPPN) statistics for 1995/96 and 1996/97.

50 Dahlan Iskan, 'Prospects for socio-political change stemming from the development of the mass media in Indonesia', paper presented at the Paradigms for the Future Conference, Asia Research Centre, Murdoch University, July 1993.

51 '"Surabaya Post" 70 per cent Berita Lokal', *Media Indonesia Minggu*, 'Special Komunikasi & Bisnis' supplement, 18 August 1996, p. 19.

52 While, to our knowledge, no statistics are available on modem use by regional newspapers, anecdotal evidence suggests that although most on Java have access to the Internet, outside Java generally only provincial papers which are part of larger conglomerates have these facilities (conversation with Slamet Riyadi Sabrawi, Pusat Media Pelatihan AIDS untuk Wartawan, LP3Y, 19 July 1996).

53 Adam, *The Vernacular Press*, p. 187, Appendix D.

54 The distinction that we are trying to make is important. Journalists had been killed during the mass murders following the 1 October 1965 coup, but they were killed not because of their activity as

journalists but because of their ostensible connection with the Communists.

55 On the Udin case, see Heru Hendratmoko (ed.), *Terbunuhnya Udin*, Aliansi Jurnalis Independen/Institut Studi Arus Informasi, Jakarta, 1997, translated by Shinta Larasati as *Journalist Slain: The Case of Fuad Muhammad Syafruddin*, Alliance of Independent Journalists/Asian Forum for Human Rights and Development/Institute for the Studies on Free Flow of Information, Jakarta, 1997, particularly pp. 4–5, 18, particularly fn 1, in Arief Budiman's Introduction. Also Noorca M. Massardi, Mega Simarmata & Salomo Simanungkalit (eds), *Udin, Darah Wartawan*, Penerbit Mizan & Pustaka Republika, Bandung, 1997.

56 Massardi, Simarmata & Simanungkalit, *Udin, Darah Wartawan*, p. 13.

57 Arief Budiman, 'Introduction: Udin: From journalist to the intelligentsia' (pp. vii–xv, p. viii) in Hendratmoko, *Journalist Slain*.

58 David Jenkins, 'Killings recalled: Promotion for man who led assault on Balibo', *Sydney Morning Herald*, 18 October 1997, captured on <http://www.smh.com.au:80/daily/content/971018/world/world3.html>.

59 Five hundred new permits were issued between 5 June 1998 and 1 February 1999, compared to only 289 prior to reform: 'Mass media: Publishing licence used for speculation investment', *Antara*, 1 February 1999, on http://www.antara.co.id/rx/art/eng/curr/national/1999/02/01/ANT20621.html, sighted on 4 February 1999.

60 Parni Hadi, 'Permen Pahit', *Republika Online*, 13 June 1998.

61 See XPOS, 'Buruk Muka, Pers Digugat', No. 37/I/12–18 September 1998, circulated by SiaR News Service and captured on 6 October 1998. XPOS has a homepage at <http://apchr.murdoch.edu.au/minihub/xp>.

3

RADIO: REVOLUTIONS AND REGULATIONS

In studies of culture and communication, radio has received much less academic attention than the press, television and more recently the Internet. Even in Indonesia, where the role of the Republican broadcaster in the history of national independence is well-documented, there are far fewer academic or popular writings on radio than on the other culture industries discussed in this book.[1] In this chapter we examine the place of radio broadcasting in the context of political transformations in Indonesia, particularly two contradictory aspects of its position: that radio is the first transborder broadcast technology, but that its technological character and its economic and legal framework, particularly in the New Order, have defined radio as a primarily local cultural medium, in contrast to film and television, which are seen as media for communication on a national scale. We suggest that these two characteristics made radio in Indonesia a significant vector of popular voices even within the much-censored mediascape of the New Order.

History

The technology of transmitting sound via electromagnetic waves was quickly seized for its strategic political and commercial applications in the Indies. The first radio broadcast facility in the Indies, a naval communication radio, commenced broadcasting in 1911 on Sabang, off the northern tip of Sumatra, the gateway to the Straits of Malacca, one of the busiest sea lanes of that era.

Because of its military application, in many parts of the world, including the Indies, until the end of the First World War it was illegal for individuals to listen to radio signals. With the relaxing of wartime restrictions, amateur broadcasters set up the Batavia Radio Society, which started regular broadcasts in 1925, six years after the world's first musical broadcasts took place, in the Netherlands. For commencing regular shortwave radio transmission from the Netherlands to their East Indies colony from 1927 (which included an address by Queen Wilhelmina on 2 June), the Dutch 'probably should be given credit for pioneering the concept of colonial broadcasting'.[2]

Over the next few years several Dutch and indigenous radio societies formed. In 1934 a Dutch community radio society, the Nederlandsche-Indische Radio Omroep Maataschappij (NIROM), was given government permission to fund operations throughout Java by a radio levy collected via the Post and Telegraph Office. But it was not a monopoly since there were about thirty stations operating independently, as well as NIROM's five. The first indigenous network, Perikatan Perkumpulan Radio Ketimuran (Eastern Radio Association Federation, PPRK) was given a limited licence in 1937 to broadcast matters of a cultural or social nature.

This official Dutch tolerance of heterogeneity ended in 1942, when the Japanese occupation forces placed all radio stations under the control of the Propaganda and Information Department, Sendenbu, which set up the Java Broadcasting Superintendent Bureau to oversee radio. Staff from the government monopoly Japan Broadcasting Corporation (NHK) were sent to manage the Bureau's eight local stations.[3] The Japanese banned the reception and relay of all overseas transmissions. The underground resistance maintained clandestine sets to keep abreast of the progress of the war. Such intelligence proved a powerful asset in the planning for independence. Radio-loudspeaker 'singing trees' (about 1500 of which had been set up by the Japanese for propaganda dissemination throughout Java) also provided an effective medium for nationalists to broadcast Indonesian programs promoting the concept of an Indonesian identity and nationhood. On the evening of 17 August 1945, the Indonesian Republicans managed to elude Japanese control of the Jakarta

Hoso Kyoku radio station and broadcast the Declaration of Independence read by Sukarno earlier that morning.[4] The following day a crackling broadcast—in Indonesian, with an English translation—was beamed around the country and around the globe from Bandung where young Republicans had hooked the local radio into the Central Telegraph Office's shortwave transmitter, telling the world that Indonesia was of age.

On 11 September 1945, the state radio network, Radio Republik Indonesia (Republic of Indonesia Radio, henceforth RRI) was established as a consortium of eight local stations formerly in the Japanese-controlled network. Their operation was placed under the Department of Information in April 1946.[5] RRI played a major role in keeping the nation and the international community informed about the struggle for independence. It established an international division, the Voice of Indonesia, to transmit shortwave bulletins directed at overseas audiences. The young republic's use of radio for propaganda purposes during the next four years earned it the disparaging epithet of the 'microphone republic' from the Dutch UN representative.[6]

Domestically, radio was a vital communication tool for the young nation. Radio ownership rose rapidly, to about half a million licensed sets by the mid 1950s. Radio was used extensively in education, especially political education, such as preparing the electorate for the country's first general elections, in 1955. Independent Indonesia followed the Japanese policy of government monopoly over broadcast. By the time of the establishment of the New Order, there were thirty-nine RRI stations around the country, broadcasting to more than a million licensed radios.[7] Major towns received RRI's national and regional programming. News and other designated special broadcasts were compulsorily relayed to all RRI stations from Jakarta. Regional stations were able to accommodate programming in local languages and of local origin. With no television (until 1962), low literacy levels and a relatively diverse and free press, the RRI was the state's primary and most centralised medium for mobilising public opinion.

The influence of RRI must have been clear to all sides in the coup and counter-coup of 1965. The first public buildings occupied by Lieutenant-Colonel Untung's troops on 1 October were the RRI and telecommunications centres on Jakarta's central

Merdeka Square. Untung's first public action was a radio broadcast announcing that a plot by the 'Council of Generals' to overthrow the President had been foiled. After Major-General Suharto's forces recaptured RRI's Jakarta studios that evening, Suharto broadcast his assumption of personal command over the Army.

Radio generally was significant in legitimising Suharto's rise to power in 1965. The political instability and dissatisfaction with government radio had fostered the growth of hobby radio stations in the early 1960s, sometimes little more than a handful of individuals operating from a private residence. Some of these became more directly politicised after the incidents of 1 October 1965 and were staffed round-the-clock by bands of student activists opposed to President Sukarno. One of the best-known, Radio Ampera, set up by activists including brothers Soe Hok Gie and Arief Budiman, broadcast for a time from the home of Mashuri, then a neighbour and trusted political ally of Suharto.[8] While technically illegal, such anti-Communist and anti-Sukarno broadcasts were not only condoned but were actively aided by ascendant factions of the military. While based at Mashuri's residence Radio Ampera was openly protected by pro-Suharto troops.

Despite low transmission power and very limited audience reach, the existence of 'hundreds of "unofficial" stations...on the air in the vicinity of the capital alone'[9] effectively broke RRI's monopoly control over broadcasted information and interpretation of the fluid politics of the time. Radio Ampera, for example, chose to broadcast its leading news commentaries at 7 p.m., precisely the time of the RRI evening news, thereby forcing listeners to choose. Student stations also flouted RRI's ban on certain types of Western pop music (see Chapter 6), by broadcasting popular songs from prohibited bands like the Beatles and Rolling Stones. The strategy drew young listeners to the fledgling non-government radio. RRI never regained its monopoly of the airwaves.

A New Order for Radio

As Indonesian politics was transformed during the late 1960s so was radio, as an industry and a cultural and political medium. In 1967 the New Order tried to regularise the non-government broadcasters by separating small hobby stations from the more formally established broadcasters. In 1968, soon after being confirmed as full President, Suharto ordered a crackdown to limit campus-based and other student stations. In 1970 private radio stations were legalised. The following year the New Order government attempted to curb their political role by obliging the now-legalised private broadcasters to relay RRI newscasts and restricting permissible transmission area and broadcast content. Also from 1970 district governments began establishing their own stations (Radio Khusus Pemerintah Daerah) independent of local RRI.

Given the active role private radio had played in anti-Sukarno propaganda, the New Order had little option but to allow its continuation in some form. In later years, many former student activists saw the legalisation as a means of controlling and restricting the function of radio by defining it as an apolitical entertainment medium. During the 1970s there was strong growth in commercial stations so that, over the next decade or so, non-government broadcasting became synonymous with commercial stations.

Regulations

In 1970, Government Regulation (Peraturan Pemerintah) No. 55 on Non-Government Radio Broadcasting set out the criteria for establishing a non-government radio broadcasting enterprise and provided the framework for the New Order's radio policy. The social function of radio was described as 'education, information and entertainment' and programs were 'not to be used…for political activities'. Foreign investment (or donation) was prohibited. Station owners had to be Indonesian citizens who had not been involved in the PKI or the Thirtieth of September Movement, and were not office-bearers in any political party or mass organisation. More contentiously (and ignored in practice), broadcasts had to be based on written script, held as documentation and noted in a daily log. Licences were issued for one year and were renewable. Initially the Department of Communications, and since 1983 the Department of Tourism, Post and Telecommunications, was responsible for the technical aspects of broadcasting, particularly the allocation of frequencies.[10] The monitoring of content to ensure 'security and public order' (*pengamanan, kea-*

manan dan ketertiban umum) was the responsibility of the military's Command for the Restoration of Security and Order (KOP-KAMTIB) and the Department of Information. Over the years, however, the Department of Information came to be seen as principally responsible for all aspects of radio other than the allocation of broadcast frequency.

A 1971 Directive of the Communication Minister[11] gave authority over non-government stations to the provincial governor and the local KOPKAMTIB. A Directive of the Minister of Information[12] in the same year emphasised the local moorings of radio, stating that 'a broadcast is local, not national, in character', and that the 'nature, content and purpose of a broadcast reflects the local relationship with the conditions and growth of the area reached by the broadcast'.[13] After 1982 shortwave broadcast by private radio was phased out. Stations opted increasingly for AM and, from 1987, FM bands, which offered clearer transmission over shorter distances.[14] Government regulation stipulated maximum transmitter power, which limited the broadcast area to about 100 km for FM and 300–400 km for AM stations.[15]

Implementation of government policy was the responsibility of the Regional Authority for the Development of Non-Government Radio (Badan Pembina Radio Siaran Non Pemerintah di Daerah, BPRSNPD, henceforth Regional Radio Authority), appointed by the governor and consisting of provincial bureaucrats. All stations had to present a monthly report to it. In 1978 this local authority was given wide powers to take both 'preventive' and 'repressive' actions, including withdrawing permission for, and closing, non-government stations which broke the law. The Regional Radio Authority also had the right to vet any 'broadcast material which originated from abroad'. While private stations were obliged to relay news and other (unspecified) government broadcasts from RRI Jakarta, the local body determined which materials were 'obligatory relay' (*wajib relay*) from RRI 'according to the interests of the region concerned'.[16] An Instruction from the Director-General of Radio, Television and Film that same year also credited the local over the national, restating the responsibility of the Regional Radio Authority to determine the suitability of 'obligatory relay' material to local conditions. In addition, it emphasised that non-government stations should give priority to programs 'whose materials are drawn from local regional cultures' and 'whose broadcast materials originate domestically and are appropriate to local conditions'.[17] The effect of such regulation was to emphasise that private radio was a local medium, over which provincial authorities held considerable sway, armed with the capacity to terminate licences.

The provincial governments' influence was largely eroded after 1983. Through the 1970s, despite state radio's monopoly on newscasting, there were great discrepancies between the amount relayed by private stations, with some relaying virtually no RRI broadcast. This was regularised in 1984 with all private stations relaying 140 minutes of RRI news in each 24-hour cycle.[18] The Regional Radio Authority was now required to enforce a 'prevailing code of ethics in accordance with the etiquette and values of the *national* character' (our emphasis). Morever, 'the use of materials which originate from abroad, in whatever form' now had to be centrally approved by the Director-General of Radio, Television and Film (in this case, the Director of Radio) in Jakarta.[19] After 1987, annual licence renewals for private stations also had to be approved centrally by the Directorate-General of Radio, Television and Film of the Department of Information.

The annual renewal of broadcast licences was an insecure process. A licence took months to obtain from Jakarta and cost Rp. 10 million (including 'unofficial' charges), in the mid 1990s—an average month's profit for small provincial stations.[20] Many small stations attempted to circumvent the regulations by going on air with only the approval of the provincial governor or broadcasting illegally over small areas without any permits at all. But they risked closure in annual surveillance, referred to as 'sweeping', carried out by the Department of Telecommunications. In Aceh, for instance, thirty-six of the seventy private stations closed in 1996.[21]

Despite the increased reach of Jakarta's arm in the last decade of the New Order, radio remained both in practice and in government policy a much more local medium than either film or television. The Broadcast Bill enacted in 1997, while noting the different spans of broadcast (local, provincial, regional, national) permissible for private television, states that radio broadcast is always restricted to the vicinity of the station. Unlike television, state-owned RRI remained the only national radio at the end of the New Order.

Industry organisation

In December 1974 representatives of 173 non-government radio stations from thirty-four cities formally established the Indonesian Private Commercial Radio Broadcasters Association (Persatuan Radio Siaran Swasta Niaga Indonesia, PRSSNI) to 'advance private radio broadcasting in Indonesia and to assist the government in making development a success, in the fields of information, education and socio-cultural affairs'.[22] As was the common New Order practice with industry bodies, in 1977 the Minister of Information formally declared PRSSNI[23] the sole recognised association for private radio stations. In 1996 the association had a membership of 449 AM and 241 FM nationally. In 1985, a Directive from the Minister of Information[24] elevated the association's authority, obliging it to 'assist the government in the development and supervision/surveillance [pengawasan] of private radio broadcasters in Indonesia'. In 1989, to further ensure the organisation's responsiveness to the regime, President Suharto's daughter Siti Hardiyanti Rukmana ('Tutut') was elected General Chairperson (Ketua Umum) of the PRSSNI, a post to which she was re-elected in 1992 and 1995. She was dumped in October 1998 after her father's fall.

Since Tutut was an office-bearer of the government's election machine Golkar, her position on the association contravened regulations prohibiting political party functionaries from holding radio broadcast permits. But the Broadcast Bill of 1997, which superseded all previous regulations, removed this restriction on ownership, stating expressly that 'Every Indonesian citizen has equal right and the broadest possible opportunity to play a role in the creative, work and business aspects...in the broadcast sector' (Ch. VII, Clause 59).

PRSSNI's leverage over private-sector radio was significant since, among the pile of letters and documents (from the local district head to the Director-General of Radio, Television and Film) required before a station could be issued with its annual licence, were letters from both the regional and national levels of the PRSSNI. Some local branches have been prepared to flex their muscle even against the Minister of Information, when the latter has issued permits for radio stations not approved by local PRSSNI.

From the state's point of view, PRSSNI's most significant role was in ensuring industry self-censorship. With little capacity to monitor directly the highly diverse broadcasting of a regionally and financially dispersed industry, the government depended on the industry's self-restraint, particularly at moments of political crisis. In the aftermath of the 27 July 1996 widespread urban riots, PRSSNI's central office-bearers reacted swiftly to curb radio coverage and analysis of the incident. The public unrest had been triggered by a military-backed takeover of the PDI (Indonesian Democratic Party) headquarters in Jakarta from the supporters of Megawati Sukarnoputri, the legitimate leader of the small opposition party, who had been unseated by government manipulation. On 31 July the association's Central Committee wrote to all PRSSNI members, endorsing the Armed Forces Commander's insistence that the unrest was masterminded by a revived Communist movement which had been banned since 1965. The letter called on all radio stations to be vigilant against attempts to 'twist the facts, as was done by the PKI in 1965', instructed them to record and archive all discussions, analyses and interviews broadcast, and effectively barred stations from broadcasting anything other than the government's interpretation of the incidents.[25]

Such calls, which cannot be backed up with surveillance, were never fully heeded by every station. In Yogyakarta, for instance, many stations, while eschewing overt political analyses, continued to broadcast stories of local student demonstrations in support of the PDI activists in Jakarta, sometimes under the guise of local traffic reports—such as information on roads blocked off by demonstrators! The issue of keeping records of programs has always been resisted by radio stations, largely because it absorbs money and space which most do not have, but also because recording is a serious restraint on the stations' ability to broadcast politically sensitive material without leaving material evidence of dissidence. Stations we observed in Yogyakarta did not change their practice in response to PRSSNI's call. Nor did they adhere to the Broadcast Bill, the Suharto government's final legislative initiative in this sector, which made recording of radio broadcast compulsory.

Ownership

The Broadcast Bill of 1997 removed some of the restrictions on ownership and management of radio stations. There was no explicit ban against suspected Communists, other than a general restriction on people with criminal convictions. As mentioned above, the ban on political party and mass organisation office-bearers investing in the industry was also removed. The prohibition against foreign investment in the radio industry (as in the print media and television) remained, only to be contested within weeks of Suharto's departure.

Unlike television, commercial radio licences were issued largely on a commercial basis, without centralised political interventions. Through the mid 1980s, deregulation of the Indonesian economy opened up new possibilities for successful companies which saw the market potentials of the mass media, including radio. In 1987 the Director-General of Radio, Television and Film, in what may be interpreted as an attempt to stem a trend towards establishment of fledgling radio networks, ruled that 'bodies operating non-government radio stations are not permitted to open branches or agencies, whether using the same company name or a different company name'. In addition, perhaps to stop stations being linked with larger non-radio conglomerates, he ruled that 'bodies operating non-government radio stations are not permitted to engage in other types of businesses apart from activities linked to the social function of broadcast radio itself'.[26] Whatever the motivation, the effort was ineffective for, covertly or overtly, there were growing numbers of radio networking and conglomerate cross-media ownerships by the early 1990s, several of them associated with the presidential family circle.

Siti Hardiyanti Rukmana's company PT Radio Citra Dharma Bali Satya acquired a private radio station in Denpasar, in a joint venture with Jakarta's Radio Trijaya, part of the Bimantara conglomerate of younger brother Bambang Trihatmodjo.[27] Trijaya, located in the RCTI television complex, was started in 1990 by Bimantara's Peter Gontha who, in 1994, expanded the network to include Radio Arif Rahman Hakim (ARH, established in 1966 as an activist student station) in Jakarta, SCFM in Surabaya (East Java) and Radio Prapanca in Medan (North Sumatra). Trijaya's weekly discussion program 'Jakarta First Channel', broadcast live from the Sahid Jaya Hotel, was reportedly so popular that advertisers had to book three months ahead for a spot.[28] The program illustrates how successfully Bimantara was able to capitalise on its growing cross-media interests: the 'Diskusi Opini Live' discussion each Monday morning was broadcast on Trijaya radio, and was sponsored by both the Nuansa Pagi program on Bimantara's RCTI TV station and by the Bimantara-affiliated daily paper, *Media Indonesia*. The latter generally provided a journalist to act as moderator of the broadcast. Bimantara's other radio station, the student-oriented Radio ARH, also had a *Media Indonesia* journalist, Achmad Fadila, as moderator of its popular Monday afternoon 'Student Debate' program.

Other media entrepreneurs, like Eric Samola, the financier behind *Tempo* magazine and *Jawa Pos* newspaper, and the owners of the Kompas-Gramedia Group (both mentioned in Chapter 2) also made investments in radio. Samola owned Jakarta's Sport-FM, a specialist sports station. Kompas-Gramedia owned Radio Sonora, one of Jakarta's most popular stations (particularly popular with older sections of the population). Similarly, the newspaper group Sinar Kasih, which owned the flagship daily paper *Suara Pembaruan*, owned the Christian-oriented Jakarta station Radio Pelita Kasih.

As we show elsewhere in this book, the Suharto family and friends acquired unprecedented financial control over print and audio-visual media from the late 1980s. While in the 1990s both Bambang and Tutut, the main media players among the Suharto children, started to acquire radio stations, their holdings (about half-a-dozen between them) remained necessarily small in the highly diverse radio industry. In the late 1970s, another member of the family, Sudwikatmono, had gained control of film import and distribution, partly through manipulation of industry organisations. Similarly, control of the industry organisation PRSSNI, rather than ownership *per se*, may have been regarded as the most efficient and fastest way to gain control of financial and political aspects of radio broadcast.

Market

The level of ownership of radio sets soared through the 1970s along with the expansion in the market for consumer goods gen-

erally, as Indonesia recovered rapidly from the economic downturn of the 1960s. Between 1970 and 1980 the number of sets in
use increased more than sixfold. In 1970 there were 2.5 million
sets in use, in 1980 there were fifteen million and by 1994, 28.8
million.[29] More than 3.1 million portable radios were sold in
1995 alone, making Indonesia one of the largest such markets.[30]
In 1994, there were about fifteen radio receivers per hundred
Indonesians, which was roughly the same ratio as in the Philippines, but less than half that of Malaysia and a quarter that of Singapore.[31] Ownership rates per head of population are lower in
Indonesia's rural areas, but in Java most households now own a
radio. Ethnographic accounts of Javanese villages suggest that
radio ownership in rural areas remains far higher than television
ownership or subscription rates for print media, and that radio is
the primary mass medium for much of rural Indonesia.[32]

Indonesia's advertising industry also expanded rapidly. Radio's
share was boosted in the early 1980s after the banning of advertisements on national television (see Chapter 4). Even in the
1990s, after the inception of private television, while radio's percentage of total revenue declined from 9.7 per cent to 4.1 per
cent between 1991 and 1996, the total advertising amount had
risen such that revenues to radio grew from Rp. 100 billion to
Rp. 190 billion in the same period.[33]

Radio stations around the country proliferated—there were
about 700 in the mid 1990s. The highest-rating station in Jakarta
(and thus the nation) reached a daily listening audience of over
half a million in the mid 1990s. Competition for advertising and
consequently for audiences was stiff. This encouraged stations to
target their programming to very specific market segments, concentrating on particular types of music such as the popular
Indonesian *dangdut* (see Chapter 6), Western rock or traditional
regional musical genres. In rural areas in particular, the most popular radio shows tended to be traditional forms of oral entertainment, 'tailored to the local cultural tastes of each region'.[34]

As Lindsay illustrates in her detailed study of radio and local
identity in Indonesia, the 'persistent survival of private
radio…indicates the vitality of the Indonesian tradition of local
community expression through radio broadcasting'.[35] Popular
stations do not simply broadcast to a given geographical area;

they attempt to create and maintain audience loyalty by manufacturing a communal identity and continually refining 'their own
interpretations of what is "local"'.[36] Promotions and 'market
mobilising' for some stations (such as Jakarta's Radio CBB *dangdut* station) included charitable and religious activities such as
sponsoring mass circumcision feasts.

The degree of specialised and localised service provided by private radio is exemplified in the tiny Radio Terunajaya in Pam-
eungpeuk, Garut district, the sole radio station for four rural
districts scattered along a 30 km span of the southern coast of West
Java. Located in a hilly region, with poor communication and
transportation, far from asphalt roads, the station's special appeal is
its broadcast of individual and community announcements. Villagers use the station to transmit urgent messages from one village
to another, knowing that, with little alternative entertainment,
someone in the target village is likely to be listening and will pass
on the message. Among its other regular broadcasts are Sundanese
folktales and other fiction, and Indonesian and Sundanese pop
music. Despite its small size, Terunajaya's captive market of 140 000
enables it to survive commercially. Set up in 1991 with capital of
Rp. 100 million, it broke even after two years on the strength of its
niche market and strong community identification.[37]

In contrast, the state radio network RRI has put much of its
resources into reaching an undifferentiated mass national audience.
The gradual expansion of RRI's reach through establishing broadcasting stations and relay facilities was boosted after the launch of
the Palapa satellite in 1976 and the more powerful Palapa generation B in 1983. By the mid 1990s, with fifty-two stations, RRI
was able to reach 81 per cent of Indonesian territory and 92 per
cent of the population.[38] Its actual audience share, however, is
almost impossible to establish. By all accounts it has been eroded
by the expansion of private radio stations through the archipelago.
Required since 1968 to raise part of its funds through advertising,
RRI has never managed to be appealing to advertisers. The Information Department's figures for the 1990s show the RRI routine
budget rising from just over Rp. 18 billion in 1990/91 to more
than Rp. 24 billion in 1992/93. Advertisement revenue fell in the
same period from over Rp. 454 million to around Rp. 390 million.
Market surveys from the 1990s (carried out on behalf of advertis-

ers) show that urban young adults, the advertisers' main target, do not listen to RRI. Some internal surveys by private radio stations, which we sighted during fieldwork in 1996, showed that urban audiences in general do not listen to the public broadcaster.

The loss of advertising revenue (always an insignificant portion of its total expenses) in the face of competition from private radio and, in the 1990s, from private television was less important for RRI than the perceived political cost of its eroded share of the national audience. To regain its audiences RRI has attempted, since the early 1980s, to replicate aspects of the commercial services. A string of city stations (Programa Kota) was set up in provincial capitals in the 1980s. While these did not top the popularity charts, their local focus seemed to appeal to larger proportions of population in their broadcast area than did the national programming. In the 1990s RRI attempted to develop a second national network, 'Programa 2 Nasional', better known as 'Pro2FM', run as a commercial network in collaboration with a large private business conglomerate.[39] It is not bound by old RRI conventions of placing advertisements only between programs, and has tried to cultivate a fashionable youthful image.[40] At a time when private commercial stations were not permitted to broadcast from outside their studios, Pro2FM acquired an outside broadcast (OB) van which it used for direct mobile broadcasts to underscore its station motto 'to present info earlier'.[41] But, as we note later, despite legal restrictions and without specialised technology, many private stations managed to broadcast events live from outside their studios. Just as RRI was 'going commercial' with Pro2FM, so were local governments increasingly having their stations (Radio Khusus Pemerintah Daerah, RKPD) 'managed' by commercial companies in the hope of making a profit for the local government.

Broadcast Content

Broadcast language
In rural areas there is an overwhelming preference for informational broadcasts (such as rural and agricultural development programs) to be in local languages rather than in Indonesian.[42]

RRI broadcasts news in twelve regional languages and village agricultural programs (*siaran pedesaan*) in forty-one local languages and dialects, in addition to some in Indonesian. Almost all private radio stations make some use of the languages of the location in which they broadcast; some broadcast predominantly in a regional language. A few even broadcast in minority languages of large city populations. For instance, there are Betawi broadcasts in Jakarta and Madurese ones in Surabaya. There is thus a proportionately greater presence of a greater variety of regional languages on radio than in film, television and the print media.

Indonesian national governments have discouraged the use of foreign language on radio. The 1971 Ministerial Directive prohibited stations from relaying foreign broadcasts, using foreign languages (except in specific language teaching programs), or even mixing languages used (*bahasa campuran*). 'Good Indonesian' was to be used at all times, except in regional cultural programs, when a regional language is permitted. Other regulations reinforced this rule. A 1987 instruction from the Director-General of Radio, Television and Film advised that 'the names of Non-Government Radio Stations may not use foreign terms or words whose meaning is not clear'.[43] But the intrusion of English has grown. It is particularly noticeable in station identification advertisements and the radio positioning statements used by the stations. Central Kalimantan's Radio Bravo Rasisonia in Palangka Raya positions itself with the English statement 'We born for this city' (sic). Manado's Radio ROM2 is 'The right radio for busy people', while competitor Radio Memora is a 'Young energetic station' to offset Radio Karya Dharma's claim to be 'The oldies station'. Radio Madina FM in West Java declared itself 'The Spirit of Moslem' (sic). In fact, of the more than 400 PRSSNI stations advertising in the 1995 handbook, about fifty-five used English slogans as their market positioning statement.[44] Some, such as Central Java's Radio Aro's 'Yang bikin happy and enjoy' (sic) (Making you happy and for your enjoyment?), defy linguistic borders.

The 1971 prohibition against broadcasting foreign programs was never effectively implemented either. Most commonly broadcast foreign programs are Western popular music. Jakarta's Radio Ramako broadcast Dick Bartley's 'American Gold' music program, purchased from US Radio Express, for four hours every Sunday afternoon. Ramako's station manager explains (with unintended irony) that 'it's not that we are wanting to show off our English, but it is so our programs have a distinctively Ramako quality and are different from other private radio stations'.[45] The sophisticated and upmarket Western classical music station in Jakarta, Radio Klasik FM, set up in 1995, broadcasts partially in English.[46] The bilingual (English and Indonesian) 'MTV Asia' which goes to air each Friday on Jakarta's Radio Hard Rock FM and is telecast on AN-TeVe at midday on Saturday is difficult to categorise as 'national' or foreign. So are a host of music and game shows on radio and television which, though produced by Indonesian personnel, are conceived elsewhere.

Foreign broadcasts

The popularity of foreign-sourced music on Indonesian stations, however, concerned the New Order government much less than the tendency for Indonesian listeners to turn their dial from local stations to foreign ones. The Suharto government, and its predecessor, were highly sensitive and generally critical of the content of foreign broadcasts into Indonesia, regarding these as serious breaches of national media borders. During the early 1960s, when Sukarno banned particular forms of Western popular music on RRI (then the only Indonesian radio), foreign shortwave broadcasts were the main source of the latest international musical trends and political news. Despite the proliferation of local private radio stations since 1966, and the considerable volume of foreign music played on them, foreign shortwave stations have retained a significant slice of the Indonesian audience. Radio Australia and the BBC appear to have had the largest following over the years, followed by the Voice of Malaysia and the Voice of America.

Estimates of the total audience for foreign shortwave broadcasts are necessarily imprecise but anecdotal evidence and survey results suggest they are substantial. Since RRI has historically broadcast on shortwave to reach distant provinces, Indonesian listeners are, on the whole, used to listening to shortwave bands which international broadcasters tend to use. A 1982 survey of graduate officials in the Indonesian government—a target group which could be regarded as well-educated, reasonably politically aware and (in the 1980s) broadly sympathetic to New Order policies—estimated that 49 per cent of men and 48 per cent of women in that group regularly listened to the radio and about half of those tuned in to overseas transmissions.[47]

Radio Australia's largest Asian audience is in Indonesia. At the end of 1965 the Australian ambassador to Indonesia suggested that 'more people listen to it [Radio Australia] than to Radio Republic Indonesia and it reaches millions'.[48] Recent surveys commissioned by the BBC indicated that Radio Australia's annual audience was about 5.6 million, down (due to closure of the Cox Peninsula transmitter, severely weakening signals to large parts of Indonesia) from 6.8 million in previous years. More significantly, the 1997 survey indicated that 30.1 per cent of university-educated Indonesians had listened to Radio Australia in the previous year.[49] There is little doubt that at times of political crisis many Indonesians, not trusting the state-sponsored version of events on RRI and TVRI (government television), turned to foreign broadcasts.

Before the advent of parabola antennae that enable reception of global televison broadcasts, certain foreign radio broadcasts were often regarded as the best source of national political news. Even in the late 1990s, shortwave radio remained far more widely available than the Internet and satellite television, and a very important source of news for Indonesian citizens. One way to wean Indonesian citizens off their foreign news habit may be a more open national media policy which permits private radio stations to openly broadcast their interpretation of political events, as alternatives to the government's versions. The other may be to redefine RRI from a government medium into a public service broadcaster. Both appear to be on the agenda of post-Suharto governments.

News

In radio, as in television, the New Order government placed enormous emphasis on its monopoly over news production. Generally, RRI broadcasts about 60 per cent music and about 40 per cent non-music information and educational programs. There is a strong conviction that a very large proportion of the population listens to radio for news. The requirement that private stations not produce their own broadcast news but relay the RRI bulletins is seen by many as a major impediment to the development of radio journalism. 'The [RRI] National News or the Regional News programs are more broadcast descriptions [*siaran pandangan mata*] of ceremonial events and ribbon-cuttings', noted one Indonesian academic.[50] Station owners and executives sought repeatedly to change the requirement to relay RRI news broadcast, not because of any critical political intent but because of the widespread belief that audiences tended to turn radio off during such relays. PRSSNI had also criticised this restriction. In 1979, its West Java branch tried briefly to produce a regional information broadcast, relayed by all PRSSNI members in the province as a counterpoint to RRI news. Most private stations had some staff with responsibility for covering 'current information' (*informasi aktual*)—in any other language, 'news'. Even senior government bureaucrats recognised that, in radio, 'although normatively there are limits...in fact they [radio stations] have extraordinary freedom'.[51]

For stations in outlying districts, the ability to broadcast up-to-date news before newspapers can is seen as radio's leading edge. Even in towns which have their own dailies, national news (by definition, news printed in Jakarta papers) is on the local radio before the newspapers from Jakarta arrive, often a full day after printing in the capital, and then only if there had been no flight delays.[52] This advantage may well be eroded by the capital-city newspapers use of long-distance printing (see Chapter 2) to publish in distant towns. During most of the New Order, however, the local broadcast medium, banned from producing news bulletins, had often been the single most important news medium.

Provincial radio, in particular, often had more latitude than other media. One well-known case in point was that of *Perspektif* (Perspective). Originally developed for SCTV, the program was withdrawn from television in September 1995 after a series of controversial interviews. It re-emerged in January 1996, without any change in its personnel or politics, as a weekly radio interview, 'Perspektif Baru' (New Perspective), syndicated on eighteen radio stations and about two dozen newspapers around the country.[53] Although the two Jakarta stations had to withdraw from the syndication network, apparently under pressure from the city's military authorities, the program continued to be broadcast in almost every other major city in Indonesia.

Provincial and local radio broadcasts were, in theory, monitored by provincial branches of the Department of Information. But the number of stations in an area frequently outweighed the capacity of the Department. In Yogyakarta in 1996, for example, the Department of Information section charged with monitoring reportedly had only a single radio receiver to follow fifteen private stations in the city and did no more than check on the compulsory news relay from RRI. Generally, the Department only intervenes if a station's programming sparks attention in the print media.

In one case in Yogya, Radio UNISI broadcast an interview in February 1995 with controversial psychic Permadi, concerning, among other things, his predictions on one of the hottest topics, the presidential succession. The interview sparked no immediate attention, but a recording of it, together with a seminar given by Permadi at Yogya's premier Gadjah Mada University, began circulating, particularly among students. Two weeks after the broadcast, the interview was mentioned in Yogya's *Bernas* and Surabaya's *Jawa Pos* dailies. The Yogya city office of the Department of Information responded immediately to the press report, writing to UNISI management requesting a copy of the interview. The following week the head of the regional office (*kantor wilayah*) of the Department also wrote to UNISI, claiming the broadcast 'had a broad impact and had been quite unsettling to all parties' and declared the station had broadcast '"political news" contravening regulations', which he then listed. He accused UNISI, in New Order-speak, of 'broadcasting information in a sensational tone, which could disturb National Security and give rise to unhealthy community opinions and [which] could unsettle the community'. The letter instructed UNISI to cease '"City Info" program on which the interview had been broadcast, as it was identical to "Straight News"' (English in the original) from 20 March. He then wrote to all non-government Yogyakarta stations condemning recent 'deviations' from government regulations, instructing them to 'eliminate broadcasts which were vulgar, and with unclear motivations and direction'. He reminded them of the government prohibition against programs on politics or which were 'politically agitative which could give rise to public opinions which contradicted the policies of the Government of the Republic of Indonesia'.[54]

For a while there was much discussion about the impact of radio broadcasts. The effect on UNISI appears to have been positive, strengthening the station's reputation in the city as critical, stirring (*mbalelo*) and informative.[55] A year later UNISI again breached censorship limits by broadcasting two extracts of a six-part interview with Sri Bintang Pamungkas, head of the then unauthorised Indonesian Democratic Union Party (Partai Uni Demokrasi Indonesia, PUDI): it canned the remainder of the series after a telephone warning from the Department of Information.[56]

The UNISI case brings into focus several problems in the government's censorship of radio broadcasts. Private radio had been defined since the 1970s as primarily a cultural medium, without the political clout of the press or the mass audience of television. There were too many radio stations, each with an insignificant share of a very local audience, for any particular broadcast to have major significance. Thus resources were never invested to develop local Information Department offices' capacity to effectively censor broadcasts.

In recognition of the appeal of news, most Indonesian stations incorporated various kinds of discussion, information or talk-back programs dealing with recent political issues. Radio Ramako's Friday morning breakfast magazine-style program was very popular until the station manager withdrew it in June 1995, in an act of self-censorship. Jakarta's Trijaya FM seemed to be constantly pushing the limits of censorship with its weekly 'Jakarta First Channel' program discussing controversial political issues, protected by the assumed immunity of owner Bambang Trihatmodjo. Its predecessor 'Jakarta Round Up', however, had been taken off air by concerned company executives in 1994 after its discussion of media bans with the editor of banned *Tempo* magazine.[57] Bandung's Radio Mara Ghita ignored the majority of broadcast regulations when it relayed various foreign transmissions for some days before the fall of President Marcos in the Philippines. Mara has broadcast talk-back programs since the early 1980s. Particular programs and anchors have had to be changed in response to government pressure, but the talk-back format remained, to the end of the New Order, not only Mara's hallmark, but was recognised by the regional authorities as a 'barometer of the dynamics of the population of Bandung'.[58]

In the last months of the New Order the ban on news was flouted openly by most broadcasters. On 27 July 1996, Radio Ramako broadcast on-the-spot reports of escalating violence triggered by the attack on the PDI headquarters, with its star presenter reporting live to air via her mobile phone. This became common practice for many stations in the final days of Suharto's rule. Some radio stations, particularly those with large student followings, used their broadcast not only to report the rapidly unfolding political saga but also to provide various kinds of support for the demonstrators.

The ban on radio stations producing their own news had always been impossible to police. Particular radio programs were closed down from time to time, only to reappear in a different guise. Current affairs and talk-back programs tended to rate well, particularly those regarded by the audiences as courageous and willing to take on the government. Through the 1990s, as the Suharto government's legitimacy was eroded, critical news and current affairs programs on radio were continually caught between their potential to generate ratings, and therefore advertising money, against increasing competition from television, and the threat that the programs might bring retribution from some section of the government. A fortnight after the resignation of Suharto, on 5 June 1998 Yunus Yosfiah, the new Minister of Information, reduced the number of required RRI relays from fourteen to four and permitted private stations to produce their own news. The latter move was simply a legalisation of a long-established practice, which the New Order had had neither the will nor the resources to prevent.

The New Order's Legacy

In spite of its mediating role in the birth of the Indonesian nation, radio operated as one of the most local of all the mass media in a number of ways. Unlike television, and even the press and publishing industries, the use of regional languages was widespread on both public and private radio. Radio station ownership was also far more dispersed than that of television or the press. Indeed, New Order policy required radio programming to be locally relevant. All these factors made radio particularly responsive to local needs, not only in the sense of promoting regional cultural specificities but also in the synergies between stations and their particular audiences at particular moments. On 12 May 1998, when security forces shot six students at Trisakti University, the most popular song on campus radio was John Lennon's *Imagine*. For demonstrating students in Jakarta, a very global song on campus radio caught the local mood of the moment. In Bandung, Radio Mara called on its older, middle-class audience[59] to signify their call for Suharto's resignation by wearing a white ribbon. The station was flooded with phone calls and ribbons.

On the other hand, the New Order government had tried to enforce a highly centralised news monopoly by obliging all stations to relay news broadcast from RRI. Since the mid 1980s, the government had strengthened the control of the central hierarchy of the Department of Information by diminishing the role of local authorities. That news monopoly, always more legal than real, was crumbling within days of Suharto's resignation. As we will see in the next chapter, in the final days of the Suharto regime, the Army attempted a final clamp-down on national television. But the continuous and contradictory radio coverage of activities on streets and campuses across the many cities and small towns of Indonesia attracted little attention from the military, which focused entirely on securing the streets of the capital.

Analyses of Indonesian politics and media focus most often on Jakarta, and, in Jakarta-centred analysis, television and the Internet are already vying for credit as the medium that brought about the fall of a tyrant. But radio, more than any other medium, has emerged from the New Order with a legal and economic framework that is resistant to monopoly control of large capital and to centralised control by Jakarta. As such, radio will be significant in the process of Indonesia's democratisation; it will be a source of diverse, regionalised public opinion and a means for political actors to reach the diverse voting publics.

Notes

1   An account of this period in Indonesian is given in 'Riwayat Ringkas Persatuan Radio Siaran Swasta Nasional Indonesia (PRSSNI)' (pp. 19–21) in PRSSNI, *Petunjuk Radio Siaran Swasta*

Nasional '95, Pengurus Pusat PRSSNI, Jakarta, 1995. The only substantial pieces of published research on Indonesian radio in English are: Drew O. McDaniel, *Broadcasting in the Malay World: Radio, Television, and Video in Brunei, Indonesia, Malaysia, and Singapore*, Ablex, Norwood, 1994; Colin Wild, 'Indonesia: A nation and its broadcasters', *Indonesia Circle*, 43, June 1987, pp. 15–40; Colin Wild, 'Radio midwife: Some thoughts on the role of broadcasting during the Indonesian struggle for independence', *Indonesia Circle*, 55, June 1991, pp. 34–42; and Jennifer Lindsay, 'Making waves: Private radio and local identities in Indonesia', *Indonesia*, 64, October 1997, pp. 105–23. In addition, Jennifer Lindsay kindly gave us copies of two earlier unpublished conference papers. Compared to film, television and popular music there is no large genre of fan magazines dedicated to radio.

2   McDaniel, *Broadcasting in the Malay World*, p. 26; Wild, 'Indonesia: A nation and its broadcasters', p. 18. Both are good sources for this period.

3   Details on the Japanese period are from Aiko Kurasawa, 'Propaganda media on Java under the Japanese 1942–1945', *Indonesia*, 44, October 1987, pp. 59–116, particularly p. 87.

4   PRSSNI, *Petunjuk Radio*, pp. 19–21, notes the circumstances of the broadcast of the Declaration. Astrid Susanto, however, implies the Declaration went to air when announced at 10 a.m. on 17 August (Astrid Susanto, 'The mass communications system in Indonesia' (pp. 229–58, p. 233) in Karl D. Jackson & Lucian W. Pye (eds), *Political Power and Communications in Indonesia*, University of California Press, Berkeley, 1978.) Other sources state the broadcast did not take place until the evening of the 17th. See also Benedict R.O'G. Anderson, *Java in the Time of Revolution: Occupation and Resistance 1944–46*, Cornell University Press, Ithaca, 1972, p. 84. Without the knowledge of the Japanese censors the text was also transmitted by Morse, using the facilities of the Japanese news service Domei, an hour after the proclamation (Adam Malik, *In the Service of the Republic*, Gunung Agung, Singapore, 1980, p. 121).

5   McDaniel, *Broadcasting in the Malay World*, p. 212.

6   McDaniel, *Broadcasting in the Malay World*, p. 215, citing Department of Information, *Sound Broadcasting in Indonesia*, Directorate of Radio, Jakarta, 1972.

7   McDaniel, *Broadcasting in the Malay World*, p. 218. McDaniel makes the point that statistics on licensed radios considerably underestimates actual usage, since many owners may avoid paying the licence fee.

8   Harold Crouch, *The Army and Politics in Indonesia*, Cornell University Press, Ithaca, 1978, p. 212. Arief Budiman describes his involvement in radio during this period un 'Umar Kayam Dia yang tidak Menyerah', *Kompas Online*, 15 June 1997, circulated via <indonesia-p@indopubs.com> on 14 June 1997.

9   McDaniel, *Broadcasting in the Malay World*, p. 223.

10 In 1982, the responsibility for allocation of broadcast frequency was given to the Director-General of Post and Telecommunication. In the new Cabinet formed in 1983 that Directorate was moved from the Department of Communication to the Department of Tourism, Post and Telecommunication.

11 SK/26/T/1971.

12 No.39/KEP/MENPEN/1971

13 *Surat Keputusan Menteri Penerangan Republik Indonesia Nomor 39/Kep/Menpen/1971 tentang Petunjuk-Petunjuk Umum tentang kebijaksanaan penyelenggaraan acara serta isi siaran bagi radio siaran non-pemerintah*, Bab II Ketentuan-Ketentuan Khusus, Pasal 4, Sifat Siaran, paragraphs 1 and 2.

14 Laws and regulations concerning radio broadcasting appear in PRSSNI, *Petunjuk Radio Siaran Swasta Nasional '95*, Pengurus Pusat PRSSNI, Jakarta, 1995 and other PRSSNI publications such as Sekretariat Pengurus Pusat PRSSNI, *Kumpulan Peraturan tentang Radio Siaran Swasta di Indonesia: Tahun 1970 s/d 1992*, PRSSNI, Jakarta, 1992.

15 Lindsay, 'Making waves', p. 114, fn. 40. These stipulations are widely disregarded: Lindsay notes that, although FM transmitters should be no more than 100 watts, 'most FM stations broadcast with at least 5 kilowatt transmitters, and some as much as 20 kilowatt'.

16 Ministerial Directive SK No. 24/KEP/MENPEN/1978 and Appendix.

17 Instruction of the Director General of Radio, Television, and Film, No.09/INSTRK/DIRJEN/RTF/78.

18 Obligatory relays included, at 3 p.m., five minutes of sports news, and at 8 p.m., ten minutes of 'Industry and Economic News',

which gives the market rate for vegetables. It was permissible to avoid relaying the hourly five-minute news summaries between 1 a.m. and 5 a.m. if this would break into a 'Cultural Broadcast' such as *wayang*. See PRSSNI, *Petunjuk Radio Siaran Swasta Nasional '95*, p. 472. The date given in this source is incorrect: it should be 11 December 1984, not 1994. Prior to general elections, the volume of compulsory relays increased dramatically as campaign events were included.

19 SK No. 226/KEP/MENPEN/1984, Article 6.3.

20 Lindsay, 'Making waves', p. 114, also notes that a larger station may make 'four times that amount, and a successful top-twenty Jakarta station can earn around up to $US100000 per month profit'.

21 'Sebanyak 36 stasiun radio siaran di Aceh, disegel', *Kompas*, 12 November 1996, p. 10. Of course, given the separatist movement in Aceh, and the consequent breakdown in law and order in many parts of the province, this large-scale flouting of broadcast regulations may not be representative of the situation across the nation.

22 'Riwayat Ringkas Persatuan Radio Siaran Swasta Nasional Indonesia (PRSSNI)' (pp. 19–21) in PRSSNI, *Petunjuk Radio Siaran Swasta Nasional '95*, quotation from p. 20.

23 At this time the name of the organisation was slightly changed, with 'Niaga' (Commercial) being replaced by 'Nasional' (National).

24 SK No. 245/KEP/MENPEN/1985.

25 Correspondence No. 153.A/PP.PRSSNI/VII/1996, dated 31 July 1996, and signed by H. Purnomo (Ketua Pelaksana Harian) and H. Shidki Wahab (Sekretaris Umum).

26 No. 1050/RTS/RSS/K/1987, 20 August 1987, II.C.4 & 5, in PRSSNI, *Petunjuk Radio Siaran Swasta Nasional '95*, p. 479.

27 The Suharto family's business dealings in Bali are detailed in George Junus Aditjondro, *Bali, Jakarta's Colony: Social and Ecological Impacts of Jakarta-based Conglomerates in Bali's Tourism Industry*, Working Paper No. 58, Asia Research Centre, Murdoch University, 1995 and in various Internet articles by him. We would like to thank Dr Aditjondro sincerely for sharing his data with us in numerous personal communications.

28 'Radio Trijaya "Jakarta First Channel"', *Kompas*, 13 November 1996, p. 19; M. Jamiluddin Ritonga, 'Radio Swasta Kita', *Media Indonesia*, 4 September 1996, p. 6.

29   See Table 'Radio broadcasting: number of receivers, and receivers per 1000 inhabitants', Asia.WT0901.e on the UNESCO Statistics website http://www.unesco.org/general/eng/stats/asia.wt0901.e.96.html (sighted 19 June 1997).

30   Euromonitor, *International Marketing Data and Statistics 1997*, Euromonitor, London, 1997, p. 389, Table 1413.

31   Unesco statistics for 1994 on the number of radio receivers per 100 inhabitants for neighbouring countries were Vietnam 10.4, Cambodia 10.8, Philippines 14.4, Thailand 19, Malaysia 43.2 and Singapore 64.5. In the disputed territory of East Timor, there was less than one receiver per hundred inhabitants, the lowest ratio of all Asian (including Middle Eastern) countries listed. See Table Asia.WT0901.e on the UNESCO Statistics website http://www.unesco.org/general/eng/stats/asia.wt0901.e.96.html (captured 19 June 1997).

32   See, for example, Salamun (ed.), *Dampak Masuknya Media Komunikasi terhadap Kehidupan Sosial Budaya Masyarakat Pedesaan Daerah Istimewa Yogyakarta*, Departemen Pendidikan dan Kebudayaan, Direktorat Jenderal Kebudayaan, Directorat Sejarah dan Nilai Tradisional, Proyek Penelitian, Pengkajian dan Pembinaan Nilai-nilai Budaya, Jakarta, 1992–93, pp. 13, 34, 37. From the late 1980s onwards University of Gadjah Mada student theses in Anthropology routinely include media habits of rural populations. Almost all of these accounts support our observation.

33   Baty Subakti & Ernst Katoppo (eds), *Media Scene 1995–1996 Indonesia*, Persatuan Perusahaan Periklanan Indonesia (PPPI), Jakarta, 1995, p. 53, Table 7.1, 'Advertising expenditures by type of media 1992–1996', which notes that the figures are 'gross advertising expenditures' excluding discounts, and those for 1996 are projections. As a percentage of total advertising revenue television increased from 38 per cent in 1992 to 50.2 per cent by 1996. With the exception of outdoor advertising, all other media declined against television.

34   Susanto, 'The mass communications system', p. 237.

35   Lindsay, 'Making waves', pp. 115–22, provides an excellent analysis of the local role of private radio, with several valuable case studies. Quotation from p. 115.

36   Lindsay, 'Making waves', p. 116.

37 Dedi Muhtadi, 'Siarannya Terdengar Hingga Pulau Christmas', *Kompas*, 25 September 1996, p. 19.

38 'RRI tetap diperlukan', *Kompas*, 4 September 1991, p. 12; 'Tantangan "RRI" di usia ke-50: Menjadi menarik tapi tetap jaga jati diri' (editorial), *Kompas*, 12 September 1995, p. 4.

39 Ign[atius] Haryanto (ed.), *Laporan Tahunan 1996: Pers Indonesia Terus di-Pres*. Aliansi Jurnalis Independen/Lembaga Studi Pers dan Pembangunan, Jakarta, 1997, Lampiran II 'Peta Kepemilikan Media Massa 1996', p. 77, lists the Aburizal Bakrie Group as 'kerjasama' (collaborating, working together with) RRI in Pro2FM. Aburizal Bakrie is an influential indigenous business person, then chair of the powerful Indonesian Chamber of Commerce (KADIN).

40 'RRI mencoba menjawab kebutuhan khalayak', *Media Indonesia*, 8 September 1996, p. 9.

41 'Pro2FM kembalikan kejayaan RRI', *Media Indonesia*, 8 September 1996, p. 9.

42 Susanto, 'The mass communications system', p. 239.

43 Director-General of Radio, Television and Film, No. 1050/RTF/RSS/K/1987, 20 August 1987.

44 See PRSSNI, *Petunjuk Radio Siaran Swasta Nasional '95*.

45 'Ramako 106,15 FM, "It's a Magic"', *Kompas*, 23 October 1996, p. 19.

46 'Classical music gets new lease of life from FM stations', *Jakarta Post*, 30 June 1996, p. 3. This source refers to the classical music station as 'TOP FM' (89.7 MHz), but the description appears to be of TOP FM's partner station Radio Klasik FM (89.65 MHz), which is also part of the MNC group.

47 Leslie Palmier, 'Mass media exposure of Indonesian graduate officials', *Indonesia*, 44, October 1987, pp. 117–28, from tables 15 and 16 on p. 127.

48 Cited in Errol Hodge, *Radio Wars: Truth, Propaganda and the Struggle for Radio Australia*, CUP, Cambridge, 1995, p. 88.

49 These figures are based on three major audience surveys commissioned by the BBC World Service Research Department, conducted by SRI, the Indonesian branch of A.C. Nielson.

50 Sumbo Tinarbuko, 'Mengoptimalkan potensi siaran RRI', *Kompas*, 11 September 1993, p. 4.

51 The former head of TVRI, Ishadi, is quoted in 'Perlu Regulasi di Bidang Penyiaran Media Radio', *Kompas*, 4 July 1996, p. 10.

52 Operations manager for Radio Pesona Amboina 103 FM, for example, says one rationale for his station's establishment was its capacity to fill the information lag that had existed in Ambon because the newspapers arrived there by 9 p.m. on the day of printing in Jakarta, but were not home-delivered to subscribers until the following morning: 'Penyaji Informasi Pagi Hari', *Kompas*, 18 December 1996, p. 19.

53 Article XIX, *Muted Voices: Censorship and the broadcast media in Indonesia*, Article XIX, London, 1996, p. 15.

54 Quotations from: Kantor Departemen Penerangan Kotamadya Yogyakarta, No. 251/VI/a/1995, dated 9 March 1995; Badan Pembina Radio Siaran Non Pemerintah, Propinsi Daerah Istimewa Yogyakarta, No. 04/BPRSNP/III/1995, dated 16 March 1995, signed by Hoetojo Hoerip; Kantor Wilayah Departemen Penerangan Propinsi Daerah Istimewa Yogyakarta, No. 300//K/III/1995, dated 20 March 1995, signed by Hoetojo Hoerip.

55 Tri Agung Kristanto, 'Radio Unisi FM Sarat Informasi', *Kompas*, 20 November 1996, p. 22.

56 Article XIX, *Muted Voices*, p. 13.

57 Article XIX, *Muted Voices*, p. 16.

58 Interview with the founder and several senior staff of the station, August 1998. The comment from a regional military commander was reported to Radio Mara staff, and later adopted by Mara as part of its station profile.

59 Radio Mara's own assessment of its audience profile based on SRI surveys: 'leading radio for the age group 34–55' and middle- to lower-middle class, based on income. See PT Radio Mara, *Laporan Tahunan 1991–1998* (Annual Reports), pp. 7–9.

4

TELEVISION:
TRANSBORDER
TRANSMISSIONS, LOCAL
IMAGES

In Chapter 3 we looked at radio as a highly decentralised sector of the Indonesian communication market. We turn now to television, the medium most firmly controlled from Jakarta, first by the New Order government and later by a small coterie of President Suharto's family and friends. Throughout the New Order, television remained expressly geared to the promotion of national integration, encapsulated in the motto of state television TVRI (Televisi Republik Indonesia): 'TVRI weaves together our unity and the union' (*menjalin persatuan dan kesatuan*). This chapter aims to unpack this idea of 'national integration', to understand what it meant in the New Order, by focusing on the two most significant shifts in television policy: satellite transmission of national broadcasts from the late 1970s and, a decade later, the privatisation of television.

Our discussion takes up one of the important debates in recent television theory. Asian governments often legitimise their national cultural policy via a critique of US or Western cultural imperialism. Within this perspective, satellites, facilitating the transport of television programs across the globe, have come to be seen as a particularly damaging source of 'Westoxification' or Western cultural domination of Asian nations. However, recent academic studies in the area of culture and communication suggest that a single US-dominated television culture is not emerging. Instead, there is a diversification in the cultural marketplace as India, Hong Kong, Japan and Brazil become significant televisual exporters in particular regions. The problem for any national policy, and of the Indonesian television policy in the last decade, was not putting up a defence against a single powerful invader, but managing an explosion of diversity.

Most of the chapter discusses privatisation of television from the late 1980s. Through the decade, partly for technological reasons and partly due to the dominant ideology of the free market, public television almost everywhere was giving way to highly commercial forms of broadcast. We look at the reasons and the political and cultural consequences of privatised television in the historical context of the late New Order.[1]

Televising Indonesia

Proposals to introduce television came as early as 1953 from sections of the Department of Information, spurred by US, British, German, and Japanese companies jockeying to sell the hardware. On the eve of the Fourth Asian Games in Jakarta in 1962, Sukarno and the Cabinet were finally convinced, on the grounds that Indonesia's international reputation depended on the Games being broadcast, particularly in Japan (which had had television since the early 1950s). In the context of Sukarno's bid for a role on the world stage, Indonesia was televised for the world to see.[2]

Television broadcasting started with the help of Japanese expertise and equipment, and some British training, under the Organising Committee of the Fourth Asian Games, on the first day of the Games in August 1962. In October 1963 its long-term organisational structure was finally in place. The TVRI Foundation (*Yayasan TVRI*) was responsible to the Department of Information for the programming content on TVRI, but autonomous in regard to funding. This was an extension of the dominant European pattern of public service broadcast partially funded through advertising, the reverse of the British model of state-funded but publicly accountable broadcast. The Foundation decided almost immediately to seek revenue through fees for television ownership and advertising. In 1966, the year after the New Order came to power, TVRI started receiving an annual government subsidy. But by 1971, with the economic reconstruction undertaken by the New Order well under way,[3] advertising revenue outstripped other funding sources.

At the time of the coup television was an insignificant medium. TVRI broadcast for only about three hours in the evenings and had only one relay station outside Jakarta, in Yogyakarta. The real growth in television in Indonesia started in the 1970s. New regional stations were added rapidly, mainly relaying Jakarta programs. In 1976 Indonesia launched a domestic broadcast satellite, Palapa, followed in 1983 by the more powerful Generation B Palapa. The technology was American and the name replete with Javanese symbolism.

In concrete terms, the satellite reduced 'variations in the broadcast of news and information programs between the regional stations of the TVRI'.[4] It also sped, expanded and regularised the flow of information throughout the Indonesian territory. In 1983 an Integrated Programming Pattern (*Pola Acara Terpadu*) was instituted: all programming for all stations was annually determined in the Jakarta headquarters of TVRI. In effect, regional stations became relay stations for TVRI Jakarta. The obligatory relay (*wajib relay*) category constituted only two or three hours a day (a decreasing proportion as the broadcast hours increased). But the budgets of regional stations rarely allowed their programming to exceed 15–20 per cent of total airtime. A very small amount of regional programming circulated nationally and was always mediated through Jakarta, never exchanged directly between regional stations. Since the mid 1970s all regional stations had local news bulletins, but hardly any segment of these ever got into national circulation.

Thus the television system which emerged in Indonesia, in the shadow of the satellite, was far more centralised than comparable, large, state-monopolised televisions in India or China.[5] Kitley summarises the symbolic implications of Palapa thus: 'The fragmented, far-flung archipelago is unified in a seamless electronic net which annihilates space and imposes its own time, drawing the vastness and diversity of Indonesia into a whole, structuring for the periphery a clear and constant fix on the centre'.[6]

By all accounts, the satellite had been named by President Suharto. It refers to the vow of Gadjah Mada, Prime Minister of the fourteenth-century Majapahit kingdom of central Java, often cited in the government's publicity documents in its original classical Javanese, but almost never in Indonesian. It can be translated thus:[7]

When the other islands [the islands beyond Java] have been conquered I will enjoy the palapa. If Gurun [either Gorong to the
west of Papua or Sorong Papua], Seran [Seram in Maluku], Tan-
jungpura [Borneo/Kalimantan], Haru [east coast of Sumatra],
Pahang [on the east coast of peninsular Malaysia], Dompo [in
Sumbawa], Bali, Sunda, Palembang, Tumasik [Singapore] have
been conquered, then I will enjoy the palapa.[8]

The references to Singapore and Malaysia would be recognised
only by scholars of classical Javanese and presumably by those
who named the satellite Palapa. The political claims of Sukarno
to 'Greater Indonesia' had been eschewed by the New Order.
However, perhaps we can see in the Palapa satellite the continuing quest for a Javanised Jakarta's cultural and ideological centrality not only within the national border but in the region beyond,
via the latest and most prestigious media technology. More
importantly, the creation of the Indonesian nation is signified not
through the symbolism of a union that always already existed, but
as an achieved state—the conquest of the periphery by the centre. If Palapa was indeed a tool to create a nation, the nation was
not a representative collection of Indonesia's regional diversities
but one created by televisual chains of command, connecting
each region to Jakarta. That relationship is symbolically acknowledged in the name 'Palapa'.

Private Television, National Vision

In November 1988 Indonesia's first private television channel
started a period of trial pay-television broadcasting in Jakarta. By
April the following year its transmission had grown to eighteen
hours a day. In the next four years every large business conglomerate, including some with a major stake in the print media, was
negotiating for a slice of the new market. Amid expectations
that a large number of private stations would be licensed to
broadcast from different regional capitals, five broadcast permits
were awarded.

Surrender of state monopoly over television was an international trend in the 1980s, occurring in neighbouring Malaysia
and later in Singapore. In Indonesia, private television was not

so much a paradigm shift towards more democratic or even market-driven media; it was a policy adjustment to a changing mediascape within the framework of central cultural control of the peripheries. The New Order's characteristic nepotism in issuing licences to private operators ensured that although the government lost some control, the Suharto regime retained its monopoly over television in Indonesia.

Family matters

The first private station, RCTI, belonged to Bambang Trihat-mojo, President Suharto's third child, at the helm of the powerful Bimantara business group with extensive interests in primary and manufacturing industries. RCTI started as pay-television, but in August 1990 it was permitted to broadcast free-to-air. Television quickly became the most prominent of Bimantara's moves into communication hardware (electronics and telecommunication) and software (newspapers, magazines, television programming).

In 1989 Surya Citra Televisi (SCTV), the second private chan-nel, went to air from Surabaya, the capital of East Java and Indonesia's second-largest city, and soon after opened a second station in Bali. Eighty per cent of the company shares were reportedly controlled by Henri Pribadi, an ethnic Chinese busi-nessman with a long association with Suharto's cousin, Sud-wikatmono, who owned the remaining 20 per cent.

The third private channel, Televisi Pendidikan Indonesia (Indonesian Education Television, TPI), started in December 1990, renting TVRI transmission facilities. Initially it offered a four-and-a-half-hour morning broadcast, to supplement school and college curricula, but quickly expanded to eight hours, with only 38 per cent educational content.[9] Suharto's eldest daughter, Siti Hardiyanti Rukmana (Tutut) owned most of TPI. TPI's declared profile as an educational channel, run by a purportedly non-profit organisation, which allowed it to use TVRI facilities, also meant that it could broadcast nationally, whereas the other two channels, RCTI and SCTV, were initially restricted to Jakarta and Surabaya. Within a year of going to air, TPI's advertising rev-enue had overtaken RCTI's.[10] TPI's national access and conse-quent advertising advantage quickly become another element in the already public family business rivalry. In 1993 a further deregulation allowed private channels to broadcast throughout Indonesia via the Palapa satellite, so they could be received by parabola antennae throughout the country and beyond.

The last two stations, AN-TeVe (which started broadcasting in 1993) and Indosiar (in 1995) were thus national networks as soon as they were launched. Indosiar was part of the Salim Group, one of the largest ethnic Chinese business conglomerates, headed by Lim Sioe Liong, President Suharto's longest-standing Chinese associate. AN-TeVe (Cakrawala Andalas Televisi) was to be restricted to West Sumatra according to its initial permit, but in fact, like all the other stations, operated from Jakarta. It was partly owned by the Bakrie Group (whose business fortunes predate the New Order and which is not seen as particularly close to the palace) and partly by Agung Laksono, closely associated with the then ruling party Golkar. All these business groups (with the apparent exception of the Salim Group) have had or acquired, since their entry into television, interests in other print or electronic media.

This powerful group of entrepreneurs resisted all attempts by the Department of Information to restrict their reach in any way. The tension was clearest in 1996–97 as the parliament completed Indonesia's first Broadcast Bill, which the President refused to sign. This was the first time that President Suharto returned a Bill for reconsideration. It was widely reported that the Bill's requirement that no station transmit to more than 50 per cent of the national population was unacceptable to the industry. Some months later, Harmoko, the long-serving Minister of Information (1983–97) was replaced. The new minister, Hartono, a close political associate of Tutut, criticised the contentious provision of the Bill. Parliament obliged by removing the offending clause. Suharto finally signed the Bill in October 1997, his last important intervention in the formation of media institutions in Indonesia. In the current financial crisis and political turmoil, some of the networks will change hands. But for the moment the ownership of these assets is set to remain close to the palace, as Habibie's son is reportedly keen to take over one of the private stations.

The market

Television was the fastest-expanding medium of the 1980s, in terms of number of sets and consumption habits of Indonesians. During the decade the number of sets grew sixfold, while radio rose only threefold. Central Bureau of Statistics (BPS) data indicate unequivocally and consistently that by the late 1980s more Indonesians were watching television regularly than were reading newspapers or magazines or listening to the radio (although, as indicated in Chapter 3, radio remained important in rural areas). In parts of Sumatra, by 1986–87 television-watching was two to three times as common as radio-listening among the surveyed populations. Consequently, producers and distributors of consumer items regarded television as the most effective means of reaching mass audiences.

As mentioned earlier, Indonesian state television had been funded through advertising revenue almost from its inception. Since the launch of Palapa, advertising revenue had grown rapidly. There was, however, a growing critique of consumer culture, particularly from Islamic groups. In 1977, as part of concessions to such opinions, commercials were restricted to late evenings. This affected TVRI's income very little. Its annual advertising revenue grew from about Rp. 368 million in 1971 to Rp. 7.6 billion in 1980. During the same period, the government's routine subsidy (despite an almost threefold increase) fell from 8 per cent to 1.4 per cent of TVRI's total earnings.[11]

But on 5 January 1981, with no prior warning, the President called for an end to advertising on TVRI. The move was an ideological sop to Islamic political groups; the Islamic party PPP, especially its women's groups, supported the ban. Advertising on TVRI ceased on 1 April. Flush with oil money, the government immediately announced an almost tenfold increase in its annual subsidy to TVRI, to Rp. 10 billion.[12]

The Department of Information had not been consulted on the issue and the advertising ban did not have the support of its senior bureaucrats.[13] Polite protests followed, spearheaded by the Advertisers Association (PPPI) and the Indonesian Chamber of Commerce (KADIN). Sukamdani Gitosarjono, a businessman particularly close to Mrs Suharto, suggested that a private television channel should be created to carry advertisements at least to

Jakarta residents. The idea received immediate support from some bureaucrats in the Department of Information.

The political decision to ban advertising did not seem to serve the interests of any significant section of the business community. Advertising industry figures in 1985 belied the expectations that a large part of the advertising funds released from television would flow into radio and the press—it did not happen. Advertising agencies shifted their attention from the broadcast media to various forms of narrowcasting, door-to-door sales, merchandising and the film and video industries.[14] In early 1987, the Department of Information reportedly became aware that advertisers who targeted consumers in certain parts of Indonesia were even taking their message and money to Malaysian TV3, as large sections of the Sumatran population were tuning into the station across the border.

The additional government funds did not cover TVRI's growing expenditure in the mid 1980s, particularly as awareness grew that more innovative programming was necessary to expand and maintain its audience base. In order to meet its growing deficit, TVRI turned to making 'sponsored' programs. Initially these were mainly from government departments and in the non-news broadcasts. The practice of running departmental messages in various forms in both film and television was an old one. But in the post-commercial era TVRI news-spots were for sale to government departments and increasingly also to businesses under the guise of 'news' of new products, seminars, new initiatives and commercial deals. TVRI stations, national and regional, were permitted to set their own price 'to cover cost of production' of 'sponsored' items.

At the end of 1987 the government announced its decision to trial a private channel funded by advertising revenue. The expansion of the Indonesian economy from the late 1980s had laid the financial basis for some sort of commercial television, funded by advertising revenue. Massive rises in advertising expenditures followed the establishment of the new television networks. Total national advertising expenditure doubled from Rp. 639 billion in 1990, when private television was available only in Jakarta and Surabaya, to Rp. 1381 trillion in 1993, when the private channels gained a national audience. In 1995, when all five private channels were in operation, the national advertising budget rose to Rp. 3335 trillion. Over the same period television's share of this revenue grew from 8 per cent in 1990 to 25 per cent in 1991, to 49.1 per cent in 1995. While the portion of advertising going to all other media fell, their real income from advertisements rose: substantially for newspapers, from Rp. 320 billion in 1990 to Rp. 1538 trillion in 1995, and nominally for the cinemas from Rp. 8 billion to Rp. 11 billion in the same period.[15] In 1995, the commercial stations together generated net revenues of $US326 million and RCTI reportedly contributed 34 per cent of Bimantara's net income.[16]

Over the borders

While domestic economic pressures were clearly pushing for the opening of a potentially lucrative market, technological change was opening Indonesia's borders to televisual incursions from outside. Almost no account of television in the Asian region in the 1980s can be written without reference to this global technological phenomenon. This section attempts to understand the implication of global television changes for the New Order's national televisual project, which we described earlier as the attempt to extend Jakarta's voice and vision to the far corners of Indonesia and beyond.

From around 1983 parabola antennae mushroomed across the skyline of Jakarta's wealthy suburbs and started spreading to other metropolitan cities. Everywhere in Asia, the coming of satellite-transmitted television programs generated new anxiety about Western cultural imperialism. While neighbouring states like Singapore and Malaysia moved quickly to ban domestic use of parabola antennae, the decision was much more complicated for Indonesia. Even after the launch of the more powerful domestic broadcast satellite in 1983 and with over a hundred relay stations, TVRI broadcasts, by its own estimates, covered only about 35 per cent of the nation's land-mass and some 65 per cent of the population. Even on the small and densely populated island of Java, there were blind-spots which TVRI signals could not reach. The parabola antenna, which threatened to allow foreign broadcasts to permeate national boundaries, also held the promise of extending Indonesian national television broadcasts to the corners of the archipelago, beyond TVRI's terrestrial signal range. In

1986, the government officially declared an 'open sky' policy, permitting private and residential use of parabola antennae, which were already in use in many cities. The Department of Information and some regional military commands provided isolated rural communities with parabola antennae to enable them to pick up TVRI signals.

The decree[17] legalising the use of parabola antennae instructed that use be restricted to receiving broadcasts from the national Palapa satellite. But no one pretended that the angle of the antennae could actually be policed. In any case, foreign programming was available on Palapa. By the late 1980s fifteen transponders were used for non-Indonesian channels, including South-East Asian public broadcasts and international operations like NBC, STAR and CNN broadcasting to South-East Asia, earning the government substantial revenues.[18] The number of parabola antennae rose quickly. According to some reports, in the mid 1980s Indonesia had the fastest takeup rate of any Asian nation, with an estimated 25 000 antennae by the end of the decade. The number does not give a full picture of how many people had access to non-national broadcasts through the antennae. Frequently, several houses—according to some estimates up to 500—are connected to a single dish. Depending on the size of the dish, a viewer in Java or Sumatra could pick up six to twenty foreign broadcasts by the mid 1980s.

Even without a parabolic device, residents on the east coast of North Sumatra and in West Kalimantan received spillover broadcasts from Singapore and Malaysia. There are no definitive estimates of the proportion of population that had access to these broadcasts. But internal research by the Department of Information produced worrying data. One study released in 1986 showed that, whereas through most of Indonesia 95 per cent of the televiewers watched TVRI, 'in one province only 41 per cent of the respondents watched TVRI, while 58.5 per cent watched broadcasts from Malaysian television'.[19]

The Sumatran scene was set by changes in regional television. In 1984, the private Malaysian television station TV3 started broadcasting. TV3 was available to much of North Sumatra with a UHF antenna (which cost only a few thousand rupiah) and did not need the far more expensive parabolic ones (in the mid 1980s Rp. 2.5–5 million). According to newspaper reports, TV3 not only decimated TVRI's Sumatran audience, it also sent cinema owners and local video-rental shops broke. Travelling through Sumatra in 1989, we saw many cheap hotel lobby televisions switched almost permanently to TV3; surprisingly, many viewers seemed unaware that they were watching foreign television. Even in Jakarta in that period, the limited capacity of antennae and viewer choice ensured that by far the most frequently picked up foreign channel was a Malaysian one.[20]

It was in the context of dealing with television spillovers from Malaysia that the discussion shifted from alternatives which would allow a government-owned channel to carry advertising (as had been in the case before 1981) to a commitment to private television. The problem was not the distant enemy, the West or the USA, beaming foreign culture, driving a chasm through national cultural and political frontiers. Rather, changes in global television technology had opened up small local footpaths via what Straubhaar has called 'cultural proximity'.[21] The problem of televisual border control for Indonesia derived not from great differences between East and West but from the proximity, the similarities, with a neighbouring country.

In an address in September 1987, the Director-General of Radio, Television and Film spelled out the political imperative upon which the television privatisation policy was grounded. He said that TVRI had reached only 35 per cent of the total area of the country, and 'more than 15 per cent of the area was dominated by foreign broadcasts'. North-eastern Sumatra, West Kalimantan and several other provinces, he said, could be called 'colonies of Malaysian and Singapore television'. He went on to suggest that television should be modelled on the national radio policy, within which private radio stations and the state-owned RRI had acted as a counter to foreign radio broadcasters such as 'BBC–London, VOA–America, and ABC–Melbourne'.[22] A month later, the Minister of Information approved in principle that a 'restricted channel broadcast' (*Siaran Saluran Terbatas*), requiring a decoder for reception, was to be permitted in the capital. The opening line of the ministerial Decree stated 'Remembering the speed of development of information and telecommunication technology, along with the limits of development funds, it is time to look again at the television broadcast that has been available so long'.[23]

From the government's point of view, the 'limits of funds' were real: 'In 1982–86…falling oil prices, rising external indebtedness and a sudden decline in economic growth in 1982 signalled an end to the period of oil-financed growth and abundance'.[24] The introduction and expansion of the private networks seemed to many to be the best option for national cultural defence, which could not be done with the limited resources of state television. In this sense, private television was not a sudden and dramatic surrender of the state's historically legitimised, 25-year-old monopoly of audio-visual broadcasting. That monopoly was threatened in any case. Private television was not a move to liberalise television (in anything but an economic sense of liberalisation); it was a scramble to woo the national audience back to a national media space, with a different kind of television from that which the government was seen as capable of providing.

Programming Changes

In 1990, as the first private channel went free-to-air, the Minister of Information's Decree No. 111 tried to set rules for the operation and programming of the emerging television institutions. Modelled on regulations for the film industry, television programs were required to support the 1945 Constitution and the state ideology Pancasila, and 'avoid issues that might give rise to SARA conflicts'.[25] Further, all programs were obliged to 'support national development plans in accordance with government policy, both domestic and foreign' and they must 'be arranged with full regard to good manners and in *Indonesian language that is true and correct (baik dan benar)*' (our emphasis). Finally, programing must avoid 'all possibility of becoming a channel for the spread of foreign ideology or culture which could weaken the national character and national defence'.

The 'Broadcast Language' section stated that 'formal Indonesian' (*Bahasa Indonesia yang baku*) was to be the principal language of broadcast, and 'English the secondary language, but with English dialogues provided with Indonesian subtitles'. Other foreign languages could only be broadcast in 'language-teaching programs'. Indonesia's regional languages were restricted: 'to be used when suitable for a particular program'.[26]

The emphasis on Indonesian over regional languages was a restatement of long-established TVRI practice, another dimension of the drive for centralisation of television. Local languages on television have always been treated as belonging only to the sphere of 'traditional' culture, strictly excluded from political participation. There have, for instance, never been news broadcasts, talk-shows or children's programs in any local language. Yogya is the most culturally proud Javanese city, with the second-oldest television station in the country. Even there, in 1996 the only Javanese-language programs were the hour of *kethoprak* (folk theatre) every Tuesday evening and an hour of *wayang* (traditional theatre) every other Thursday on the local TVRI, and Saturday late-night *wayang* on Indosiar. With the exception of some popular music programs occasionally featuring a regional-language song, no regional language other than Javanese (in the rare instances mentioned above) was ever heard. On television, local languages are marked as archaic, belonging to traditional cultures of particular geographical areas; they are the museum exhibits of national television.

Foreign content

Although the ministerial Decree stated in general terms that Indonesian television must 'prioritise' domestic productions, private television was introduced with no specific requirement on domestic content. RCTI started broadcasting with almost 90 per cent imported programs (the other 10 per cent relays from TVRI), and quickly earned the nickname Rajawali Citra Televisi *Impor* (instead of *Indonesia*). Even before it went to air Indosiar Visual Mandiri (which could be translated as 'Indo-broadcast Visual Self-reliance) was being denigrated as Indosiar Visual *Mandarin*, partly because its owner is Indonesia's most powerful Chinese businessman, but more because it emerged that the company had a deal with Hong Kong's TV-B under which a group of Hong Kong Chinese producers were to help prepare Indonesian broadcast material for Indosiar.[27] But the proportion of foreign programs on private channels decreased fairly quickly. In 1996, most stations claimed to be broadcasting 35–40 per cent local material. Remarkably, and perhaps a little ironically, given the anxiety about its Chinese connection, within a year of going to air Indosiar was presenting 45 per cent domestic material.

When RCTI first went to air, its 90 per cent imported material was largely American, including old serials like *MacGyver* bought at bargain prices (under $US3000 an episode). But the numerical dominance of US imports was soon challenged. SCTV turned to Hong Kong and Taiwan films. TPI started screening Indian films in early-afternoon slots, some reportedly bought for around a hundred dollars. By 1996, US imports still held the largest share of television hours, but among the thirty most popular programs there were more Asian imports (from Hong Kong, Japan and India) than US ones. Taken together, there were more feature films from India and Hong Kong than from the USA. In daytime soapies, on SCTV Latin American telenovela were dominant. In the lucrative Sunday morning children's hour, Japanese cartoons had overtaken American ones on Indosiar, and on RCTI the two had about equal time (on Japanese cartoons, see Chapter 1).

These calculations of foreign content do not, however, take into account advertisements, which contain some of the most powerful and by far the most expensive, high-production-value images and take up 20 per cent of screentime on all private channels. Legally, all advertisement on television must be produced domestically, using Indonesian backgrounds and artists. This regulation is frequently ignored. But even when advertisements are domestically produced in Indonesian language, their creative control is largely in the hands of foreigners. Indonesia's twelve largest advertising agencies are all affiliated to multinational advertisers and all employ foreigners (mainly Western, but recently some non-Indonesian Asians) as creative director. We could argue that this 20 per cent purportedly Indonesian and most expensive material on television is mainly under foreign creative control.

State television, TVRI, continued to broadcast almost 80 per cent domestic production, with a small amount of English-language imported programs, mainly feature films and serials. But commercial television decimated TVRI's audience. Figures from Survey Research Indonesia (the only ratings agency in Indonesia, henceforth SRI), show that TVRI's peak-hour audience in large cities was about 6 per cent of the population. SRI surveys only five cities and the figures may be slanted in favour of commercial stations which pay for the agency's services. But a 1995 study by the government-funded Indonesian Institute of Scientific Research (Lembaga Ilmu Pengetahuan Indonesia, LIPI) showed that the TVRI following had fallen to 9 per cent among the urban young (aged fifteen to twenty-four). Internal research by the Department of Information in 1996 suggested even lower figures.[28] There is almost no market research on rural audiences, where according to TVRI's own assessment its following remains much higher. The Indonesian Advertisers Association estimated this audience at about 47 per cent in the mid 1990s.[29] Even though imported programming on the private channels declined gradually, by the end of the New Order a far greater percentage of Indonesians were consuming a proportionately greater amount, and variety, of foreign televisual images than in the days of TVRI monopoly (even given the access to parabolic antennae and cross-border spillovers).

While this foreign content on private television may be somewhat domesticated by its passage through formal and informal censorship processes, the state's censorship system was breaking down under the enormous explosion of audio-visual material in the 1990s. As mentioned earlier, Decree No. 111, the first attempt to regulate the content of private television, was modelled on the system of film censorship. In 1993 the government's Board of Film Censorship was recast as an autonomous body, the Institute of Film Censorship (Lembaga Sensor Film, LSF), ostensibly to be more open and accountable to the community but in effect a dumping-ground for retired bureaucrats.[30] The LSF had two viewing rooms operating for six hours each, five days a week, to look at all film, video and television broadcast material. The massive task would have involved reviewing, on average, about eighteen hours of broadcast from each private station (not including approximately two hours of TVRI relay) seven days a week, and (annually) around three hundred films and videos of various types and lengths.[31] Many television programs (such as game shows and talk-shows) were almost impossible to pre-censor. Also, unlike films, which are rechecked by provincial authorities before release in each province, there could be no double-checking of television signals, as they are relayed simultaneously throughout the country.

In the privatised television system, censorship worked much as it had always done on TVRI (most of its programming is exempt from censorship), through self-censorship based on an understanding within senior management about the parameters of tele-visual discourse. As the discussion of news later in the chapter shows, the New Order government was, in any case, far more anxious about domestic information content on television than about imported foreign entertainment.

Local content

Summing up research on national television in the era of satellites, a group of Australian scholars have concluded: 'Television is still a gloriously hybrid medium, with a plethora of programming of an inescapably and essentially local, untranslatable nature'.[32] Whether or not the Indonesian case fits this generalisation depends largely on how we categorise the 'local' in domestic programming. Much domestic programming, as we have indicated, is national in the sense that it is in the national language, formal Bahasa Indonesia, and its content is designed to be acceptable to all its culturally var-ied audiences. TVRI's failure to maintain its audience is, to some extent, evidence that 'national' programming could not compete against imports. There are indications, however, that when domes-tic programming breaks out of the state-imposed national mould to express the 'inescapably...untranslatable' local language and image, it is embraced by audiences.

In 1994, *Si Doel Anak Sekolahan* (Doel the Uni Student) was screened on RCTI. A domestically produced serial, it not only topped the ratings for the year but exceeded all previous ratings for television in Indonesia. Two other kinds of domestic pro-gramming rose to the top of the rating chart in the next two years: Indonesian copies of kung fu films based on old legends, and comedy.

A significant element in *Si Doel*'s appeal for urban audiences (no rural statistics exist) is its emphasis on local specificities, which had been continually pushed aside to valorise the 'national' in Indonesian television. *Si Doel* was set largely in an old Betawi *kampung* (lower-class housing).[33] The Betawi are indigenous residents of the Jakarta area, who have not shared in the economic growth or political power of the city.[34] Much of the serial's dialogue, in the peculiar Malay dialect spoken by this group, is not fully accessible to those who have learnt only formal Indonesian. As the urban youth slang, *prokem*, is a variant of Betawi, the language is understood in Jakarta and other large cities beyond the small Betawi community.[35]

RCTI's first Bahasa Betawi success was *Lenong Rumpi*, a twelve-part comedy program which went to air on 22 June 1991. *Lenong* is a Betawi performance form and the Rumpi group had had enormous success in Jakarta with their live performances. They had initially hoped for a spot on TVRI but were turned down. RCTI not only accepted the series but launched it, symbolically, on the anniversary of the city of Jakarta, amid great publicity for its promotion of a regional culture. *Si Doel* was more remarkable in that it was the first modern television drama substantially in dialect, breaking away from TVRI's practice of programming in a particularly formal version of the Indonesian language. The success of *Lenong Rumpi* and later the outstanding success of *Si Doel* point to the televisual potential of localised speech. In Jakarta, the site of *Si Doel's* language and its story, the series has rated more highly than elsewhere. In its first run in 1994, its rating in Surabaya was about half that of Jakarta. When it started its third run, with two years of national promotion as the 'highest-rated program' ever broadcast in Indonesia (demographic factors ensure that the top of the charts in Jakarta is inevitably the top of the national ratings), the series was only sixth on the ratings card for Medan and second for Surabaya. Even in Bandung, a few hours drive from Jakarta, its ratings were about fifteen points behind those in Jakarta. At the end of its run in December 1996, the series was still top in Jakarta but was not among the top ten in any other city. *Si Doel* was a very local program for Jakarta—not Jakarta as the national capital, but as a particular linguistic and cultural space.

In Indonesia, as elsewhere, television is a medium of the domestic, in the sense of 'near to home, local, parochial'. Measured in terms of any particular locale in Indonesia, the national discourse controlled by a centralised state may be almost as distant and alien as some of the images and messages from across borders. Programmers within TVRI have long been aware of the importance of regional languages and local issues in the battle to win back audiences. Even in the early 1980s there were internal documents pleading for more provincial autonomy. In TVRI Yogyakarta, there was a strong conviction that local language and local performance forms drew large audiences not only in surrounding rural areas but even in the city. The Yogya station ran its regular *wayang* and *kethoprak* broadcasts in the peak viewing period following the evening news.

As TVRI lost its audiences to private television, there was heightened recognition of the need for more localised programming. Despite the centralising drive of the New Order's televison policy, TVRI's funding structure was changed in 1997 to allow regional stations more autonomy. In effect, the production budget of most regional stations increased more than threefold. After Suharto's resignation, decentralisation not only of the public broadcaster but of Indonesia's television institutions as a whole was publicly on the agenda. The new Director-General of Radio, Television and Film used his address on TVRI's 1998 anniversary (often used to informally announce government policy) to indicate a change of direction:

> In the current state of communication and our geographical position, it is appropriate that TVRI...orient itself to the locality where the station is situated, because it is the local stations which most fully understand the situation and condition of the local community. Also the implementation of the concept of 'affiliated station' will make possible the spread of television stations in the regions, carrying locally oriented programming alongside transmissions from relevant [national] broadcasters.[36]

News

Of all televison texts, news was the most directly controlled from Jakarta. Modelled on the regulation for private radio stations, private television broadcasters were not only barred from producing news but were obliged to relay TVRI's national news broadcast from Jakarta. The central TVRI produces four half-hour news programs. The 7 p.m. national and the 9 p.m. international news had to be relayed at the same hour on all channels, barring exceptional circumstances such as ongoing direct telecast of a major event via satellite. The TVRI late news, which closes its daily program, was generally relayed with a few hours delay by the commercial stations. TVRI's two regional news broadcasts (one for the east, one for the west) were relayed only on its regional stations. Each TVRI regional station also broadcasts half an hour of local news, not relayed on any other channel. Commercial stations followed the private radio practice of casting their own news in the guise of 'information'. All had at least one such evening bulletin, before the 7 p.m. news; some rated highly.

The 7 p.m. and 9 p.m. TVRI news roughly marked the two ends of the peak viewing hours and remained important moments at which the whole nation could be addressed.[37] Frequently, particularly at times of political tension, government propaganda programs such as speeches, special reports or 'entertainment' were obligatory relay items for an additional part of peak viewing time. Ratings indicate that during these peak hours, most viewers, including those with parabola antennae, watched an Indonesian channel, whatever the program, thus effectively delivering a large captive national audience.[38]

No news is good news

Other than foreign sourced international news, on the 9 p.m. bulletin we identified four categories of news: state matters that TVRI had been instructed to broadcast, departmental and business publicity that it was paid to broadcast, soft news, and news of the past and the future.

Domestic news on TVRI was almost always 'old news', in the sense that it had already appeared in the papers. Hardly any news was broken on TVRI. This may be because the bulletins appear at the end of the day. But it may be because TVRI news producers had to ensure that no political sensitivity was involved. This judgment was based on how important government departments and senior functionaries reacted to the news in the papers. The pattern was not enforced through external censorship measures, but developed and reproduced in newsroom practices for over thirty years.

By an unspoken but rarely ignored rule, no political incident was covered by TVRI without quoting a government source.[39] For instance, Yogyakarta television was unable to report the murder of a local journalist, Udin (see Chapter 2), although his death was making headlines in the press and the story had appeared on national TVRI bulletins. TVRI Yogya did prepare a report when the National Human Rights Commission was investigating the Udin case, but could not air it because the local police refused to provide TVRI with a comment. In contrast, the local police were extensively interviewed in the local print media, which would have reported on the issue with or without their comments. But police silence effectively muzzled the local broadcaster.

Typically, each item on the TVRI 7 p.m. national bulletin started with a general statement: 'The impact of international culture sometimes brings negative consequences which lead to the flourishing of teenage delinquency. This is being monitored by Golkar'. This was the second item on 27 July 1996, leading into a report on the Minister of Women's Affairs visit to Bengkulu the previous day. Item three on the same day: 'The government will continue to find ways to improve the departure for Haj [pilgrimage]'—linking yesterday's efforts with tomorrow's promises. On most days, every item on the daily national news fitted easily on a continuum where 'today' has no news value, except as a time to recall what happened yesterday and will happen tomorrow—a daily metonymic reminder of the smooth unfolding of national development. We will return shortly to Item One on 27 July 1996, the day of the biggest riots in Jakarta since 1974, which was more difficult to fit into TVRI's normal framework.

What difference did private stations make to the kind of television news that could be produced in Indonesia? The expectations that private television might follow Western conventions of balance in political reporting was not fulfilled. The election campaign of 1997 drew renewed attention to the issue of balance in television coverage of the three political parties, particularly because of the severe restrictions on outdoor campaigning which made radio and television far more important in that campaign than in any previous election. In previous elections TVRI allocated far greater amounts of time to the ruling party, Golkar, than to the two minor parties. The monitoring by AJI (Alliance of Independent Journalists, see Chapter 2) of RCTI, AN-TeVe and TVRI news during the 1997 campaign shows similar discrepancies in election coverage by all stations. From January to March 1997 for instance, AN-TeVe gave 5.58 minutes to Golkar and none to the other parties, RCTI 9.29 to Golkar and just over three to other parties together, and TVRI almost an hour to Golkar and under five minutes to the other two parties combined. Not one mentioned the large political rallies by supporters of ousted PDI leader Megawati, although these featured in the domestic and international press.[40]

Differences between private channels and TVRI emerge, however, when we turn from the content of the story to the formal characteristics of its presentation. The difference is immediately obvious in the mode of address. '*Saudara*' (brothers/sisters/relatives), the address to the national family with which the TVRI news invariably opens, was dropped by the private stations in favour of '*pemirsa*' (viewer or spectator), a functional rather than relational term. The private channel news also resembled Western television news in their use of eyewitness accounts. The RCTI program *Seputar Jakarta* (Around Jakarta), the first of private television's covert news programs, was constructed as a series of vignettes of Jakarta streets, including large segments of vox-pop material, focusing on the 'ordinary citizen'. In contrast, as Kitley points out, in TVRI news the eyewitness and indeed the 'ordinary citizen' construct of Western media is largely absent. When this 'ordinary citizen' is present they are depicted in a structured hierarchical relationship to a dignitary—usually one visiting from Jakarta—who is the focus of the camera and the news commentary.[41] In the news program, called *Seputar Indonesia* (Around Indonesia), which replaced *Seputar Jakarta*, the person on the street, now not only in Jakarta but around the nation, was both visible and vocal. The coverage of the 27 July riots in Jakarta on TVRI and RCTI indicate that these formal differences might have modified viewers' interpretation of news items even when the story content was much the same.

Today's news: or is it?

In 1995 private stations were allowed to produce their own news as long as the incidents reported were more than twenty-four hours old. In effect this was a formalisation of TVRI's practice of presenting political news after official reactions were known. In fact, the private channels covered news on the same day as TVRI, often earlier, as their news slot preceded TVRI's 7 p.m. news. On

27 July, when the supporters of Megawati were ousted from the PDI headquarters and rioting spread through Jakarta, the first television footage was seen nationally on RCTI and SCTV bulletins, preceding the first TVRI national bulletin at 7 p.m.

The Jakarta riot story headed both RCTI's *Seputar Indonesia* and TVRI national news. RCTI gave it six minutes, 4.5 minutes comprising shots of rioting crowds, schoolchildren pouring into streets and snippets of a fiery speech by a member of the government-endorsed faction of the PDI. It gave twenty-three seconds to a government representative (a police lieutenant-colonel). TVRI gave the item 7.5 minutes, an uninterrupted four minutes devoted to the government voice represented by Jakarta military commander Major-General Sutiyoso's briefing to the media on what had happened and how the government had re-established control. The report contained just under three minutes of street scenes, comprising long shots of the rioting crowds, medium shots of the army in riot gear (which could have been stock film) and panning shots of smoke in the sky. Commentary on both stations provided the government's interpretation of the event: that the riots were the result of internal conflict in the PDI, joined by irresponsible elements from outside the party.

The items opened and closed with very different wording. RCTI's opening comment was 'The physical confrontation could not be prevented when the Medan group came to the PDI headquarters occupied by the supporters of Megawati'. Its closing comment was 'As the news of rioting at the PDI headquarters spread, hundreds of people wishing to learn of the situation gathered near Diponegoro Road, which was blocked by security forces'.

TVRI's opening comment was 'The PDI headquarters is now in status quo under police supervision'. It closed with General Sutiyoso speaking direct to camera: 'To officials and the security forces I instruct "Do not hesitate to react in a manner that is professional and proportional"'.

In the RCTI account *something had happened*: despite the best efforts of the government 'the physical confrontation' *had taken place,* resulting in disruption of schools, traffic (roads closed by military) and work (people gathered on the street, not at work). In the TVRI account *nothing had happened after all*: in spite of irresponsible masses status quo existed and the Army would be in control following instructions from above. On 27 July, 'today's news', the biggest riots in Jakarta for twenty-two years, could not be left out of the 7 p.m. bulletin. But it had to be textually transformed into a relative non-event, another exercise in military control and self-control, a story of continuity, of status quo, rather than disruption.

Over the following few evenings, while TVRI news concentrated on senior military officials reassuring citizens of the return to normalcy, RCTI's roving cameras constantly showed empty streets and burnt shops, even though the commentary never expressly deviated from the official position. While television was out of step with the rising dissent, which was more visible in other media forms, the private stations' news format signalled cracks in the didactic monotone of TVRI, if only through the differences between street pictures and official interpretations. And the cracks appeared not only at moments of political upheaval. On any day there was more about criminality or accidents on RCTI's bulletin than on the TVRI national news. In other words, RCTI's reports acknowledged a degree of chaos which was absent from state television national news.

The 'politics of pictures'[42] became evident in the final weeks of Suharto's rule in the private channels' drive for good footage. Student activists were highly critical of the unsympathetic way television was reporting their movement. In contrast, sections of the government were anxious about the constant images of student campuses in city after city, close-ups of the faces and banners of the protesters, letting students on one campus know what was going on in another, letting rioters in one city know what could be got away with in another. The Army considered the private stations' coverage of the events as unacceptable. On 16 May, the day after President Suharto returned from his last overseas trip, General Wiranto's office informed the Minister of Information that the Army would shut all private stations unless they could be brought into line. The newly appointed Director-General of Radio, Television and Film moved to impose the TVRI model on all television. Private stations were instructed not to send cameras to cover riots and student demonstrations, except as part of a team led by a TVRI camera crew. It was a last-ditch and ineffective attempt to replace close-up pictures of chaos with modulated long shots taken by the national broadcaster.

As with radio, so with television. Private stations' practice of news-casting was legalised in the post-Suharto period. At the same time, the obligatory relay was reduced from three TVRI bulletins to two. TVRI's news text itself is beginning to show signs of change, though these are much slower and more erratic than the legislative moves of the new government. As we put the finishing touches to this chapter, some months before the East Timor ballot a senior community leader was interviewed on the 7 p.m. news in the Timorese language, Tetum. It is hard to read an isolated instance such as this, particularly in the context of a highly contested debate over East Timorese independence. The presence of Tetum in a formal interview on national news could signify acknowledgment of Timor's foreignness, or it could be an early sign of a different linguistic regime emerging in a changing political regime.

Conclusion

Television, more than any other medium discussed in this book, was a creature of the New Order. Insignificant in the 1960s, its institutional and textual strategies developed alongside its increasing importance as the key propaganda tool for government policies, and as the site for the regime's definition of Indonesian national culture. We have argued that television was privatised in order to retain central control over cultural consumption of Indonesian citizens, in an era of government financial constraints and an increasingly strong business sector. With operators picked from around the presidential palace, private television may have been expected to deliver to the Suharto regime an audience that was tuning out state television.

On the other hand, the very expansion of the televisual sphere loosened the state's grip over it. Born in an atmosphere of competition, not only against each other but also, against international providers such as CNN, BBC and so on, private television's programming was honed to a quite different purpose: getting audiences to advertisers. In a time when political dissent against the

Suharto leadership was increasingly fashionable among the middle classes, including media professionals, an increasing distance from the official voice was profitable, not-withstanding the owners' closeness to the regime.

We have argued that the New Order government's control over television and its audiences had been eroding since the 1980s. On 3 February 1999, the Minister of Information, Yunus Yosfiah, announced a dramatic expansion of the broadcast sector and the establishment of cable television. Any bona fide business was permitted to establish either free-to-air or cable channel, limited only by available frequencies. Eight new broadcast channels and seven cable channels are already registered, even though the existing private channels are reportedly struggling to survive in the economic downturn since mid 1997. It is unlikely that the market potential of this policy change will be realised without a further policy shift to allow foreign investment in the media.

While President Habibie's family appear keen to enter the televisual fray, it will be impossible in a bigger and more open market to establish the kind of control that the Suharto family had. In any case, the Suharto experiment with private television in Indonesia suggests that ownership gives only incomplete control over the political implications of the medium.

Notes

1   For a detailed account of Indonesian television, including the introduction of private television, see Philip Kitley, 'Television, nation and culture in Indonesia', unpublished PhD thesis, Murdoch University, 1997, an indispensable source for anyone wishing to understand the history and political economy of Indonesian television. We have referred to this and other works by Kitley at several points in this chapter. But beyond that, as we have mentioned in the Acknowledgments, a large part of our engagement with television was shaped during one author's supervision of Kitley's thesis. This chapter thus owes a special thanks to Philip Kitley.

2   J.D. Legge, *Sukarno: A Political Biography*, Penguin, Harmondsworth, 1972, pp. 358–84.

3   Richard Robison, *Indonesia: The Rise of Capital*, Allen & Unwin, Sydney, 1986, pp. 132–53; Hal Hill, 'The economy' (pp. 54–122),

in Hal Hill (ed.), *Indonesia's New Order: The Dynamics of Socio-Economic Transformation*, Allen & Unwin, Sydney, 1994, pp. 61–71.

4   *Laporan Pengembangan Siaran Nasional TVRI 1980–1981*, prepared by the Pusat Penelitian Dan Pengembangan Media Massa (based on several government-funded research reports on television after 1976), Jakarta, 1980/81, p. 8.

5   In India 70–80 per cent of airtime in regional broadcasts is filled with regional-language material produced in the provinces. In China, factory-based and other local stations have created anarchy beyond the control of the central government's CCTV. See Anura Goonasekera & Duncan Holaday (eds), *Asian Communication Handbook*, Amic (Asian Mass Communication Research and Information Centre), Singapore, 1993, p. 116.

6   Kitley, 'Television', p. 92.

7   'Lumun huwus kalah Nusantara, isun amukti palapa, lamun huwus kalah ring Gurun, ring Seran, Tajungpura, ring Haru, ring Pahang, Dompo, Bali, Sunda, Palembang, Tumasik, Samana isun amukti Palapa'. *Sumpah Palapa Gajah Mada*, cited in J.B. Wahyudi, *Televisi Republik Indonesia dan Televisi Siaran*, Mitra Citra Mulia, Jakarta, 1989, p. 21. Our translation is based on the Dutch translation in J.L.A. Brandes, *Pararaton (Ken Arok) of Het Boek der Koninger van Tumapel en van Majapahit*, Martinus Nijhoff, The Hague, 1920. We are grateful to Dr Supomo for his help with interpretation of the quotation.

8   There appears to be some uncertainty about what 'palapa' is. Classical Dutch scholar Zoetmulder says 'I assume that palapa of Pararaton has arisen through metanalysis from palapan, and means "pleasures, relaxation", enjoyed after one has completed one's work, which took all one's time and energy (to rest on one's laurel)': P.J. Zoetmulder, with S.O. Robson, *Old Javanese–English Dictionary*, Martinus Nijhoff, The Hague, 1982, p. 1240.

9   P.T. Cipta Televisi Pendidikan Indonesia, *Company Profile of Televisi Pendidikan Indonesia*, no date (possibly 1992), p. 4.

10 Media Kerja Budaya editorial committee, 'Televisi: Mesin Kebudayaan', *Media Kerja Budaya*, Jakarta, Vol. 2, 1995, p. 9.

11 The figures are *Tempo* magazine's estimates, 17 January 1981, cited in Aloysius Pitono Adhi, 'Gagasan "Pembangunan" dalam TVRI: Analisa Discourse atas Program Siaran TVRI', unpublished Honours (S1) thesis, Department of Communication, University of Indonesia, 1993, pp. 56–7.

12 Adhi, *Gagasan*, p. 61.

13 Interview (Jakarta, June 1998) with Sumadi, who was Director-General of Radio, Television and Film in 1981.

14 See Krishna Sen, 'Si Boy looked at Johnny', *Continuum*, 4:1, 1991, pp. 136–51.

15 Figures taken from Baty Subakti & Ernst Katoppo (eds), *Media Scene 1991–1992 Indonesia*, PPPI, Jakarta, 1992, p. 47, and Baty Subakti & Ernst Katoppo (eds), *Media Scene 1995–1996 Indonesia*, PPPI, Jakarta, 1996, p. 53.

16 Susan Berfield, 'Asia's no pushover', *Asiaweek*, 8 November 1996 on <http://pathfinder.com/@@cKcCMwQAdb@WrYyJ/Asia week/96/1108/cs1.html>; Faith Keenan, 'Murdoch's gambit', *Far Eastern Economic Review*, <http:/www.feer.com/Restricted/july_18/media_ju18.html>.

17 Decree of the Minister for Tourism, Post and Telecommunications, Republic of Indonesia, No. KM 49 Year 1986, on Parabola Antenna Reception of Television Broadcast. Like radio and the Internet, responsibility for the television broadcast system lies with the Department of Tourism, Post and Telecommunications (Deparpostel). Like the Internet (discussed in Chapter 7), television policy in the 1980s was caught between the outward-looking economy- and technology-driven Deparpostel, and the ideological control-driven Department of Information.

18 William Atkins, *Satellite Television and State Power in Southeast Asia: New Issues in Discourse and Control,* Centre for Asian Communication, Media and Cultural Studies, Edith Cowan University, Perth, 1995, p. 25.

19 Cited in Gati Gayatri, 'Apresiasi Masyarakat Terhadap Siaran TVRI', paper presented on behalf of the Research and Development section of the Department of Information at the Seminar Membangun Citra Aara Seni dan Budaya Media Televisi, Yogyakarta, 21–22 August 1996.

20 See for instance T.A. Puri, 'Penggunaan Antena Parabola Di Kalangan Pemirsa Televisi Di Jakarta', unpublished Honours (S1) thesis, University of Indonesia, 1988.

21 Joseph Straubhaar, 'Beyond media imperialism: Asymmetrical interdependence and cultural proximity', *Journal of Critical Studies in Mass Communication*, 8:1, 1991, pp. 39–59.

22 M. Adhi Wibowo, 'TVS: Menuju Masyarakat Informasi', *Merdeka*, 5 September 1987.

23 Decree of the Minister of Information of the Republic of Indonesia, No. 190A/KEP/MENPEN/1987, dated 20 October 1987.

24 Hal Hill, 'The Indonesian economy: The Strange and sudden death of a tiger; (pp. 95–103) in Geoff Forester & R. J. May (eds), *The Fall of Soeharte*, Crawford House, Bathurst, 1998.

25 The term 'SARA' was coined to refer to anything likely to exacerbate tensions based on ethnicity (Suku), religion (Agama), race (Ras) or between social groups or classes (Antar golongan).

26 Minister of Information's Decree No. 111, 1990.

27 For details see Kitley, 'Television', Ch. 9.

28 Last two sets of figures cited in Gayatri, 'Apresiasi'.

29 Koes Pudjianto, 'TVRI Sebagai Inisiator Pengembangan Industri Pertelevisian Nasional', paper presented at the Seminar Membangun Citra Acara Seni dan Budaya Media Televisi, Yogyakarta, 21–22 August 1996.

30 In its 1996 membership there was not one person born since 1955, and several born in 1925.

31 In the financial year 1996/97, the Institute claimed to have 'censored 68 national commercial films and 184 imported commercial films, 78 national non-commercial films and 58 imported non-commercial films' plus '6865 national commercial and non-commercial video films, and 10478 imported commercial and non-commercial videos': Department of Information, *Indonesia 1998: An Official Handbook*, Jakarta, 1998, p. 223.

32 John Sinclair, Elizabeth Jacka & Stuart Cunningham (eds), *New Patterns in Global Television: Peripheral Vision*, OUP, Oxford, 1996, p. 10.

33 For a discussion of what *kampung* housing represents socially and its implication in Indonesian audio-visual media representations, see Krishna Sen, *Indonesian Cinema: Framing the New Order*, Zed Books, London and New Jersey, 1994, pp. 115–16.

34 For a history of the Betawi people in Jakarta, see Susan Abeyasekere, *Jakarta: A History*, OUP, Oxford and New York, 1987, particularly pp. 64–7, 191–6, 232–7.

35 Henri Chambert-Loir, 'Those who speak *Prokem*', *Indonesia*, 37, April 1984, pp. 105–17; Prathama Rahardja & Henri Chambert-

Loir (eds), *Kamus Bahasa Prokem*, Pustaka Utama Grafiti, Jakarta, 1988.

36 S.K. Ishadi, 'Implementasi Kebijakan Penyiaran Menghadapi Tata Masyarakat Baru' in Retno Intani (ed.), *Sarasehan Nasional Pertelevisian*, papers from seminar on the 36th anniversary of TVRI, 1998, Aditya Media, Yogyakarta, 1998, p. 31.

37 Analysing TVRI news, Kitley makes a cogent argument about the 'ritual-like' structure of Indonesian news which distinguishes it from the kind of text that is seen as 'news' in the West. In Kitley's terms, this ritual reinforces the cohesion of Indonesian society both vertically (across hierarchical categories) and horizontally (across geographical distances): see Kitley, 'Television', Ch. 6, particularly p. 237. That ritual of physical cohesion begins to unravel a little when, for instance, the RCTI audience watching the World Cup Soccer does not watch the 7 p.m. news until a few hours after the rest of the nation and TVRI's 10.30 late-night news does not appear on other stations till 2 a.m the next morning.

38 We base this conclusion on SRI ratings (which we sighted) during a two-part drama *Terjebak* (Trapped) relayed simultaneously on all channels, 28–29 September 1996. It was a fictionalised account of the 27 July 1996 incident as a neo-Communist plot.

39 This analysis is based on observations and interviews in the TVRI Yogyakarta newsroom, but appears to be a common condition throughout regional stations. The Jakarta situation is slightly different because intense attention from national and international press occasionally forces issues onto the national news broadcasts.

40 Alliance of Independent Journalists, 'Monitoring television for the general elections', unpublished report circulated by e-mail, May 1997.

41 Kitley, 'Television', Ch. 6, particularly pp. 219–25.

42 This phrase is from the title of John Hartley's *The Politics of Pictures: The Creation of the Public in the Age of Popular Media,* Routledge, London and New York, 1992.

5

NATIONAL CINEMA: GLOBAL IMAGES, CONTESTED MEANINGS

Since the advent of video in the early 1980s what constitutes film, where and how it is watched and therefore how it might be regulated and governed have become open questions. Further, as indicated in Chapter 4, since the late 1980s national (though not state-controlled) television with its fast-expanding audiences has taken centre-stage in the discussion of national culture. Indeed, it is on the small screen that most Indonesians see films: American, Chinese, Indian and Indonesian.[1] In the 1990s, with the rapid decline in the number of Indonesian films, television absorbed the former workers of the film industry, now turning their hands to producing telefilms on videotapes, called *sinetron* in Indonesia. The number of companies making features (on celluloid) for cinemas fell from ninety-five in 1991 to just thirteen in 1994. Over the same period, feature video producers rose from sixty to eighty-nine.[2]

This absorption of the film industry, its workers and its functions into television means that the practices, codes and rules (aesthetic and political) developed within the New Order's film industry are shaping the highly popular television *sinetron*. So, though the Indonesian film industry may be comatose, in its history we discover the formation of the archetypal national audio-visual fiction which, revised for a different medium,[3] is getting wider circulation via televison. In this chapter we analyse the predominant patterns and forms of this 'national fiction', produced and reproduced in film in the New Order.[4] Much of this history predates video technology and private and global television unsettling the methods of cultural border control. In the first half of the chapter we argue that as the film industry expanded in the 1970s, in a new political context, it developed a particular social vision and a narrative form predicated on the vision of 'order' that legitimised the repressive New Order regime. The second half of the chapter charts the changes of the 1990s as the New Order's grip over cultural institutions slowly slipped. Though the institutions and regulations of the 1970s remained, new communication technologies, the increasing circulation of global imagery and the mounting local discontent against the New Order and its mechanisms of control, transformed the way in which Indonesian film texts were constructed/encoded and received/decoded.[5]

The Film Regime of the New Order

The key institutional structures through which cinema was governed and controlled in the New Order were partly inherited from the colonial period—the board of film censorship set up in 1925 and the state-owned ANIF (Algemeen Nederlandsch-Indisch Film) which started producing features and documentaries in 1936. The Japanese period (1942–45), though brief, further strengthened the state's role in film production,[6] training native Indonesians in news and propaganda films. The national government maintained both institutions and in the Guided Democracy (1957–65) era the state film company (now called Perusahaan Film Negara, PFN) churned out reels of Sukarno images while the Board of Film Censorship (Badan Sensor Film, BSF) took a leading role as the ultra-nationalist gatekeeper of Indonesian culture, keeping out the political and sexual 'excesses' of Hollywood cinema.

Much more than television and even more than radio (under state control until 1972, see Chapter 3), cinema was laden with a political history by the time of the New Order. Ideals about film content were shaped largely by the perception of cinema as a site of political discourse in the last years of Sukarno's rule and the violent anti-Communism and indeed the anti-politics ethos of the early New Order period. Cinema was deeply implicated in the political polarisation of the early 1960s. Hollywood films were a key symbol in the hyper-nationalist critique of Western imperialism, and were banned in October 1964.[7]

In the purges that followed the accession of Major-General Suharto, all left-wing elements were excised from cinema (and from the rest of Indonesian cultural life). Prominent leftist film-makers were jailed or, at the very least, they were excluded from all media—leftist cultural organisations were destroyed, their films and ideologies banned. However, the institutional basis for controlling film content, devised in the closing months of Sukarno's government was retained. A presidential Decree in 1964 placed all aspects of cinema (previously overseen by four different ministries) within the Department of Information. Cinema became defined as a 'mass medium', like radio, press and television, while other cultural activities like the arts, theatre and literature remained under the Department of Education and Culture. This institutional demarcation between 'media' and 'art' became more marked later in the New Order when, in 1978, the Department of Information was placed under the aegis of the Coordinating Minister of Politics and Security, and the Culture portfolio in the jurisdiction of the Coordinating Minister of People's Welfare. Positioning cinema within the state apparatus emphasised the ideological and propaganda aspects of films, rather than their artistic and creative dimension.

Institutions of order

The New Order, as we suggested in the Introduction to this book, represented itself as a political foil to the revolutionary excesses of the Old (dis)Order of Sukarno's government. In this context, New Order Indonesian film policy moved from the nationalist rhetoric of guarding against foreign film incursions to policing the works of Indonesian film-makers.

In a dramatic reversal of the ban on Hollywood films, the film market was thrown open to foreign imports. In 1967 the annual number of imported films rose to about 400 and nearly doubled in 1969. The removal of political constraints on business relations with Hong Kong and Taiwan allowed Chinese business contacts to be revived, so Chinese films (from these two countries) became a major part of the import sector for the first time since the 1930s.

There was, however, no rethinking about censorship, and other than the removal of left-wing board members, no immediate change to BSF's structure. Pre-censorship as a condition of production has always distinguished films from all other private sector media. Inherited from the Dutch era, the BSF is the oldest and most persistent institution of Indonesian cinema. But new layers of pre-censorship were added in the first decade of the New Order, which resulted in locally produced films being even more stringently censored than imported ones. From 1976 onwards every person working on a film needed to obtain permission from a professional organisation authorised by the government.[8] Since the early 1970s film scenarios required approval from the Directorate of Film in the Department of Information before shooting could start. At the completion of shooting, the rush copy (unedited prints) had to be submitted to the same authorities for 'guidance' about what might have to be edited out. These informal (but never disregarded) stages of censorship became discreet modes of government control over local production.

Until the early 1960s the composition of the BSF was such that censorship could be, and often was, responsive to popular pressure and the socio-cultural sensitivities of Indonesia's diverse communities. Under the New Order the institutional control of censorship passed gradually from community representatives to government departments, particularly security agencies like the police department and the Intelligence Agency (BAKIN). Through the 1970s and 1980s, the BSF's openness to society in general and its willingness to accommodate pressures, apart from pressure by state functionaries, declined markedly. To all intents, administrative changes during 1978–82 (with the Information portfolio in the hands of former Intelligence Chief, General Ali Murtopo) returned film censorship to its colonial function—as an arm of the government's internal security apparatus.[9] In 1992, the Board of Censorship was renamed Lembaga Sensor Film (LSF, Institute of Film Censorship) and became in theory a quasi-government agency, but with little real change in its practices or structure. It remained responsible to the Minister of Information and its proceedings were strictly confidential. While the LSF is responsible for censoring all audio-visual material distributed, screened or broadcast in Indonesia, television news, current affairs and live broadcasts are exempt from pre-censorship requirements. By all accounts, the censorship of television advertising and video clips is more nominal than real. Generally, censorship only affected films and telefilms.

Rules of order

There were various attempts to codify censorship practices after 1965. In 1977 the first systematic Censorship Guideline laid down in a ministerial Decree practices that had become the norm since 1965. In 1981 the National Film Council (the government-funded industry advisory body) published its Production Codes. Government Regulation No. 7 of 1994 was the final restatement of those provisions, until the end of the New Order. Although the government's public relations pronouncements emphasise censorship of sex and violence and protection of national culture, these elements occupy a comparatively small portion of regulatory documents.[10] The 1977 Censorship Guideline, for instance, has only one direct reference to sex in its list of twenty-four criteria for banning or cutting films: a warning to 'films which emphasise sex and violence'. The 'general principles' in the Introduction to the Censorship Guideline states, 'As a consequence of our involvement in international communication, we cannot isolate ourselves from the influence of foreign culture entering Indonesia through film [among other means], be they foreign or national films containing foreign ingredients. This has both positive and negative elements'. There is no further reference to foreign culture in the list of criteria, other than the banning of ideologies of 'colonialism, imperialism, fascism' and all forms of Communism, which in Indonesian political discourse are often seen as foreign.

The strongest theme in the regulatory documents is an injunction to avoid all reference to social conflict or tension in Indonesia. Thus films are to be banned or excised if they are deemed likely to destroy the unity of religions in Indonesia, harm the development of national consciousness, exploit feelings of ethnicity, religion or ancestry, even arouse sentiments of ethnicity, religion and race, or engender social tension, including between social classes. Films are forbidden to express dissent against government policies or anything that could cause damage to persons or institutions associated with the state. Government Regulation No. 7 of 1994 states that films promoting 'an analysis or political ideology of false accusations which might be seen as disturbing the stability of the nation' will be automatically banned.

The Production Codes developed in 1981 by the Film Council, a body with a promotional rather than policing role in the industry, recast the censors' proscriptions as positive prescriptions. Accordingly, Indonesian films 'need to express' the 'harmonious coexistence of religions' and 'mutual respect for the practice of faith in accordance with the religion and belief of each person'. Films are also urged to show 'how Indonesian people put unity, unification as well as the well-being of the nation and the state above personal and group interests' and to include episodes 'which emphasise the values of…national unity'. Films are not to include 'any statement which may lead to the decline of the community's trust in the organisations of justice', they may not deride the 'upholders of law and order', nor show police officers being killed by criminals. Indeed, crimes may only be depicted if they are shown as being punished, and in stories involving kidnapping the child must be returned unharmed by the end of the film.[11]

The foregoing account suggests that restrictions were not so much against foreign cultural imports as they were against the political and cultural options of Indonesian film-makers. Censorship regulations and processes were designed primarily to shape the narrative of Indonesian films—to produce film texts that would show a state in total control and a nation united. The state institutions of particular concern were the justice and police departments—institutions which tame citizen dissent. These controls seem even more odious when we recognise that since the late 1970s (after a period of import reduction in 1974–78) successive government legislation had strengthened the hands of importers and permitted imported films to take an increasing share of the market.[12] Ironically, the assumption that national cinema had the power of political persuasion worked against the commercial viability and the artistic freedoms of Indonesian national cinema in the New Order.

Texts of order

We have argued so far that the New Order's concern with an ordered politics was reflected in its censorship practice, the primary aim of which was to control the message of locally made films. Censorship and trade do not, of course, make up the entire 'media ecology' in which films are made and consumed. Channels of aesthetic judgment such as film festivals and critical acclaim, state and private funding, and the political and cultural context generally, all affect the formation of screen texts. Indeed, any textual formation is so complex that it is impossible to isolate the precise factors that may have shaped it. We argue that the archetypal film text of the New Order is, like the legitimising rhetoric of the regime itself, about the 'restoration of order'. This constant reiteration of 'order' in film texts is maintained to some extent by censorship, both the actual intervention of censors and self-censorship driven by the threat of intervention. We will look closely at one text, a much-censored film about contemporary social issues, to unpack the metaphor of order that runs through New Order films.

In its most productive years, mid 1970s to mid 1980s, the Indonesian film industry spawned a great variety of genres. We could have chosen any number of films from that decade for the purpose of our analysis. *Perawan Desa* (*Village Virgin*), which we discuss in some detail, is exemplary in that it provides a model of cinematic excellence in a period which was not only the high point of Indonesian cinema, but also the mid-life of the New Order. There were of course exceptions to the archetype, both during that period and before and after; we discuss these later in this chapter.

The most controversial film of 1978, *Perawan Desa* was held by the BSF for a year and substantially changed before release. At the 1980 Indonesian Film Festival (FFI), the film won the three most coveted awards, Best Director, Best Scenario and Best Film. Neither before nor since has any film which had so much difficulty getting through the censorship process been so richly rewarded by the festival jury.[13]

The film was based on a criminal law suit. Sumariyam, seventeen years old, from a village near Yogyakarta, was pack-raped by well-connected young men in September 1970. But the police produced false evidence in preliminary hearings, so that the culprits were never brought to court. Even their names were never made public, although there were hints about their identities in press reports.

The film closely followed popular knowledge and popular perceptions about the rape incident. Sumira, a schoolgirl from a poor village family, sells eggs in the city of Yogyakarta. There are rumours in her village and in the city marketplace that there have been several rapes in town, all committed by the same group of young men, who are protected by their fathers' high offices. Early scenes establish the city-slick, would-be rapists and their friends as rich, immoral and Westernised (which in the language of the film are identical), and the villagers as ethical, communal and Islamic. About twenty minutes into the film, Sumira is dragged into a jeep, raped by four men and dumped on the roadside. Sympathetic students, journalists and lawyers come to her aid and rally public opinion against the criminals. Meanwhile, the rapists use their contacts in the highest quarters of the police force to get protection from publicity and prosecution. The Yogya Police Commissioner obliges by arresting students and journalists. Failing to stem the tide of public sympathy for Sumira, the Commissioner takes her into custody, claiming it is for her own security. Isolated from her friends and supporters and under police pressure, Sumira not only withdraws the rape allegation but agrees to falsely confess that she concocted the rape story. Sumira then stands trial on the charge of misleading the public.

In court, the police produce false witnesses who collapse in the face of the defence lawyer's cross-examination. Finally, the terrified defendant is put on the stand and breaks down sobbing: 'I was raped by long-haired boys. But I was forced to say things that were not true'. The case against Sumira is dismissed for lack of evidence. She leaves the court supported by her parents and her lawyer. The final shot shows a fainting Sumira against a hazy background of the sympathetic, critical and curious public, and pages of newspapers, carrying her story, scattered across the screen.

That is how *Perawan Desa* originally ended: an indictment of the law-enforcing authorities and, by extension, of the state which favours the rich and powerful. The middle-class professionals, despite their best efforts, can do little against the travesty of justice. The closing images, of a disorderly street with crowds almost bursting the borders of the screen, printed pages in disarray and a chaotic soundtrack, might easily be read as a cinematic metaphor of social disorder. The film came to BSF in 1978. The three board members who initially viewed the film, rejected it. It went to a plenary session on appeal from the producer. An addition to the ending was devised that would substantially change what the censors considered an unacceptable conclusion.

The added sequence takes only about seven minutes. After Sumira's trial, three of the criminals are irate as they listen to news of the trial, on the radio. The fourth member of the gang, who has been out pushing cocaine (for the first time in the film!), rushes in, announcing that he has been spotted by the police. All four then jump into a car and try to make a getaway with the police in hot pursuit. The chase ends with a car crash that severely injures the four criminals. As the wailing ambulance draws up in front of the hospital, Sumira emerges in a nurse's uniform. She is telling an old friend how wonderful everybody has been to her and how new opportunities have opened up because of people's sympathy. She sees the blood-drenched and groaning accident victims being brought in and recognises them. Asked whether she is still bitter about those who caused her to suffer so much, she says, looking at the men on the stretchers: 'They have already received the punishment they deserve'.

The new ending thus carried reassurance about the maintenance of natural and social justice even when institutions have failed. It ensured that Sumira saw and accepted that her tormentors had received their punishment. Though the rape went unpunished, the police were, in the end, instrumental in retribution for the criminals and agents of the restoration of order. The new closing scene, a striking contrast to the old one, showed the serenely confident heroine, in pristine white, with well-modulated speech (in the classic moralising tone of Indonesian cinema), standing at the centre of the screen framed by the walls of the hospital: the disorder triggered by the excesses of the wealthy and the breakdown of the institution of security were resolved in the image of another respectable institution.

This implausible 'happy ending' tacked onto a narrative of tragedy and disaster was not invented by the censors for this film. Since the mid 1970s, when films began to address issues of social conflict, there were many films that dealt with poverty and exploitation but resolved all contradictions in the last moments. Indeed, that became the formula for dealing with social issues while evading censors' cuts. In 1981, with the experience of *Perawan Desa* and the government's intervention in its production, the film industry finally codified that formula in the Production Codes discussed earlier, as the requirement that crimes in films must be shown to be punished. With few exceptions, films made between the mid 1970s and the mid 1980s followed a narrative structure from order, through disorder to restoration of order. This formal characteristic was not altered substantially by differences in themes, genres or other aesthetic attributes.

Disorderly Readings

How were these 'orderly' texts read by their audiences? The fact that Indonesian cinema has never had a large national following may suggest a degree of resistance to the kind of texts it produces. More importantly, those who watch the films may interpret them in ways that vary greatly from the views of bureaucrats at BSF or producers who only want to fund politically safe films. In some cases, critical opinion provides a clue about how a film might be read. For example, the seven-member jury (including prominent writers and intellectuals) who awarded the 1980 'Best Film' to *Perawan Desa* evaluated the film without reference to the tacked-on happy ending:

> *Perawan Desa* is a film of very high social relevance, extremely relevant in the efforts of the Indonesian people to search for and establish truth and justice and [it] depicts clearly the fate of the little people (*rakyat kecil*) who suffer trampled by injustice. The film also shows the courage of the citizens, both men and women, including journalists and youth, who become involved, individually and socially, in the defence of someone who becomes the victim of arbitrary authority.[14]

No mention of the narcotics, the good work of the police or the punishment of the criminals!

However, most of what we might call 'reading against the grain'[15] appears not in formal reports but in what Ben Anderson dubbed 'direct speech': 'gossip, rumours, discussions, arguments, interrogations, intrigues',[16] in other words, the major part of the 'fluid and ephemeral' day-to-day communication between citizens, which is generally inaccessible to academic discourses. Contemporary audience research almost unanimously suggests[17] that state control (or control by producers, creators or encoders) over the meaning of screen texts is never perfect or complete. Yet this level of spectatorial autonomy seems politically insignificant when the contradictory meanings made in the privacy of individuals' reception have no public or collective resonance.

In the 1990s the advent of the Internet made it possible to access some forms of informal speech, eroding some of the demarcation between formal (written or broadcast) speech and informal, ephemeral, direct speech, by making certain gossip and chat available beyond face-to-face conversation. We will return to this issue in Chapter 7, but here we want to draw attention to the relatively wide circulation of 'readings against the grain', readings that resist the official interpretations of a particular film.[18] We argue that circulation on the Internet of dissident readings of a propaganda film, *Pengkhianatan Gerakan 30 September (Treachery of 30 September Movement)*, makes these readings at once accessible, collective and political.

In 1981, the state film company Pusat Produksi Film Negara (PPFN) assigned the controversial director Arifin C. Noer to work on a docudrama of the events of 30 September 1965. *Pengkhianatan* was a colossal, big-budget production—five-and-a-half hours of violence and political speeches. This was Arifin's second propaganda film for the government; the first, *Serangan Fajar (Dawn Attack)* was a fictional film about Indonesia's 'war of independence', with Suharto as military hero.[19] *Pengkhianatan* was the first full-length feature on the events of 1965 funded by the New Order government. For all practical purposes, the film was the work of Brigadier-General G. Dwipayana, who was then Director of the PPFN and a member of the President's personal staff. He was especially responsible for matters relating to the mass media. Any summary of the film, taken from the press, would sound like a repetition of the story told often by New Order authorities and historians about what happened in the early hours of 1 October 1965 and its aftermath: a group of Army officers under the leadership of Colonel Untung planned a coup to overthrow the Sukarno government and install the Communist Party of Indonesia in power. Untung's men, together with members of the Communist Party, kidnapped six top generals and brutally slaughtered them. Chaos followed, until troops under the control of Major-General Suharto captured Untung and destroyed the Communist leadership.

Pengkhianatan was not released through normal commercial channels, partly because PPFN was not willing to risk its commercial failure and the significance of such audience apathy. Instead, the film became compulsory screening for schools and government departments, and from the mid 1980s to 1997 was broadcast annually around 30 September on TVRI and relayed on every private station since their establishment. It is the single most-broadcast Indonesian film and, if the ratings for 30 September 1997 can be trusted, it is also, almost without doubt, the single most-watched Indonesian film.

There had been some debate in the media about the historical accuracy of the first Suharto propaganda film (*Janur Kuning (Yellow Coconut Leaf)*, 1980) depicting his role in military battles against the Dutch. But carefully orchestrated media coverage and the extreme sensitivity of its subject-matter prevented immediate public questioning of the historicity of *Pengkhianatan*. In the 1990s, the previously muted discussion about the incidents of 1965 became increasingly public in small publications, pamphlets and the Internet.[20] It is in the context of this increasingly open political dissent that disorderly, 'against the grain' readings of some films become visible and viable as political activity.[21]

In February 1996, the Solo branches of all three political parties called for the banning of a James Bond film, *Golden Eye*, on the grounds that it contained the image of a hammer and sickle, a symbol associated with the banned Indonesian Communist Party (PKI). The parties expressed concern that exhibition of the symbol might 'provoke the community' (*meresahkan masyarakat*).[22] In response, one university student wrote to the Apakabar Internet mailing list: 'Does a symbol as a mere symbol have the magical power to turn viewers into Communists?...Even the film G30S/PKI [*Pengkhianatan*] which clearly depicts the hammer and sickle flag? Indeed the film is broadcast every year'. The writer disputed official readings of other banned films and pointed out the failure of censorship:

> I have seen the film *Schindler's List* (banned in Indonesia). And I can judge that what is intended as its message is not just a defence of the Jews repressed by the Germans. But more than that it can also mean a defence of any nation repressed by another. And that can be Palestinians repressed by the Jews, Indians by Yankees and Spaniards, Aborigines by Australians, also Indonesians repressed by other Indonesians.[23]

A year later, discussion about *Pengkhianatan* reappeared in much greater detail in the context of another failed government propaganda exercise. The Minister of Youth Affairs proposed a seminar to discuss Sukarno's 1967 speech to the parliament as part of the reignited anti-Communist, anti-Sukarnoist propaganda in the aftermath of the 27 July affair. The idea of the seminar was abandoned after a few weeks for fear of raising controversial issues, but there was a certain amount of historical reassessment in the print media and more on the Internet, including expressions of doubt about the historical accuracy of *Pengkhianatan*. On the *SiaR* mailing list, on 16 September (a fortnight before the inevitable television screening of the film), a long message declared that 'critical opinion' had assessed Arifin's film as a 'double-edged sword'. A typical chatty posting, it did not identify its sources or distinguish between analysis and opinion, conversation and printed material:

> In the last seven years there have been various new assessments [of the film] which seem to have escaped the attention of the Department of Information. For instance...the film shows that only a few people knew of the G30S plans...If only a small section of the PKI leadership and military agents knew about it, how is it that over a million people were killed and thousands of people who knew nothing had to be imprisoned, exiled and lost their civil rights?
>
> Secondly, the film showed more the involvement of the military...rather than of the PKI mass organisations. Thirdly, when the film was shown at some of Jakarta's most popular state high-schools, where students come from families of civilian bureaucrats

and military, they cheered [*bersorak-sorai*] when they saw that our revolutionary heroes were being tortured. They were pleased that there had been people who could oppose the military, and even Generals.[24]

The writer questioned the value of broadcasting the film 'again in a few days', wondering how many people would watch the film and what 'their comments and opinions might be'. He concluded that the PKI leadership, were they able to, should give 'the "PKI Award" to the Minister of Information who continues repeatedly to broadcast this film of national tragedy'. Other contributions over the next few days added to the dissident reading, thus turning anonymous individual interpretations into collective social meaning defying the film's propaganda purposes.

A number of related points need to be made. There is little doubt that spectators, Indonesian spectators included, make different sense of films from those prescribed by official institutions. In the mid 1990s in Indonesia these counter-readings were entering public political discourse not only because there was a new technology that operated without the structural and aesthetic constraints of older media,[25] but also because new readings 'against the grain' of propagandised and censored films were emerging in the context of heightening political dissent. The dissident readings and their circulation on the Internet indicated some of the cracks in the New Order's methods of media control, including its governance of cinema through censorship and propaganda.

We have argued that the archetypal New Order film moves from order to disorder to restoration of order. Disorderly readings are not the only threat to this authorised story in the New Order films. The arrival of video technology in Indonesia not only temporarily eroded the cinema market but, as in every other market, put new choices in the hands of the Indonesian viewers—of watching a film where and when they liked, turning it on and off, fast-forwarding, watching the film in bits and out of sequence. In theory, the video had the potential to severely disorganise the narrative order (and the ordered narrative) of Indonesian films. Whether and to what extent this actually happens is not easy to establish. But the advent of video did provide a way to beat censors' bans on particular films and the monopoly of one import and distribution company (partly owned by the President's cousin Sudwikatmono) in the industry. It became increasingly common and fashionable to organise video screenings of foreign films that had been banned by censors or not imported into Indonesia for commercial reasons. In elite circles in Jakarta, it had always been possible to watch films banned for the general public. It is said that Sukarno himself made sure that he saw the Hollywood films that his lieutenants declared unsuitable for the nation. Since the mid 1980s videos and laser discs have put officially banned foreign films within relatively easy reach of the well-travelled urban middle-classes, particularly students, intellectuals and cultural workers. Screenings of uncensored material frequently took place in public venues such as NGO offices and were advertised through posters, on campuses and at open gatherings.

Changing Formats

In the late 1980s a new film form—serialised films—grew enormously in popularity. *Catatan Si Boy* (*Boy's Diary*) (first episode released in 1987) and *Saur Sepuh* (first episode in 1988) set the pattern for two very different kinds of serials, and remained among the top-grossing films for the next five years, reportedly outselling all imported films in 1988–89.[26] The serialised film form was born partly out of advertisers' need to reach a growing market, after the best access had been severed in 1981 by a government ban on television advertising. Since video players and video rentals were rapidly expanding in the Indonesian market, advertisers quickly turned to video magazines with serialised stories to keep viewers returning for the next episode. Serialised films shown in cinemas were an extension of this video advertising experiment. *Saur Sepuh*, a fantasy set in the last days of Java's Majapahit empire (fifteenth century), a refinement of earlier Indonesian films about mythical and mystical heroes of the past was, on the surface, an unlikely vehicle for advertising messages at the end of the twentieth century. But it was partially funded by a national pharmaceutical company producing traditional cures, which were advertised on the film's posters and at screenings.

The better vehicle for advertisements, *Catatan Si Boy,* had a very different heritage. It started as a weekly hour-long radio serial in 1985 on a commercial station which played the 'top 40s' and had a strong following among young Jakartans. The story centred on Boy, a smart secondary-school kid from a super-rich family, and his friends. There were similar teenage heroes in serialised books. The most successful of them, *Lupus* (discussed in Chapter 1), was filmed in a series of five episodes, starting the same year as *Si Boy.* Lupus, Boy and similar characters could be related to the rise of the teenage market generated by the growth and prosperity of the upper- and middle-classes in the 1980s—a market that advertisers were keen to reach. Boy, the super-rich kid with a taste for brand-name products, was a good way to reach consumers, particularly in a serialised story which could depend on a regular following, both in terms of a specific demographic and regular access. The soap opera, in its original sense of a play that included advertising (initially on radio, later on television), was thus reinvented for the big screen in Indonesia. Many imitations followed, one even called *Catatan Si Doi.*

Each *Si Boy* segment ends with the possibility of another beginning. *Si Boy I* ends with Boy's break-up with a girlfriend, *II* starts with new girl Vera and ends with a tiff about Boy's plans to go to Los Angeles to study. *III* takes us through Los Angeles tourist sites and lots of simulated US television advertising (mostly Pepsi, which partly funded this production), small skirmishes and a new friendship with a Filipino girl. The film ends with Boy and his new and old friends skylarking in a park. End of film, but clearly not of the story. *Si Boy* films always end with 'see you later' (*sampai ketemu lagi*) never the usual *tamat* (the end).

It is not so much that the narrative has an open ending that leaves the audience to imagine various and contradictory closures, but rather that the film stops at a particular point in the story that we know will keep on going. This lack of closure in *Si Boy* sagas marks a change from what we have described as the archetypal audio-visual text of the 1970s and 1980s. As we have shown, how a story ends was very important in the making of Indonesian films, because censorship codes and practices insisted on a certain kind of closure to ensure a morally correct, politically convenient interpretation. Like television soaps, *Si Boy* films are filmed in present continuous, rather than the past perfect tense of the typical Indonesian film which starts with a crisis that is resolved at the end of the film.

In terms of its settings, images, stars, characters and audiences, the *Si Boy* series belongs to the *film remaja* or 'teenage film' genre, which has grown in popularity since the mid 1970s. In keeping with the dominant formal character of Indonesian cinema, *film remaja*, which depend on the construction of teenagers visually, socially and linguistically as a distinct group, generally conclude with their assimilation into the adult world, either through the teenage lovers getting married (thus graduating into orderly adulthood), resolving their conflict with their parents, or both. Teenage is defined as a phase of life, which might involve unruly behaviour and conflict; these problems are resolved through growing up, which means accepting social rules. This narrative device simultaneously acknowledges and denies generational conflict. By avoiding closure Boy escapes the need to accept the orderly life of adulthood. The film can allow aberrant practices, and plain bad behaviour, without having to condemn them in a morally correct conclusion. Boy's best friend Emon's effeminate behaviour is sometimes the brunt of jokes, but it is never 'reformed' or 'forgiven'—it does not even have to be 'accepted' in some generous gesture—as any sign of homosexuality must be in the average Indonesian film. Emon and the Filipino girl (in *Si Boy III*) who make passes at both Boy and his girlfriend are accepted with no more comment than 'they're both a bit off'.

Boy's unending story leaves options for the film's characters and viewers that the constant pressure to resolve conflicts in favour of the older generation and the 'establishment' does not. Epri, a young college student who played Boy in the radio serial, said of himself and his alter ego, '*hobinya ngtrend*' [favourite pastime, being trendy]. Boy is always dressed in the latest fashions, eating the latest fashion foods and using trendy 'Engdonesian' language (Indonesian peppered with English expressions). Boy's defining characteristic is that he is 'in', he is 'now'; past and future are both much less important than the 'current'. The structure of the films and the characterisation of Boy make them perfect vehicles for a consumer culture, and, at the same time, a breach in the discourse of order in New Order cinema.

Much of what we have argued about *Si Boy* holds true for the most popular genre of audio-visual texts of the 1990s—the *sinetron* or telefilms, which generally take the serial form and can leave conflicts and contradictions unresolved until the next episode. These texts are not designed as a political or cultural critique. But the soap opera form has too many loose ends, too many byways, for its conclusions to be controllable by the institution of censorship—especially one designed for narrative feature films.

The Cutting Edge

The New Order allowed little space for experimentation in cinema. The relatively small industry, censorship, the stranglehold of the distribution monopoly and the historical definition of Indonesian cinema as the entertainment choice of the poor and the uneducated all acted against experimentation. The art film circuit in Indonesia is virtually non-existent. The handful of films that gained some international recognition not only failed in the popularity stakes, they also frequently failed to get mainstream critical acknowledgment in Indonesia (best represented by the Annual Film Festival Awards). It is those films, however, that were most closely aligned to political critique of the New Order. We have argued elsewhere that middle-class political challenges to the government in 1974 and in 1978 produced their own resonances in cinema.[27] Following Anderson we could suggest that films, like other 'visual condensations of significance',[28] give insights into a mood that we might miss in the overt political discourses of the New Order state and opponents. With that in mind, we now look at *Surat Untuk Bidadari*, the only Indonesian film of the 1990s to gain a degree of international critical acclaim.

Surat Untuk Bidadari (*Letter for an Angel*) was directed by Garin Nugroho, who rose to prominence with his first feature film, *Cinta Dalam Sepotong Roti* (*Love in a Slice of Bread*), winning several awards at the 1991 Indonesian Film Festival, including the coveted Best Film. He also received the Best New Director prize at the Asia-Pacific Film Festival in Seoul in 1992. The film did relatively well at the box-office, and was the most popular of all films nominated for the Best Film award. This combination of popular and critical acclaim brought the new director funding for his second feature *Surat Untuk Bidadari* from the state film company PPFN, then anxious at the downturn in production,[29] and the newly established educational television channel, TPI (see Chapter 4). Internationally, *Surat Untuk Bidadari* was Indonesia's most successful film of the 1990s, receiving three international awards in 1994, one at the prestigious Berlin Film Festival, the Caiddi d'Oro award for Best Film at the Twenty-fourth Taormina Film Festival in Italy, and winning gold in the Young Cinema competition at Tokyo. The National Film Council (*Dewan Film Nasional*), recognising the international potential of Nugroho's work, funded his third feature, specifically to represent Indonesia at the 1995 Asia-Pacific Film Festival. However, *Surat Untuk Bidadari*, unacceptably experimental for the distributors, never had normal commercial release in Indonesia. It was also rejected by the Film Festival jury. But Indonesia's longest-standing literary journal, *Horison,* gave the film a special commendation for its artistic experimentation.

Part ethnography and part fantasy, the film broke most norms of Indonesian film-making. Set in a small village on the island of Sumba, it told the story of a pre-teenage boy—but with violent sexual scenes, it was not a children's film. Nugroho went to Sumba with a storyline about a young boy's search for identity, but without a fixed script or cast. The fiction was written into an ethnographic film that he shot entirely on location, with long scenes of local rituals. There are only three professional actors in the film; most of the rest of its large cast, including the boy hero, came from local villages. The hereditary village chief (*raja*) was played by a real *raja* from the area. Several scenes contain dialogues which are partly in Sumbanese dialects. Some characters, including the boy hero's father, speak exclusively in Sumbanese. No film in the New Order had used local casting to this extent. Although in the 1990s a small number of popular television series (like *Si Doel,* mentioned in Chapter 4) and films were starting to use the Betawi dialect of Indonesian or Javanese, this was the first film to substantially use a minority language from an outer island.

Jakarta-dominated since the 1940s, during the New Order the film industry became entirely concentrated in Jakarta, the city which also dominated as the setting for films. At least three-quarters of films made since 1970 are implicitly or explicitly set in Jakarta and its surrounds. Most of the rest are set in rural or mythical Java. Since the late 1970s a small but growing proportion have been set in foreign locations, usually large cities in Europe, the USA or South-East Asia. Films set on other islands of Indonesia are extremely rare, even more so when they constitute anything other than an extended setting for Jakartan protagonists (such as Si Boy setting up shop in Bali in *Catatan Si Boy V*).

1977, when more films were produced than in any other year, provides a good example of this Jakarta-centricism. Of the 124 films that year, only eleven were explicitly set in cities other than Jakarta. Of those, one was in Paris, one partially in Korea, one in Kalimantan, one in Bali, two in Sumatra and four in other cities in Java. Only *Mandau Dan Asmara* (*Sword and Love*), set in Kalimantan, and *Para Perintis Kemerdekaan* (*The Founders of Freedom*), set in West Sumatra, focused on the local community of those provinces. *Mandau Dan Asmara* was a story of the tragedies caused by Dayak headhunting practices. *Para Perintis Kemerdekaan* was a serious historical film directed by senior poet and intellectual Asrul Sani, which recounted the rise of nationalism in the early twentieth century. Both films shot on location and used regional music, but professional (by definition, from Jakarta) actors and formal national language. Of the remaining 115 films, most were set in Jakarta or in 'the city', conceived visually on the outskirts of the capital.

An older tradition of depicting regional cultural forms by using locally specific images and casts all but disappeared after 1965. In the 1950s, arguably the most innovative period of Indonesian national cinema, Bachtiar Siagian and D. Djajakusuma,[30] from very different political and aesthetic positions, had experimented with incorporating regional content into feature films and using non-professional casts from the local population where the films were set and shot. But Nugroho's film is not a direct descendant from either of these engagements with the local. Unlike Siagian (and Sani in *Para Perintis Kemerdekaan*), Nugroho is not seeking regional revolutionary credentials. Like Djajakusuma's most famous work, *Harimau Campa* (*Campa Tiger*, 1953), *Surat Untuk Bidadari* shows the violence at the heart of a local community. But unlike *Harimau Campa*, in *Surat* the institutions of the nation-state do not offer any solution, nor are the 'local' and the 'traditional' there to be found in purity.[31] Foreign symbols which littered Nugroho's filming location found their way into the film. The

Batman t-shirt worn by Lewa, the film's young hero, and the Elvis portraits painted on minibuses were ethnographic material the director found on the island and included in his particular view of the local, the national and the global.

Between scenes of ritual practices, the film tells the story of Lewa and the small village community on the island of Sumba in eastern Indonesia. The other central figures in the film are the village madman Malaria tua (Old Malaria, who suffers from chronic malaria), Berlian Merah (Red Gemstone), the village beauty who becomes the prey of the villainous village strongman Kuda Liar (Wild Horse) and the well-intentioned young schoolteacher who comes from outside the village and is later raped by Kuda Liar. Lewa is motherless and later in the film is orphaned, when his father is killed by Kuda Liar's men. Early in the film, Lewa meets the crew of a fashion-shoot on the edges of the village and acquires a Polaroid camera in exchange for a piece of traditional material needed as a prop. For the rest of the film the camera becomes Lewa's tool in the search for his mother and for his own identity.

Lewa's mother died when he was an infant. Her memory becomes important to him when his schoolteacher, using a textbook, tries to teach the class to read. The class read aloud the caption '*ini ibu*' (this is mother) under the drawing of a woman in Javanese clothes, projected as 'national costume'. But the alien image does not fit Lewa's view of his mother. He runs out screaming, 'This is not mother. The book lies'. His father, an unschooled horse grazier, cannot say whether the picture in the book looks like Lewa's mother. Lewa goes to look at the bus in which his mother was killed, which lies rusting in a gorge. He finds a poster of popstar Madonna pasted on the bus. He returns with his newly acquired Polaroid to take his first photograph. He sticks the photo of the Madonna poster in place of the 'mother' in his textbook and, the following day at school, happily says '*ini ibu*'. He has constructed a mother from an image which is simultaneously local (found on a rusting bus in Lewa's surroundings) and global, in defiance of the 'national' construction. But he is immediately confronted by the next image, the national urban male in trousers and shirt, captioned as '*ini bapak*' (this is father). Lewa again runs out of the class screaming, 'This is not my father's face'. He tries to find his father to take his photo to correct the book, but his father has just been killed. During the elaborate burial ceremony which occupies the villagers' attention, Lewa steals the body, drags it to the edge of the village, where his father spent most of his time, and takes a photograph to place in his schoolbook.

A second Western pop icon features through Kuda Liar, a devoted fan of Elvis Presley. Kuda Liar wears an Elvis hairstyle and costume (sometimes in combination with traditional clothes), has Elvis songs blaring from his car and has pictures of Elvis pasted all over his room and car. There are also older foreign symbols that are part of the village—Lewa and Malaria Tua spend their happiest hours playing on an old plane downed during the Second World War. And there is Lewa's friend Kakek Jepang (Japanese Grandpa), left over from the same period, though it isn't clear whether he is Japanese or a former collaborator who speaks Japanese. Towards the end of the film, while attempting to hide from pursuing men from a neighbouring village, Lewa fleetingly puts a Ned Kelly bucket on his head.

The signifiers of the outside world coexist with the very parochial signifiers—traditional clothes, rituals, village wars and, most importantly, the structure of legitimate rural authority still epitomised by the *raja*—without seeming to disrupt local cultural practices. The icons of global culture, like the local practices, are not inherently good or bad. The criminal Kuda Liar is an Elvis devotee, but Madonna is more acceptable as a mother-image than the Javanese woman of the national school curriculum. It is the institutionally imposed 'national' culture that poses the real threat to the local. Lewa's problem starts when the 'national' image of the family—men in trousers, women in *kebaya* (Javanese blouse), children in neat dresses—confront his own reality of dead mother, illiterate father and life on horseback among hill-tracks. In the closing sequence of the film the nation intrudes with more destructive effect, in the form of the court that removes Lewa from his natural and communal surroundings and puts him inside the institutional walls of a detention centre.

Through the film Lewa's battle against Kuda Liar escalates, as the latter rapes and murders those whom Lewa loves. Lewa's camera captures evidence of some of Kuda Liar's crimes, and he repeatedly becomes the target of Kuda Liar's fury. Finally, during a ritual dance that occupies the attention of the villagers, Lewa slays the drunken Kuda Liar with an arrow through his heart. Unlike the murders committed in the village by Kuda Liar and his men, his murder brings national law into the village. A prosecutor and judge arrive, speaking in formal official Indonesian never before used in the film, to establish law and order in the village. Though villagers turn out in force to support Lewa, the court finds evidence of the boy's delinquency in his photographs of women's breasts, his attachment to Berlian Merah (who has allowed him to photograph her breasts) and of course his killing of Kuda Liar. Lewa is sentenced to time in a detention centre. In the last scene he lies still in a windowless room facing a wall, refusing to acknowledge Berlian Merah, who has come to visit. This is the first time we see Lewa inside a closed room, the first time we see him still and speechless. As in the archetypal New Order text, the state institution has finally established order out of Lewa's chaotic search for identity and justice. But this order saps the spirit of youth, it breaks the ties of local culture. The threat to local, even traditional, culture comes not from global cultural forms brought in by the media and the markets (Elvis records, Madonna prints on buses, Polaroid from the fashion industry); it comes from the more motivated incursions of the nation-state. Indeed, global icons like the Polaroid and Madonna become weapons in the local's struggle for survival against homogenised images of national identity imposed by the national centre.

Global icons, like Pepsi and McDonalds, and even the more territorially situated imagery of the outside like the Hollywood Hill, Sydney Harbour Bridge and Perth cityscapes have often appeared in films without being defined as particularly foreign— they are just elements in the lives of contemporary Indonesia. What distinguishes Garin Nugroho's film is not that the foreign is made familiar (familial? Madonna as mother), but that the foreign is explicitly more familiar than the powerfully intrusive 'alien' national culture. Lewa's Batman t-shirt, his Madonna-mother, the Polaroid camera extension of his eyes, his Ned Kelly mask, even his Elvis-enemy, do not represent incursions from another place: they are deterritorialised signifiers which can mean anything the user wants them to. The court and the school textbook, in contrast, do arrive from a particular, faraway place, with hegemonic and destructive power.

Conclusion

Technological change (producing new ways of encoding and decoding film texts), changes in global media economies, the government's media policies and the growing dissent against Suharto's long repressive rule since the late 1980s were all factors in eroding the dominance of the myth of 'order' in the cinema in the middle years of Suharto's rule. In its twilight, its power of propaganda and censorship were fraying. What was emerging through the rips, however, was not the demand for democracy, justice and the end of Suharto's reign that marked the discourse of political opposition in the 1990s (the censors, alert to overt politics, would not allow that), but a complex reassessment of the legitimising discourse of the New Order and of Indonesian nationhood itself. The Jakarta-dictated, Java-centric national cultural identity was being challenged by local, global and what Robertson has called 'glocal' possibilities,[32] even in the discourse of a film industry which was almost totally centralised in Jakarta.

Notes

1   This becomes evident when we look at the distant provinces. In East Timor, for instance, there appears to be only one movie theatre, with a single screen—in Dili (see Departemen Penerangan Republik Indonesia, *Data Dan Fakta 1993/1994 Program Tahun 1 Pelita VI*, Direktorat Jenderal Radio, Televisi, Film, Jakarta, 1994, p. 147). According to the latest figures available from the Indonesian Central Bureau of Statistics, only 0.41 per cent of the East Timorese population watched films and nearly 24 per cent watched television (see Biro Pusat Statistik, *Statistik Indonesia 1995*, BPS, Jakarta, 1995, p. 116, Table 4.1.18).
2   See Departemen Penerangan, *Data Dan Fakta 1993/1994*, p. 137.

3   The filmic and televisual modes of reception of text are very differ-
     ent and change the way texts are created and understood. See J.
     Ellis, *Visible Fictions: Cinema, TV & Video*, Routledge & Kegan
     Paul, New York and London, 1982, pp. 23–37.

4   The idea of 'national fiction' derives from Ben Anderson's seminal
     work *Imagined Communities: Reflections on the Origin and Spread of
     Nationalism*, Verso, London and New York, 1991, extended by tex-
     tual theorists to look at the way any narrative fiction is constantly
     implicated in constructing and contesting the way any nation is
     pictured, imaged and imagined. See Homi Bhabha (ed.), *Nation
     and Narration*, Routledge, London and New York, 1990.

5   For a clarification of the terminology 'encoding/decoding' see
     Stuart Hall, 'Coding and decoding in the television discourse'
     (pp. 197–208) in Stuart Hall et al. (eds), *Culture, Media, Language*,
     Hutchinson, London, 1980.

6   Aiko Kurasawa, 'Propaganda media on Java under the Japanese
     1942–1945', *Indonesia*, 44, October 1987, pp. 59–116.

7   See Krishna Sen, 'Hidden from history: Aspects of Indonesian cin-
     ema 1955–65', *Review of Indonesian and Malaysian Affairs*, 19:2,
     1985, pp. 1–50.

8   Krishna Sen, *Indonesian Cinema: Framing the New Order*, Zed
     Books, London and New Jersey, 1994, pp. 55–6.

9   See Sen, *Indonesian Cinema*, pp. 66–9.

10   The 1994 presidential Decree has greatly expanded the clauses
     relating to sex. It includes for the first time an explicit ban on
     homosexuality, lesbianism and the depiction of masturbation.

11   Departemen Penerangan RI, *Kode Etik Produksi Film Nasional*,
     Jakarta, 1981.

12   See Sen, *Indonesian Cinema*, pp. 56–66.

13   Some aspects of *Perawan Desa* are discussed in Sen, *Indonesian Cin-
     ema*, pp. 114–20.

14   'Pertanggungan Jawab Penilaian Oleh Dewan Juri FFI 1980
     Semarang', in a special edition of *Bulletin KFT*, 3:VIII, pp. 28–9.

15   This term was made popular in the 1970s in feminist, gay and les-
     bian readings of Hollywood cinema, encoded from a heterosexual
     perspective but decoded from within a different sexuality. Since
     then much other work has been done which suggests discrepancies
     between those who produce media texts and those who consume,
     about the meaning of the text.

16   Benedict R. O'G. Anderson, *Language and Power: Exploring Political Cultures in Indonesia*, Cornell University Press, Ithaca and London, 1990, pp. 153–4.

17   For an excellent summary, see Ien Ang, *Living Room Wars: Rethinking Media Audiences for a Postmodern World,* Routledge, London and New York, 1996, Part I, pp. 19–84.

18   Research into audience responses such as Liebes & Katz and Ien Ang's studies of Dallas have required extensive interviews (in Ang's case, correspondence with respondents). Recent ethnographic theory suggests that such investigation is likely to affect the response. It is possible that Internet bulletin-boards and news-groups will give researchers different access to audience response, rather than interviews that directly involve the researcher in the production of the text that is being analysed. See T. Liebes & E. Katz, *The Export of Meaning: Cross-Cultural Readings of Dallas*, Oxford University Press, New York, 1990; Ien Ang, *Watching Dallas: Soap Opera and the Melodramatic Imagination*, Methuen, London and New York, 1985.

19   See Sen, *Indonesian Cinema,* Ch. 4.

20   In the years after the civil war of 1965–66, while state-controlled radio and television were used for ritual reminder of the evils of Communism, no media discussion of the historic events was permitted. It is commonly accepted that the history of the political turmoil of the early 1960s was suppressed. But the memories were not completely obliterated and they surfaced in public discussion in the late 1970s as former political prisoners were released. In the late 1980s and early 1990s pre-1965 history repeatedly surfaced in the press, as octogenarian politicians on both sides of politics published their memoirs. In the mid 1990s the shroud over this history was ripped further by the government's own propaganda war identifying the new illegal political party PRD (Democratic People's Party) with the old banned PKI.

21   This is not an argument about authorial intention. Indeed, if we think of the director as the author of the film, Arifin C. Noer's ambivalence towards it was well-known. The film has none of the aesthetic hallmarks of an Arifin film. It is possible that he was fully aware or even intended that the propaganda should be obviously contradictory. The point is that the government funded it and continues to broadcast it as the New Order's authorised history, and yet some readings find quite different messages in the film.

22 'Film Golden Eye Diprotes Tiga Orsospol Solo', *Republika Online*, 22 February 1996, listed on <apakabar@access.digex.net> on 21 February 1996, and accessed via gopher://gopher.igc.apc.org:2998/OREG-INDONESIA/ r.884503858.25391.8 (read 11 January 1998).

23 Posting by Arya Perdana, on <apakabar@clark.net>, dated 23 February 1996, and accessed via gopher://gopher.igc.apc.org:2998/OREG-INDONESIA/ r.884505228.27117.1 (read 11 January 1998).

24 Hamtut Haeng, 'Film "Pengkhianatan G30S/PKI" Menguntungkan Siapa?' posted on <SiaR@mole.gn.apc.org> on 16 September 1997.

25 Newspapers, for instance, are not only politically censored, they are also constrained by journalistic ethics of having to 'tell a balanced story' to be accountable to the public and to the owners, and so on. The Internet does not suffer most of these constraints.

26 *Saur Sepuh* episodes 1, 2 and 3 were the most popular films three years running. The five episodes of *Catatan Si Boy* released between 1987 and 1991 never dropped below number five in the popularity ratings.

27 Sen, *Indonesian Cinema,* Ch. 5.

28 Anderson, *Language and Power*, p. 155.

29 According to Department of Information figures, 112 films were produced in 1990/91, forty-one in 1991/92 and twenty-eight in 1992/93. At the same time the number of imported films had risen slightly (see Departemen Penerangan, *Data Dan Fakta 1993/1994*, pp. 137–44).

30 Bachtiar Siagian was closely aligned to the Communist Party of Indonesia (PKI). D. Djajakusuma was associated with Usmar Ismail, 'the father of Indonesian cinema,' and deeply committed to anti-Communism. However, Djajakusuma was relatively apolitical even in the highly political early 1960s.

31 For summaries of films mentioned here see J.B Kristianto, *Katalog Film Indonesia 1926–1995*, PT Grafiasri Mukti, Jakarta, 1995.

32 Roland Robertson, 'Glocalization: Time–space and homogeneity–heterogeneity' (pp. 25–44) in Mike Featherstone, Scott Lash & Roland Robertson (eds), *Global Modernities*, Sage, London, 1995.

6

THE MUSIC INDUSTRY: PERFORMANCE AND POLITICS

Music constitutes a large part of television content and an even larger part of radio's content. This chapter will look at two main commercial structures through which music becomes available to other media and to consumers—public performances and recording. The chapter is divided into two parts. The first focuses on the structure of the industry. The second looks at the political implication of some of the industry's products.

We want to make two related arguments. First, that musical performances and texts were important sites for signifying opposition to the New Order discourse of 'order' and stability. Such musical transgressions were not subtle, as occurred in Indonesian films' social critique, nor did they use the kind of cultural guerrilla tactics that the press or radio had to use to 'get away' with adverse political commentary. Indeed, in the music industry, the line between mainstream-profitable and counter-cultural was very thin. Second, we suggest that, in this work of cultural opposition, 'foreign' (overwhelmingly, though not exclusively, Western or Westernised) musical codes and icons were frequently indigenised into conscious political opposition to the New Order, and more frequently into disorganised, carnivalesque disorderliness that showed up the cracks in the New Order's attempts to control cultural production and create 'cultural order', an 'ordered culture'.[1]

The image of a 'carnival' is drawn from Bakhtin's work on medieval Europe, which has become a significant point of reference in analysis of popular culture in recent years.[2] Bakhtin conceived of carnivals as brief but necessary moments in which the dominant cultural values were allowed to be overturned. Carnivals thus both expressed, and contained, counter-hegemonic values.[3]

The last section of the chapter is conceived partly around the image of musical events (sometimes with huge audience participation) as carnivals. We try to understand how the New Order state attempted to mobilise musical performances in its own interest and simultaneously tried to contain its performative excesses within particular times and spaces (where, when and whose performance is permitted) and within the regulatory limits of the media industries, such as radio, television and recording companies.

History

The music genres of Indonesia have always been syncretic and absorbed outside influence. Indigenisation of foreign music started long before contemporary 'world music' or 'globalisation' or the recent interest in international marketing of recorded music.[4] In the twentieth century, changing recording technologies and Western marketing practices also influenced musical production and consumption patterns in Indonesia.

US-made Colombia phonographs were imported to the Dutch East Indies in the early 1900s. In the pre-war years there were three Chinese-owned recording companies in the colony—two in Batavia and one in Surabaya—with a tiny market among the urban elite.[5] In 1951 a *pribumi* (indigenous) Indonesian company, Irama, began producing phonogram records, and was followed in 1954 by Remaco and Dimita. Lokananta, the state recording company established in Solo in 1955, quickly came to dominate the domestic recording industry, concentrating almost exclusively on Javanese music.[6] Its dominance was brief, as technological changes in the late 1960s brought new players with new methods into the industry.

President Sukarno, in his 17 August 1959 National Day address (when he outlined a 'Political Manifesto', or Manipol),[7] urged the country's youth to oppose the culture of what he dubbed the *nekolim* (*Neo-Colonialist and Imperialist*) countries of the West:

You, young men and young women, you who are certainly
against economic imperialism and oppose economic imperialism,
you who oppose political imperialism—why is it that among you
many do not oppose cultural imperialism? Why is it that among
you many still like to indulge in rock'n roll, to 'dance' a la cha-
cha-cha, to make crazy mixed-up noises [ngakngik-ngek] called
music?[8]

This critique became the stimulus for a more nationalistic
'Indonesian pop music'. There followed a search for indigenous
musical forms which could be transformed into vehicles for contemporary youth music. Bands revived old songs in contemporary
style. The famous keroncong[9] standard, 'Bengawan Solo', was rendered in a rock style with a twelve-bar interlude and Elvis-style
singing (e.g. 'BeHengAwan').[10] In the wake of the September
1959 decision by the Supreme Advisory Council (DPA) to adopt
the President's Manipol principles as the Broad Outlines of State
Policy (GBHN), there followed a ban on Western songs regarded
as ngak-ngik-ngok. This effectively excluded from state radio (the
only radio at that time, see Chapter 3) popular Western rock by
performers like Elvis Presley and the Beatles. Rock music records
were gathered up and publicly burned. But official censure turned
rock into a symbol of defiance against state authority: foreign
albums were smuggled in and young Jakartans tuned into overseas
shortwave radio broadcasts. In New Order iconography, the
burning of records became one of the signifiers of the political
excesses of the Old Order. The propaganda film Pengkhianatan
Gerakan 30 September (mentioned in Chapter 5), for instance,
opens with the image of a fire engulfing a Beatles album.

In the early 1960s, domestic producers were recording either
modifications to established genres like keroncong, or imitations of
middle-of-the-road Western performers such as Pat Boone,
which were still permitted in Indonesia. The most durable band
which emerged in the early 1960s featured the Koeswoyo brothers (known initially as Koes Bros, then Koes Bersaudara, then as
Koes Plus), who played an Everly Brothers style of pop. When
the popularity of the Everly Brothers declined in the West and
then in Indonesia, the Koeswoyo brothers band started copying
the Beatles. Accused of playing ngak-ngik-ngok music, they were

arrested on 29 August 1965 and detained for three months—until after the 30 September coup. The Koeswoyo brothers turned a combination of apolitical lyrics and rock tunes copied from the West into a symbol of political radicalism. They became one of the biggest bands of the 1970s and their re-released albums sold well even in the mid 1990s.[11]

Some Indonesian 'pop' persisted in the political turbulence of the mid 1960s. Eugene Timothy's Remaco studio, for instance, recorded an album in 1965 by a band called Trio Bintang, led by President Sukarno's son, Guntur Sukarnoputra, then a popular drummer and student at the Bandung Institute of Technology. Although the lyrics were Indonesian, the style was strongly influenced by contemporary popular Anglo-American trends. Timothy later reflected that 'Because I was regarded as a friend of the President's son, none of my other productions faced any obstruction...I don't know whether my productions then were *ngak-ngik-ngok* or not. But the community certainly liked them a lot'.[12]

The political shift in 1965–66 reopened the Indonesian market to Western musical products, and stimulated a crop of new pop bands and performers, who incorporated previously proscribed Western rock into their repertoire. Songs 'of Western rock groups like the Rolling Stones and Deep Purple, and of Indonesian counterparts like the Rollies and God Bless, were played constantly over amateur radio stations, and performed live in the rock concerts which started to be staged in large Indonesian cities'.[13] Rolling Stones lead singer Mick Jagger had a profound effect, particularly on Bandung bands: 'the name, habits, and even the titles of the Stones' songs became a kind of "cultural" standard for young people in Indonesia'.[14] The Stones' influence permeated the youth language (*prokem*) of the streets. A 'Jagger' (*jeger*) was 'cock of the walk', a tough streetfighter (*jagoan, tukang pukul*).[15] The persistence of Stones iconography is demonstrated by underground band Koil which, in 1997, was selling mail-order t-shirts with the Stones' slogan (and song title from the 1968 album *Beggars' Banquet*), 'simpathy [sic] for the devil'.[16] The fold-out cover on rock band Slank's 1995 album *Generasi Biru* (*Blue Generation*) features the top of a pair of jeans, with the red circular emblem of 'Slank' appearing from the open fly—evoking the Andy Warhol-designed cover on the 1971 Rolling Stones

Sticky Fingers album. The creative alliance of two key Slank members was likened by journalists and fans to the Stones' partnership of Mick Jagger and Keith Richards.

Early in the New Order, the appearance of portable, battery-operated cassette players and relatively cheap cassettes expanded the market for recorded music of all kinds and made it accessible to the majority of the population. Domestic production of music cassettes began around 1966. 'Pirates' led the change from more cumbersome vinyl records to the more economical new technology. Remaco moved to cassette production in 1966, after discovering that several of its distributors were making, and selling much more cheaply, thousands of pirated cassettes from Remaco's vinyl records.[17] Lokananta produced its first cassettes in November 1971 and within three years had ceased record production entirely, increasing sales twentyfold from 42000 records in 1970 to 890000 cassettes in 1975.[18] In 1970 a one-hour cassette cost only US50c. By 1981 the cost had risen to $US1.75, which was more than the daily minimum wage, but there were plenty of buyers among the growing urban middle-classes and the emerging rural market.[19]

Recording successes of popular bands like Koes Plus in the early 1970s demonstrated the market's potential and stimulated the multiplication of recording studios and distribution networks. New companies emerged to take advantage of lax copyright regulation by bringing out cheap pirated versions of popular overseas recordings. All that was required was a single original, a bank of cassette recorders, some blank tapes and photocopied labels.

The new replay technology encouraged musical experimentation and ushered in a new generation of musicians and performers, who displaced phonograph artists. It became common for community events and public performances to use portable public address amplification systems and to record these performances for later replay or reproduction and distribution.[20] The portability of the new equipment enabled local bands to produce simple master recordings which they could hawk to commercial studios, many of which were simultaneously producing pirate copies of imported records.

New Order officials periodically denigrated particular genres of music, generally on nationalist grounds, but without the conviction of Sukarno's rejection of rock. In 1988, in his speech on the twenty-sixth anniversary of the state television channel, TVRI, then Minister of Information, Harmoko, attacked 'soppy' songs (*lagu cengeng*) as 'appealing to low taste, weakening the spirit of the people, making them defeatist and sapping their commitment to the national effort for progress'.[21] TVRI promptly banned such songs but for only a few months, Harmoko's criticisms unable to stem the commercial dominance of love themes in a musical style that was a 'direct descendant of American white pop of the 1950s…wispy, disembodied, without tension or defiance, without edges'.[22] A constant stream of young solo performers, generally women, were produced by the cassette industry to perform sentimental songs, promoted to the public via television music programs and constituting one of the most lucrative genres in Indonesian pop. In 1995, B.J. Habibie (then Minister of Research and Technology) targeted 'rap' as without any artistic value, declaring it 'dirty' and 'disgusting'.[23] The lyrics of some Bandung underground black metal bands (discussed later) have occasionally provoked responses from the local military. But such infrequent interventions by state functionaries are of little importance in the development of the recording industry overall.

The Industry in the 1990s

In financial terms, the music industry in Indonesia is small by world standards, but the largest in South-East Asia. Official (not including the pirate sector) 1995 figures showed that total retail sales of recorded music in Indonesia amounted to approximately $US290 million, less than 3 per cent of the USA's $US12 880 million or Japan's $US10 019 million.[24] But sales in the Philippines were 16 per cent of Indonesia's, in Singapore 31 per cent, Malaysia 50 per cent and Thailand 65 per cent.[25]

The Sound Recording Industry Association of Indonesia, ASIRI (Asosiasi Industri Rekaman Indonesia), was established in 1978, as 'the only sound recording representative recognised by the Indonesian Government'.[26] In 1997 ASIRI had over a hundred members. Reflecting the economic concentration of most media industries in Jakarta, 84 per cent of ASIRI's membership was based there. The only members outside Java were two companies in Bali and one in Padang.[27] Hidden from institutional view, scattered throughout the archipelago, were small producers who were not ASIRI members.

In the 1990s approximately 20 per cent of the legal recordings were classified by ASIRI as 'foreign music', mostly Anglo-American, but also a sprinkling from Europe and Asia. Imported cassettes sold for under $US5, including government taxes and royalties. An additional Rp.1200 for censorship by the Attorney-General's office was levied on Mandarin-language cassettes (but not other languages), since the New Order restricted the circulation of all materials in Chinese. Sales of Mandarin recordings were low; even bestsellers, such as *The Best of Jacky Cheung*, reaching only 6000.

Eighty per cent of the recorded market is Indonesian music. According to ASIRI's generic categories, 45 per cent of this is 'Western-style pop music', followed by '*dangdut* music' (35 per cent) and 'ethnic music' (15 per cent).[28] Unlike films, where imports dominate, domestic musical products rule. For instance, the most popular US offering, Michael Jackson's *Dangerous*, sold half a million copies over four years[29] whereas top-of-the-charts Indonesian recordings can sell three or four times that many in a single year. Even regional-language pop releases, such as the Sundanese *Kalangkang*, have sold two million.[30]

In contrast to other culture industries, there is no direct government censorship of the recording industry, no restriction on foreign investment and little investment by politically well-connected conglomerates,[31] though some members of the President's family dabbled in music. Siti Hardiyanti Rukmana (Tutut) wrote the lyrics for the discreetly titled *10 Karya Cipta Yanti R.* (*10 Creative Works of Yanti R.*, 1996)—and put her unmistakable photograph on the cover. The album was produced by CIRI Records (PT Cipta Isthika Rucitra Indonesia) connected to Tutut's Citra Lamtoro Gung Persada conglomerate. Tutut and CIRI Records also marshalled singers to compile an album to commemorate the hundred-day anniversary of her mother's death. The President's grandson, Ari Haryo Wibowo Hardjojudanto (Ari Sigit), released an album in late 1996, called *Mungkinkah Kan Kembali* (*Will You Ever Come Back?*).[32] However, these were personal pop ambitions, not the large economic or political interests of conglomerates or the government.

Multinationals

Indonesia's music business has been highly successful, domestically and regionally, subverting the marketing strategies of the Western recording industry through pirating. Major multinational recording companies, whose products were being reproduced without royalty payments, complained incessantly in the 1970s and 1980s. In 1982 Indonesia's first copyright law was promulgated. It was tightened in 1987 and extended to include recorded music, partly in response to international condemnation of Indonesia pirating the 'Live Aid' concert for famine relief in Africa. In 1998 the Indonesian government signed an agreement with the European Economic Community guaranteeing royalties on recorded music. ASIRI claimed that by 1995 pirating levels had declined to 17 per cent of the early 1980s levels. But the Association of Indonesian Composers and Musical Arrangers (Persatuan Artis Pencipta Lagu dan Penata Musik Rekaman Indonesia, PAPPRI) calculated that in 1996 for every legitimate cassette there were up to five pirated copies.[33]

In early June 1994 Indonesia's key economic Ministers approved a deregulation package (known as government Regulation No. 20) opening the recording industry and certain other fields of entertainment (not press, radio or television) to direct foreign investment. Multinationals which had previously been content to work through Indonesian representatives jockeyed to transform local licensee companies into branches of their empire. In the first such takeover, in June 1996, Hemagita Records was absorbed into the Warner Music International group, with Hemagita's original owner, Sanjaya Wijaya, taking 5 per cent of Warner Music Indonesia and Warner Music International holding 95 per cent. The Time-Warner group, which includes HBO cable TV, CNN television news, the Warner Bros film empire and *Time* magazine, invested $US1 million in the venture.[34] In addition to reproducing its own US and European records, Warner gained the rights to record all Indonesian artists contracted by Hemagita. By July 1997 four other major multinational companies, BMG, PolyGram, EMI and Sony Music, were also producing and marketing their products in Indonesia.[35]

Some Indonesian licensees believed that absorption into multinationals would increase access to the latest technologies and the potential for Indonesian performers in the growing Asian regional markets.[36] There had long been a small specialist international audience for traditional music like Javanese or Balinese *gamelan* (gong-chime orchestra) or Sundanese *angklung* (shaken bamboo tube) ensembles. *Dangdut* was common in Malaysia, which shares a common national language and hosts a large population of Indonesian temporary workers. In the 1980s some Indonesian composers and arrangers worked for Malaysian bands, which occasionally toured and even used recording facilities in Indonesia.[37] In the 1990s the growth of the 'world music'[38] industry opened up small local pockets in the global market for a variety of Indonesian musical styles. Albums by popular *dangdut* queen Elvy Sukaesih became available in Japan, where occasional tours by big-name Indonesian *dangdut* bands are reportedly well-received. Islamic-influenced *qasidah* band Nasida Ria Group had an album on sale in Germany, and Sundanese singer Detty Kurnia was marketed in the UK. Such music is usually distributed by small independent (indie) labels like Wave (Japan), Piranha (Germany) and Flame Tree (UK).[39] But multinationals like Sony have also started to test the international market for Indonesian popular music, with Indonesian performers recording in Tokyo with Japanese musicians, in Sydney with an Australian orchestra.[40] Transnational television, carrying shows like *MTV* around the world, and global communication generally (including the Internet) add to this articulation of Indonesian music to the world markets.

In 1997 there were about fifty Internet sites on Batavia.net promoting Indonesian music, often with audio-files that could be played and downloaded. 'Syahreza's Radio Station', which called itself 'the First Indonesian Live Internet Radio Station', had audio (MIDI) clips, the latest Indonesian Top 10, a 'live chat-show' and links to various music sites.[41] A music mailing list, <nusa-musik@nusanet.com>, was started in early 1997 with a strong interest in underground, heavy/death metal, punk and thrash genres including Indonesian bands like Rotor, Suckerhead and Alien Scream. Bandung underground band Koil is one of a growing number of bands with its own webpage, showing lyrics, biographies, mail-order paraphernalia, quizzes and demo audio-clips of unreleased songs.[42] Also on the Internet was the California-based independent record label, Ragadi Music, 'formed primarily as a vehicle for Indonesian artists to market their music in the US...and around the world'.[43] Individual composers and singers are also putting their work on the Internet, testing their global market.[44]

Playing provincial

At the least internationalised end of the market is provincial cottage industry producing local music with local performers for a local audience. These companies have emerged since the early 1970s. They are generally not members of ASIRI and survive largely due to their ability to cater to the forms of music or performance most popular in their local areas, a niche not served by large national and multinational companies. Most recordings produced by the provincial sector could be categorised as traditional entertainment forms, but there are also current popular Western or Indonesian-language songs, sung by local artists in a regional language, transplanting the songs into local musical genres (and avoiding copyright laws). Such producers are scattered through provincial cities and small towns. Some, particularly in Java, serve substantial rural markets.[45]

Local performances provide an obvious source of material for these companies. Recordings are made with simple technology for relatively little cost. In central and east Java it is common for a traditional (*karawitan*) ensemble to record three albums in one session to reduce expenses. Ensemble members (ten to fifteen people) would share the very modest Rp.1 million honorarium (1992 figures) for the three albums. Recordings of shadow-play (*wayang kulit*) performances, such as those by well-known puppet-master Anom Suroto, may sell 20000 copies, well over the usual break-even point for operations of this kind (at about 3000 copies).[46] Big provincial companies like Fajar have collaborative arrangements with operators in smaller towns, who have artists but no recording equipment.

Even outside Java, in the small town of Biak in West Papua, whose population is among the poorest in the country, a shop sells a selection of locally produced cassettes of mainly local folk-music and folk-songs. Most cassettes, however, come from Jakarta, including those of the province's most successful band, Black Brothers.[47]

In a 1992 report in *Kompas,* provincial recording companies were dubbed 'cultural guerrillas' who maintain local culture in the face of national and global commerce.[48] The provincial industry is made possible by the global technology of compact cassettes and recorders. Beyond that, these very parochial sites have largely escaped the national and transnational economies of the recording industry, and the cultural codes generated by those markets.

Genres

We have noted some of the music genres produced and distributed by the industry. We have also noted the overt politicisation of some of these, since Sukarno implicated music in his radical nationalist discourse. We now look at two categories of recordings and performances, in an attempt to understand the articulation of musical genres into particular kinds of political practices in the New Order.

Dangdut: hybrid and national

Dangdut is arguably the musical genre most clearly associated with the New Order. A minor genre before 1965, by the mid 1970s it had become the identifiably national, modern Indonesian popular music. As mentioned earlier, *dangdut* comprises over a third of the domestic market for musical recordings. Many television hours, whole feature films and radio stations have been dedicated to *dangdut.*

By all accounts Rhoma Irama is the central figure in this invention of *dangdut* (dubbed onomatopoeically after its syncopated drumbeat, *dang* then *dut*) as national-popular music. He transformed older-style *orkes Melayu* (Malay orchestra) and combined it with the rhythmic style of Indian film songs, popular with urban working-class audiences, into up-tempo *dangdut*, acceptable across society and patronised by Cabinet ministers. In so doing he became 'one of the best-paid and most widely recognised contemporary Indonesians, and a musician who changed the face of Indonesian music'.[49] In many of his lyrics and, from 1976 onwards, in a series of films, Rhoma expressly defined *dangdut* as a national foil to Western music and to traditional regional musical genres.

Dangdut was adopted into the repertoire of established pop singers and played by military bands. University students saw it as a way of playfully adopting lower-class tastes as a gesture against commercial pop.[50] State functions began to include *dangdut* entertainment. By the mid 1980s *dangdut* had become an established vehicle for populist politicking, endorsed by the highest levels of government. In 1995, at the opening of a nationally televised *dangdut* concert celebrating the fiftieth anniversary of Indonesian independence, Secretary of State Moerdiono declared that *dangdut* was 'very, very Indonesian': 'This country [is] of the people, by the people, for the people. And so is *dangdut* of the people, by the people, for the people'.[51]

Rhoma Irama's attempt to use music as a medium of Islamic evangelism also made *dangdut* a point of party-political contention. His lyrics, rhythms and performances tapped the early 1980s Muslim resentment against the New Order. He campaigned for the Islamic opposition political party, the PPP, and sang at its election rallies. For this, TVRI blocked his television appearances for most of the 1980s and strict security conditions applied to his public performances. But in the 1990s Rhoma was back on television, as his party-political shift to Golkar linked *dangdut* to the New Order's *rapprochement* with Muslims.

The nationally celebrated, politically pliant, morally Islamic *dangdut*, however, also has a secular and very sexual face, seen in mild forms on television but usually performed in humble venues by unnamed artists.[52] This *dangdut* is performed at local fairs, festivals like Yogya's *Sekaten*, or in open-air entertainment centres like Yogya's Purnawisata. Heavily made-up bespangled female singers in body-hugging micro-minis, some as young as fourteen, perform to the backing of an all-male band.[53] The singers are almost exclusively women from *kampungs*, their audience predominantly (90 per cent) young, lower-class males. The singers' stylised pelvic gyrations (*goyang pinggul*) are ritualised flirtation in a matter-of-fact, even bored, manner. They periodically bend backwards, legs apart, pelvis thrust forward, as the audience cranes to view a sequinned g-string. The songs performed are mostly current hits. But what Pioquinto calls the 'genital focus' of these acts strips *dangdut* both of Irama's religiosity and of the cute televisuality of singers who make it into the national media. On television, the *goyang pinggul* is toned down and sequinned underwear is covered by calf-length glamorous dresses, modifying the implications of the love-lorn lyrics through a very different embodiment of the songs.

The self-conscious construction of *dangdut* as an Indonesian national foil to Western music is disappearing. *Dangdut*'s valorisation as 'the authentic music of the Indonesian people'[54] (*musik asli rakyat Indonesia*) had always been moderated by its acknowledged inheritance from Indian film music, making this 'national' music quintessentially hybrid and trans-medium. Indeed, its persistent popularity is partly due to its hybrid character, constantly incorporating and synthesising other musical genres that may compete with it, in any section of the Indonesian market. Many provincial popular music forms have spawned *dangdut* variants, like '*dangdut* Sunda' and '*dangdut* Jawa'. So have new imported musical genres. In the 1980s there was 'disko-*dangdut*'. In 1996 *Remix Dangdut House Mania*[55] was all the rage, as *dangdut* adjusted to internationally trendy house music.

The lyrics on the *House Mania* album point to the diverse sources of *dangdut*'s inspiration, and the hybrid character of the genre. The song titles are Indonesian but the refrains are all in American English. The collection even includes a devotional song from a 1950s Indian film sung entirely in its original Hindi, interrupted briefly by English phrases 'now what do you think of the women's liberation' and the 'let's, let's, let's do it now' and 'all aboard now' repeated throughout the album!

This is not to argue that an Indonesian cultural form is being overwhelmed by foreign cultural imports. Rather, *dangdut* is an instance of a particular localisation of codes circulating in global cultural markets. The *House Mania* album is a hybrid which would not make sense in either of the linguistic and cultural contexts (India or the USA) from which it, and *dangdut* generally, draws its elements. On the other hand, we also need to understand that *dangdut*, one of Indonesia's most successful national popular cultural forms, cannot be fully explored within the bounds of the nation alone.

Underground

More self-consciously articulated into Western music were the alternative or underground rock bands, closely following global trends in youth culture. They were anti-establishment, both in terms of their politicised anti-New Order lyrics and performances, and in their operation outside mainstream recording companies. Using the strategies and technologies of the pirate cassette producers in the early 1970s, they produced their own albums, in small production runs sold by word-of-mouth, through a local radio station, at gigs or by mail-order.[56] They adopted 'creepy, "whitey-sounding" names',[57] like Closeminded, Full of Hate, Insanity, Sonic Torment, Trauma, Koil and Sadistis.

Bandung, known for its art and engineering schools and student radicalism, was home to one of the first successful indie bands, Pas,[58] whose initial album *4 Through the Sap* was produced in 1991 by a musical director of the local Bandung rock radio station GMR, who arranged to have the cassette distributed in Jakarta and West Java. After its initial success Pas was contracted by the major label Aquarius Musikindo, which re-released the first album and followed it with a second, *In (No) Sensation*, and a third, *IndieVduality* (whose cover image incorporates Australia's AC/DC and alludes to the Beatles' *Abbey Road* pedestrian crossing). Most of the tracks on the second album (and several on the third) are in English, increasingly common among underground bands.[59] Like their 'whitey' names, the use of English lyrics was part of the bands' arsenal, enabling them to express the kind of political and cultural critique impossible in New Order Indonesian.[60]

Other underground bands have been absorbed into the mainstream media. Surabaya band Boomerang opened the live Indosiar broadcast of the Gong 2000 concert (staged to celebrate Armed Forces Day) at the former Ancol Racing circuit before a crowd of 50000 on 12 October 1996. But institutional co-optation does not appear to tame either the radical message of the lyrics or the anarchic message of the performance. The first track on Boomerang's 1996 cassette *Disharmoni* is a Who-like rock anthem, 'Generasiku' (My Generation), whose refrain yells:

> Raise your hands high
> Yell out 'This is my generation'
> Raise your hands high
> This is my generation.

It challenges:

> those who are sharp-tongued, poisoned
> by ambition and crazy for power
> Don't be taken in by their tricks
> This world belongs to us![61]

Another track, 'OKBM', expressly attacked Indonesia's leaders:

> a million dreams you've offered
> but you've only left frustration
> you've tricked and destroyed me
> you've sucked all my blood dry.
> It's false…everything that you have done for me
> desire [nafsu]…it's only to satisfy your own desire
> …
> where are you taking the kids of our country?

Boomerang advises its fans on the cassette cover: 'enjoy and play it loud, stay crazy okay…!!!'(in English).

Perhaps the most successful band bridging underground and commercial genres of popular music was Slank.[62] Most popular with eighteen- to 25-year-olds across the country,[63] it had a string of 'best-selling album' awards. *Generasi Biru* went 'double platinum' as BASF's largest-selling cassette across all musical categories in Indonesia in 1994/95. Slank maintained a hold on the commercial Top Ten listings with a mixture of soft sentimental songs like 'Kamu Harus Pulang' (You Must Return) and 'Terbunuh Sepi' (Killed by Loneliness) and growling angry protests like 'Feodalisme' (Feudalism).

The lyric of Slank's 'Blues Males' (Lazy Blues) plays on sleep/sleeping around (*tidur/tidurin*) and tells of the pleasures of finding a 'friend' in high places:

so life wouldn't be destitute any longer
waiting for inheritance while sleeping around
…
If you know the most powerful people
you can let troubles pass you by
you can get a well-placed position to sleep around
…
A water-bed to sleep around
A [five] star hotel to sleep around
a stack of money for whoever you're screwing.

In the scribbled lyrics on the cassette cover, the final line is *'Punya jabatan…Buat nidurin bawahan*!!!'(Got a [high] position to screw the underlings!)—the word *nidurin* struck out but visible through the pen-stroke. On the audio-track, in place of the word *nidurin* (screw, sleep with) there is only the sound of a piercing 'beeeeeeep', deleting the offending word but simultaneously drawing attention to it. It is not a form of audio censorship generally used in Indonesia, where anything unacceptable is editorially omitted without any indication of intervention. Slank's beep signified explicit sex, its political use in the lyrics and its censorship, while managing to stay within permissible limits of broadcast language.

Further from the commercial scene, the 1996 Bandung Underground II concert drew about 4000 to the local badminton stadium. Among the bands there was Jasad (Corpse), which established an independent recording studio, Palapa. 'We want Palapa to have a broad scope, ranging from punk to grindcore. Basically the idea is to work with all those genres thought to be anti-social by the mainstream', said guitarist Yayat. 'Most of us underground musicians feel now that we've got to start building up a system that's independent of all the snaky fucks with the major labels.'[64] In an ironic play on symbols, Jasad's studio Palapa, through which Bandung's underground bands sought to circumvent commercial companies and reach a rebellious youth subculture, shared the name of the New Order's communications satellite, which was central to government control of the national electronic media (see Chapter 4).

In their lyrics, the projected personalities of band members and their mode of address, this underground music is intensely conscious of its identification with the young and obsessed with the generation gap. The concept of a generational identity as political ideology goes back to pre-independence nationalist discourses, which gave the *pemuda* (youth) a revolutionary anti-Dutch role.[65] This role was reinforced by the part played by university and highschool students in their crucial support of the Army in the establishment of the New Order.[66] But by the mid 1970s the New Order had depoliticised campuses, breaking—at least in official political discourse—the long-established identification of youth and political mobilisation.

As Siegel has pointed out, in the New Order young men and women were redefined from *pemuda* to *remaja*, more recently dubbed 'ABG' or '*Anak Baru Gede*' (a child just grown). The *remaja* 'comes as a result of the depoliticisation of youth in the New Order. In that sense it replaces the Indonesian term *pemuda* [youth], a term whose sense always includes political activity of the sort that the Suharto regime has made difficult'.[67] A person is not *remaja* by being a certain age: 'It is by having certain "tastes" [*selera*] and certain aspirations that one is or is not a *remaja*'.[68] Writing on Solo in the mid 1980s, Seigel noted the centrality of music and various discourses surrounding it in the definition of *remaja*. Writing of a punk concert in Bali in the mid 1990s Baulch similarly observed that '"alternative" music has fast become an integral part of what it is to be an ultimately modern teen'.[69]

Politics and fashions or tastes are not, however, clearly distinguishable. Musical messages about bosses screwing everyone, and indeed screwing up the younger generation, are fashionable, bought and listened to by the thousands of *remaja* fans of the alternative music scene. The anti-authority message, the invitation to disorderliness, underlying Indonesia's alternative, underground and rock music in general, may well be more important than the actual lyrics. As one death metal musician expressed it, 'Most of us are not so much inspired by the themes of death metal lyrics...The attraction is more the music itself, it gives us hope, it's about freedom, it's an expression of our soul'.[70] Disorder, always the political antithesis of the New Order, is 'in' for the younger generation. But we need to look beyond the confines of recordings, to live performances, to understand the politics of this disorderliness.

Ordered concerts

Dangdut performances were so integral to Golkar rallies that *Tempo Interaktif* dubbed it the 'official music' of the 1997 election campaign: 'the *dangdut* singers...have rendered the greatest service in attracting the masses in their thousands to the rallies...All the top *dangdut* singers came to strengthen the ranks of [Golkar]'.[71] Rhoma Irama had appeared at PPP rallies in previous campaigns. He appeared this time for Golkar, reportedly causing rioting by his disappointed Muslim fans.

But even apart from the contrived general elections, which passed as a five-yearly 'festival of democracy', the New Order promoted vast public spectacles, centred on musical entertainment, as displays of the regime's 'popular' support. The celebration of the fiftieth anniversary of independence involved a twelve-city Rp.3 billion concert tour, the '95 People's Celebration' (Pesta Rakyat 95), the hundreds of tonnes of equipment moved by Indonesian Air Force planes. Major national anniversaries were often celebrated with huge concerts broadcast live on television, such as the *Dangdut Ria HUT ABRI*, celebrating Armed Forces Day in October 1996. Under the banner of the 'National Discipline Movement' and the Jakarta Military Command, the audience was treated to synchronised dance displays by armed men in uniform alongside bespangled female and male *dangdut* singers. Soldiers gyrated with some of the biggest names in *dangdut*, to the catchcry 'Long Live the Armed Forces!' (*Hidup ABRI*). For the finale, the Jakarta Commander himself joined the act. A few weeks later an Army-sponsored, but less successful, rock concert was also nationally televised. The tameness of the performance and its live audience indicated perhaps that Indonesian rock was an uneasy cultural tool for the New Order.

Disorderly performances

Popular rock concerts were more often venues for expressing popular discontent. In October 1988, after more than two decades as rebel hero, Mick Jagger finally performed in Jakarta. On the day of the concert slum youths stormed the huge outdoor venue, charging the security cordon and swarming over middle-class patrons who had bought expensive tickets. Rocks were thrown, cars (a symbol of middle-class achievement) torched and the entrance damaged as the gatecrashers surged inside. It took several hours for the military to re-establish law and order.

After a February 1989 concert in central Jakarta's Senayan stadium by the immensely popular Indonesian rock musician, Iwan Fals, and his band Swami, some of the estimated audience of 100 000 stormed down Jakarta's main boulevard, Jalan Sudirman. Iwan's group was banned from touring Sumatra in March 1989, a prohibition extended briefly by the Jakarta police commissioner to 'all rock performances...for an unlimited period'.[72] Iwan Fals later joined several other well-known musicians and rebel poet Rendra to form the Kantata group. Their first album, *Kantata Takwa* (Cantata of Piety), embraced something of the Islamic lyrical iconography employed so effectively by Rhoma Irama. It included several of Rendra's poems, which had been periodically banned. The musical style was dubbed '*rebana* rock' (after a traditional tambourine) and described as 'a blend of Jimi Hendrix and Rick Wakeman, to a Betawi "rebana"'.[73]

Kantata performed in Jakarta in 1990 to an enthusiastic crowd estimated at more than 100 000. It briefly seemed that a short power black-out in the stadium would erupt into arson, as the crowd ignited cigarette lighters and matches to illuminate the arena. Three older Iwan Fals songs had become anthems; fans sang and screamed to 'Badut' (Clown, interpreted by many as satirising the Minister of Information, Harmoko), 'Bento' (about a spoilt young tycoon, said to be directed at President Suharto's youngest son, Hutomo Mandala Putra) and 'Bongkar' (Rip it Down), whose stirring lyrics include exhortations to take to the streets:

> Obviously we must take to the streets to
> Overthrow the devil that stands over us
> Oh...Yes...Rip it down!

It was another two years before Fals was permitted to perform in Jakarta again, and then only for two benefit concerts (December 1992 and January 1993) for victims of an earthquake that devastated Flores. The January 1993 concert was held, not at the central Senayan stadium, but at Lebak Bulus on the southern outskirts of the city 'for security reasons', possibly (according to some young fans) because Senayan's plastic seats were more susceptible to arson than Lebak Bulus' concrete tiers.[74] Tickets for the main arena were Rp.4000 (about $A3). Constant drizzle did nothing to dampen the exuberance of the fans, mostly males between fifteen and thirty. Iwan's voice was often drowned out by the mass chorus of fans, who had memorised his anthems of opposition: 'Bongkar', 'Bento', 'Wakil rakyat' (Representatives of the People—a caustic comment on the lives of parliamentarians) and 'Penguasa' (Power-holder).

Patrons had been thoroughly frisked several times before entry. All cigarette lighters, glass bottles, heavy belt-buckles and sharp objects were confiscated. Antagonism was evident towards the estimated 2000 troops present, particularly during songs with overt political messages. Patrolling police were jeered and occasionally showered with plastic bottles or discarded sandals. Fals tried to calm people, urging the audience to 'dance, not fight'. The drenched crowd surged out at the close of the performance, piled on the roofs and bonnets of passing cars and some hurled rocks at glass windows in multi-storey buildings. There were no taxis or public transport, reportedly for fear of rioting. A church was pelted and private cars had windows smashed.

Probably the worst such riot was at the April 1993 concert by US heavy metal band Metallica, when 'about seventy people were injured, a mini supermarket was looted and scores of cars were vandalised'.[75] The crowd, many without tickets and hoping to gatecrash, had become impatient as they waited for the Lebak Bulus gates to open. They pelted security guards and, when anti-riot police arrived, began a running battle and rampage as they retreated towards the elite suburb of Pondok Indah, stoning and looting houses, shops and cars along the way. The Minister of Justice was trapped in his car by the crowd, his windscreen smashed, the driver attacked. Police arrested eighty-eight people.

Discussion in the news media widely interpreted the riots as an expression of class resentment, partly triggered by exorbitant ticket prices (from Rp.30000 to Rp.150000, ten to fifty times the Rp.3000 minimum daily wage for a factory worker) and the location of the venue on the edge of Jakarta's wealthiest suburbs.[76] But the discussion was quickly silenced by the Jakarta Region Military Commander's (Panglima Kodam Jaya) 'appeal' to academics and intellectuals not to analyse the riot 'excessively'.[77]

Since the 1993 Metallica riots, most mass public concerts (both *dangdut* and rock) have been under the auspices of a government instrumentality or military division. In the case of Iwan Fals, such arrangements are no guarantee of public order. His Bandung concert in January 1996, sponsored by the local military command, ended with rioting. Later in the year, in Ujungpandang, at the eleventh hour local police withdrew permission for him to play at an 'Environmental and Musical Appreciation Performance' because of concerns at the 'community order and security situation' *(situasi kamtibmas)*.[78]

Conclusion

The undirected communal passions of live concerts, much more than even the most political lyrics in recordings, seemed to represent both the threat and the promise for the New Order state. The record industry is the least censored of those discussed in this book, and least used for state propaganda. Performers from Rhoma Irama and Iwan Fals to some of the more radical alternative bands have been banned from television and live appearances, but never stopped from producing or marketing records. Thus, while the New Order paid scant attention to recorded music, it attempted to mobilise the communally felt and expressed pleasures of live performances for its own benefit. The political power of the performances in generating communal expressions of pleasures and frustration was always just a breath away from exceeding the orderly bounds of time and space into which these musical carnivals were restricted through permits, procedures and military guards at the venues. In a way the records are just that—records, accounts, memories of the real thing, far less potent than a performance which audiences can turn into communal dissent whatever the politics of the performer.

Notes

1   This idea of popular music as 'disorder' in New Order culture was suggested by Vedi Hadiz, in a lecture *Popular Music and Youth Culture* at Murdoch University, 27 April 1992.

2   See for example Peter Stallybrass & Allon White, *The Politics and Poetics of Transgression*, Methuen, London, 1986.

3   See 'Introduction' in Mikhail Bakhtin (trans. Helene Iswolsky), *Rabelais and His World*, Indiana University Press, Bloomington, 1984.

4   Ethno-musicologist Jaap Kunst opens his two-volume text, on Javanese music by stating that Indonesian music had never been 'autochthonous in the (relatively) pure sense of the term, except to a very limited degree'. See *Music in Java: Its history, Its Theory and Its Technique*, 3rd edn, Martinus Nijhoff, The Hague, 1973, Vol. 1, p. 1. For excellent overviews of contemporary music in Indonesia and a description of many of the styles, see Margaret J. Kartomi, 'From Kroncong to Dangdut: the development of the popular music of Indonesia', in Franz Foedermayr and Ladislav Burlas (eds), *Ethnologische, Historische and Systematische Musikwissenschaft: Oskar Elschek zum 65 Geburtstag*, 1998, pp. 145–66; Martin Hatch, 'Popular music in Indonesia' (pp. 47–67) in Simon Frith (ed.), *World Music, Politics and Social Change*, Manchester University Press, Manchester, 1989; Suzan Piper & Sawung Jabo, 'Indonesian music from the 50s to the 80s', *Prisma*, 43, March 1987, pp. 24–37.

5   *Ensiklopedi Musik*, PT Cipta Adi Pustaka, Jakarta, 1992, Vol. 1, pp. 237–8, 338.

6   K.S. Theodore, '25 Tahun industri kaset rekaman: Pembajakan masih merajalela', *Kompas*, 29 March 1992, p. 6; Efix, 'Bisnis musik rekaman, bisnis kagetan', *Kompas*, 7 July 1991, p. 6. On Lokananta, see Philip Yampolsky, *Lokananta: A Discography of the National Recording Company of Indonesia 1957–1985*, Center for South-East Asian Studies, University of Wisconsin, Madison, 1987. Yampolsky (p. 1) notes that Lokananta initially only supplied recordings to state radio stations around the country, and did not start producing discs (in 78 rpm format) for sale until about 1958.

7   In the 17 August 1959 speech referred to as his 'Political Manifesto' (Manipol), Sukarno stressed social justice, revolutionary
spirit and 'retooling' of state institutions. The following year he
appended five additional principles (collectively known by the
acronym USDEK): the 1945 Constitution, Indonesian Socialism,
Guided Democracy, Guided Economy and Indonesian Identity
(Robert Cribb, *Historical Dictionary of Indonesia,* Scarecrow Press,
Metuchen and London, 1992, p. 285).

8   Sukarno, *Penemuan Kembali Revolusi Kita: Manifesto Politik Bung Karno
pada 17 Agustus 1959*, Penerbitan Chusus Pemuda, Jakarta, c. 1959, p.
27, but quoted here from the official translation, Sukarno, *Political
Manifesto Republic of Indonesia of 17th August 1959*, Department of
Information, Republic of Indonesia, special issue No. 53, Jakarta,
1959, p. 67. Although in the original speech Sukarno apparently used
the term '*ngak-ngik-ngek*', in later usage this became '*ngak-ngik-ngok*'.

9   *Keroncong* is a style of popular Indonesian music, incorporating gui-
tars and violins, with strong Portuguese influences going back to
the sixteenth century.

10   *Ensiklopedi Musik,* Vol. 2, pp. 69–70.

11   The five brothers from the Koeswoyo family established 'Kus Bros'
in 1960, becoming Kus Bersaudara (in 1963), Koes Bersaudara (in
1965) and finally in 1969 Koes Plus. Koes Plus remains one of the
country's most productive bands, with more than fifty albums.
Having commenced its recording career on vinyl in 1960, its
popularity increased dramatically throughout the cassette years and
in 1992 its former hits began reappearing on CD, eight of which
had been released by April 1996. In 1996 the band appeared frequently on Indosiar's weekly *Tembang Kenangan* (Hits and Memories) music show (K.S. Theodore, 'Setelah Piringan-Hitam dan
Kaset: Sekarang Fenomen "Compact Disc" Koes Plus', *Kompas*, 30
April 1996, p. 19). See entry on Koes Bersaudara in *Ensiklopedi
Musik*, Vol. 1, pp. 296–7.

12   K.S. Theodore, 'Eugene Timothy, Kontroversi Industri Musik',
Kompas, 3 October 1996, p. 24 and personal communication with
K.S. Theodore, 15 November 1996. In the 1970s Remaco also
recorded several albums by The Crabs, featuring President
Suharto's son, Bambang Trihatmodjo.

13   Barbara Hatley, 'Cultural expressions' (pp. 216–66, p. 241) in Hal
Hill (ed.), *Indonesia's New Order: The Dynamics of Socio-economic
Transformation*, Allen & Unwin, Sydney, 1994.

14 *Ensiklopedi Musik*, Vol. 2, p. 174.

15 *Ensiklopedi Musik,* Vol. 2, p. 174; Vol. 1, p. 252.

16 The t-shirt appears on http://geocities.com/SunsetStrip/Palms/
    2122/thingy.htm (sighted on 18 May 1997).

17 Theodore, 'Eugene Timothy', p. 24.

18 Yampolsky, *Lokananta*, p. 2.

19 Hatch, 'Popular music in Indonesia', p. 52.

20 For example, 'Jaya karena kaset, jatuh karena kaset', *Kompas*, 14
    June 1992, tells the story of Muslimin, who built his small cassette
    sales and public address rental business in Sragen into a small-scale
    recording venture, in collaboration with a Semarang recording stu-
    dio, Pusaka Record.

21 Philip Yampolsky, 'Hati yang luka: An Indonesian hit', *Indonesia*,
    47, 1989, p. 6.

22 Yampolsky, 'Hati', p. 2.

23 Vedi Hadiz, 'Rappers give New Order an attack of nerves', *Aus-
    tralian*, 17 August 1995, p. 7.

24 International statistics in this paragraph, sourced to Euromonitor/
    International Federation of the Phonographic Industry, are from
    Euromonitor Table No. 1414, 'Personal and Leisure Goods: Total
    Retail Sales of Selected Personal and Leisure Goods 1995', *Interna-
    tional Marketing Data and Statistics 1997*, Euromonitor, London and
    Chicago, 1997, p. 389. K.S. Theodore, 'Kaset musik Jepang meram-
    bah Indonesia', *Kompas*, 17 June 1996, p. 21, gives Indonesia's 1995
    turnover as about Rp.1.14 trilyun (about $US475 million) from the
    sale of more than 70 million cassettes (95 per cent of total sales) and
    CDs (5 per cent), roughly equal to one-thirtieth the US market.

25 Euromonitor, *International Marketing Data,* p. 389. The Malaysian
    comparison is drawn from 1993 figures in 'Vital Statistics' tables
    accompanying Mike Levin, 'Despite '93 figures, Asia's markets have
    momentum', *Billboard*, 106:34, 20 August 1994, p. 47 (sighted on
    <http://sbweb2.med.iacnet.com/infotrac/session524/806/
    3621992/5?xrn_1> on 24 May 1997). See also Johannes Simbolon,
    'Indonesian music industry survives foreign invasion', *Jakarta Post*, 3
    December 1995, p. 7. Generally, sales figures are jealously guarded
    by recording companies, so figures in this chapter can be assumed to
    be estimates published by journalists writing about the industry.

26 ASIRI, *We Were Playing Music Even Before the Borobudur Temple was
    built*, ASIRI, Jakarta, c. 1995.

27 ASIRI, *We Were Playing Music.*

28   ASIRI, *We Were Playing Music*. Hatch, 'Popular music', p. 58, notes
     that 'By the end of the 1970s about 50 per cent of new cassette
     tapes were *dangdut* releases. There were indications that in the early
     1980s the percentage was falling'. Ceres Pioquinto claims that
     'Current trends in the recording industry show *dangdut* dominating
     nearly 70 per cent of the total sales of cassettes in Indonesia'
     ('*Dangdut* at Sekaten: Female representations in live performance',
     RIMA, 29:1–2, Winter/Summer 1995, p. 86, fn. 3). However,
     ASIRI statistics would suggest that, while *dangdut* performances
     may still be extremely popular, 1995 statistics bear out the claim
     that *dangdut* constitutes a much smaller market than Western-style
     pop (by Indonesian performers), that is, 35 per cent compared to
     45 per cent of total sales.
29   Cassettes remain the cheapest and most popular form of recorded
     music. In 1992, when Michael Jackson's *Dangerous* cassette had sold
     300000 copies, the CD version had sold about 10000. At that time
     most foreign CDs sold only 1000–2000 copies and cassettes less
     than 50000 ('Bisnis kaset lagu barat: Michael Jackson pecahkan
     rekor', *Kompas*, 1 March 1992, p. 6).
30   Simbolon, 'Indonesian music industry'.
31   Efix, 'Bisnis musik rekaman'.
32   'Akan saya cari (penyebar isu itu)' (interview with Ari Sigit), *D&R*,
     21 December 1996, pp. 64–8, quotation from p. 67. Suharto's
     granddaughter, Eno Sigit, was also planning an album in 1996. In
     addition to a television station and an English-language newspaper,
     Peter Gontha, business associate of President Suharto's son, Bam-
     bang Trihatmojo, has an interest in Jakarta radio station Trijaya and
     upmarket nightclub Jamz, with a well-equipped recording studio
     for direct recording of live performances (K.S. Theodore, personal
     communication, 15 November 1996).
33   PAPPRI representatives made this claim to a subcommittee of the
     Jakarta Regional Parliament (DPRD DKI Jakarta) in July 1996
     ('Produksi kaset bajakan 5 kali dari yang resmi', *Suara Pembaruan
     Online*, 26 July 1996, <http://www.SuaraPembaruan.com/News/
     1996/07/260796/Kesra/kaset/kaset.html>). This compares with
     Malaysia where in 1987 there were four pirated cassettes for every
     legitimate one produced. See Craig A. Lockard '"Hey, we equato-
     rial people": Popular music and contemporary society in Malaysia'

(pp. 11–28, especially p. 16) in John A. Lent (ed.), *Asian Popular Culture*, Westview Press, Boulder, 1995.

34 K.S. Theodore, 'PMA menantang dan ditantang industri musik Indonesia', *Kompas*, 17 September 1996, p. 25.

35 S. Rakaryan, 'Gairah Idealisme dalam Musik Produser Independen Bermunculan', *Kompas Online*, 20 July 1997.

36 Levin, 'Despite '93 figures'. For a discussion of an emerging Asian music scene encompassing Japan and South-East Asia, see Koichi Iwabuchi, 'Return to Asia: Japan in the global audio-visual market', *Sojourn*, 9:2, October 1994, pp. 226–45.

37 Lockard, '"Hey, we equatorial people"', p. 16.

38 For an explanation of this term, see Simon Broughton et al. (eds), *World Music: The Rough Guide*, Rough Guides, London, 1994.

39 Broughton et al., *World Music*, p. 432, lists among other international releases the following: Elvy Sukaesih's *Elvy Sukaesih* and *Return of Diva* (Wave, Japan); Detty Kurnia's *Coyor Panon* (Flame Tree, UK/Wave Japan); Nasida Ria Group's *Keadilan* (Piranha, Germany); Maryam Mustafa's *Kau Mulai Tak Jujur* (Sony, Japan).

40 See K.S. Theodore, 'Baru: *Dangdut* made in Japan', *Kompas*, 10 March 1991, p. 6; K.S. Theodore, 'Kaset Baru: Akustik, Jazzy, Nostalgia, dan Parodi', *Kompas*, 8 April 1996, p. 19. A number of albums have been mastered at Studio 301 in Sydney, including *Uthe* by Ruth Sahanaya, *Biar Sepi Menyanyi* by Chintami Atmanagara, *Kantata Samsara* by Kantata, *Kahitna II* by Kahitna and *IndieVduality* by Pas (K.S. Theodore, 'Kaset baru, didominasi yang cantikmanis', *Kompas*, 14 May 1996, p. 19).

41 Syahreza's radio station is located at <http://www.hway.net/syahreza> (sighted on 14 May 1997).

42 <http://www.melsa.net.id/~karatan> (sighted on 18 May 1997).

43 Ragadi Music's website is <http://members.aol.com/ragadi/home.html> (sighted on 15 May 1997). <http://www.batavianet.com> (sighted in May 1997) provides links to various sites related to Indonesian music.

44 For example, Budi Rahardjo's music page has links to songs he has composed on <http://www.ee.umanitoba.ca/~rahard/music.html> (sighted on 15 May 1997), and singer Irma Pane, whose 1979 album got into the Top Ten charts, marketed her third album, *Haruskah,* released on her own independent Indonesian music label

IPB-Disc Productions, via her homepage <http://users.aol.com/hbraam/musicians.htm> (sighted on 15 May 1997).

45　See R. Anderson Sutton, 'Commercial cassette recordings of traditional music in Java: Implications for performers and scholars', *World of Music*, 27:3, 1985, pp. 23–43.

46　'Cakrawala Kesenian Rakyat: Dari *dangdut* sampai jazz', *Kompas*, 14 June 1992, p. 6, which also gives examples of local adaptations of international and national successes. For example, Michael Jackson's 'Black and White' was recorded in the *dangdut* style by vocalists Novi Arini and Samantha on Pusindo Records. In 1983, when Aryo Group's song 'Rewel' was popular nationally, Pusaka Records in Semarang brought out an adaptation in the *tayub Sragen* (or *badutan*) style, by Karno KD.

47　Observations made during a visit to Biak in December 1989. Of the twenty-four tracks on the Black Brothers *Special Album: 24 Seleksi Special* (produced by PT Irama Tara, Jakarta) all but three are in Indonesian. The Black Brothers greatly embarrassed the Indonesian government in the mid 1980s when they sided with the Free Papua Movement (OPM) seeking independence from Jakarta, and sought political asylum abroad.

48　Bre Redana & J.B. Kristanto, 'Industri rekaman daerah sebagai gerilya kebudayaan', *Kompas*, 14 June 1992, p. 1.

49　William H. Frederick, 'Rhoma Irama and the *Dangdut* style: Aspects of contemporary Indonesian popular culture', *Indonesia*, 34, October 1982, pp. 103–30 is the most comprehensive study of Rhoma Irama and *dangdut* in English. Quotation is from p. 108.

50　By the late 1990s, however, the interest in *dangdut* as a rebellion against commercial pop may have receded. In 1997 Eddy found that none of the fifty Yogyakarta university students in his sample listened regularly to a *dangdut* radio station, or preferred *dangdut* to rock or alternative music (see Matthew Eddy's excellent study of the Yogya music scene, 'Music tastes and their expression: University students in Yogyakarta, 1997', unpublished BA (Hons) thesis, Monash University, Melbourne, 1997, pp. 46–7, 51).

51　These arguments and Moerdiono's statements are taken from Lono L. Simatupang, '"Dangdut is very...very...very Indonesia": The search of cultural nationalism in Indonesian modern popular music' [sic], *Bulletin Antropologi*, XI:20, 1996, pp. 55–74. The translation of Moerdiono's speech is slightly adapted from originals on p. 55. We would like to thank Made Tony for providing a copy of this article.

52 On regional *dangdut* performances and its working-class female singers, see Ceres Pioquinto, '*Dangdut* at Sekaten', pp. 59–89; Made Tony, 'Bius Sosial di balik goyang *dangdut*', *Basis*, 3–4:45, May–June 1996, pp. 42–51; Budi Susanto '*Dangdut* Sekatenan: Penguasa, "Agama" dan musik rakyat di Yogyakarta' (pp. 195–224) in G. Moedjanto, B. Rahmanto & J. Sudarminta (eds), *Tantangan Kemanu-siaan Universal: Antologi filsafat, budaya sejarah-politik & sastra: Kenan-gan 70 Tahun Dick Hartoko*, Kanisius, Yogyakarta, 1992. We would like to thank Made Tony for giving us a copy of this last article.

53 One *dangdut* singer we spoke to privately after her performance at the Yogya Purnawisata in 1996 admitted to being only fourteen years old and still in junior high school. In a separate conversation the middle-aged male leader of the backing band had earlier told us she was 'about seventeen'.

54 Abdul Rivai Harahap, 'Rhoma Irama (1): Surat Terbuka', *Forum Keadilan*, 14:5, 21 October 1996, p. 11.

55 *Remix Dangdut House Mania: Madu Merah Berdarah Lagi*, PT Sani Sentosa Abadi, 1996.

56 Thanks to David Bourchier for bringing to our attention various articles on the underground scene, including 'Musisi Underground dan industri tergantung telinga', *HAI*, XIX:29, 23 July 1996, pp. 4–8; Emma Baulch, 'Bandung Underground II: a subcultural smorgasboard', *HM,* December 1996, pp. 32–5. These two articles provide much of the information included in the following para-graphs.

57 'Musisi Underground', p. 6.

58 There is even a 'Bandung Underground Bands Page' on the Inter-net at http://bdg.centrin.net.id/~okipwn/bands.html (sighted on 21 January 1999), which lists fifty-nine Bandung groups, in addi-tion to several 'outsider' bands from Jakarta.

59 Theodore, 'Semakin Banyak', p. 25. As a member of one alterna-tive Yogya band explained, 'if Indonesian were used we'd be afraid of what might happen. With a political content' (original and translation in Eddy, 'Musical tastes', p. 73).

60 Emma Baulch ('See Bali and Die' on ABC Radio National's *Radio Eye* program, 7 June 1998), interviews Bali's rock bands who write in English. For a more theoretical discussion of the linguistic

coercions of the New Order see Ariel Heryanto, 'Discourse and state-terrorism: A case study of political trials in new order indonesia [sic] 1989–1990', unpublished PhD thesis, Department of Anthropology, Monash University, Melbourne, 1993, especially Ch. 2.

61 'mulut-mulut tajam berbisa/ambisi dan gila kuasa/jangan hiraukan ulah mereka/dunia ini milik kita'.

62 The name 'Slank' derives from the youth slang expression *slenge'an*, meaning 'whatever I want' (according to Nug Katjasungkana, 'Slank's music: A portrayal of current-day youth culture', typescript dated Sunday, 7 April 1991, photocopy provided by Bimbim Sidharta, 22 May 1997).

63 Statistics on Slank provided by Bimbim Sidharta (by fax dated 21 May 1996) to whom we would like to express our appreciation for supplying detailed background information on the band.

64 Details on Jasad and quotation from Baulch, 'Bandung underground', pp. 32–3.

65 See Benedict R. O'G. Anderson, *Java in a Time of Revolution*, Cornell University Press, Ithaca, 1972, pp. 1–16.

66 On the anti-Sukarno and anti-Communist student movement, see François Raillon, *Politik dan Ideologi Mahasiswa Indonesia: Pembentukan dan Konsolidasi Orde Baru 1966–1974*, LP3ES, Jakarta, 1985.

67 James T. Siegel, *Solo in the New Order: Language and Hierarchy in an Indonesian City*, Princeton University Press, Princeton, 1986, pp. 224–5.

68 Siegel, *Solo*, p. 204.

69 Emma Baulch, 'Punk, rastas and headbangers: Bali's Generation X', *Inside Indonesia*, 48, October–December 1996, pp. 23–5.

70 Quoted in Baulch, 'Punk', pp. 24.

71 'Ikke Nurjanah: "Saya di-booking Pak Ginandjar"', *Tempo Interaktif*, May 1996, at <http://www.tempo.co.id/har/970527_2.htm> (sighted on 28 May 1997).

72 Andreas Harsono, 'A star is banned', *Inside Indonesia*, 21, 1989, pp. 14–15.

73 *Ensiklopedi Musik*, Vol. 2, p. 171.

74 The following comments are primarily based on the 30 January performance, which one of us attended.

75 'Youths go on rampage before heavy metal rock concert', *Jakarta Post*, 12 April 1993, p. 1; 'Riotous youths turn rock concert into a nightmare', *Jakarta Post*, 12 April 1993, p. 3.

76 'Social envy cited as cause of riot', *Jakarta Post*, 13 April 1993, p. 1. See also editorial, 12 April 1993.

77 'Insiden Metallica Jangan Dijadikan Bahan Polemik', *Kompas*, 14 April 1993, pp. 1, 10.

78 'Ribuan Penonton Kecewa', *Kompas*, 17 June 1996, p. 9.

7

THE INTERNET: VIRTUAL POLITICS

If radio was the communication medium of Indonesian independence, then the Internet might well vie for top billing in the fall of Suharto. There is little doubt that, in the last two years of Suharto's rule, the Internet was used extensively by the urban middle-class opposition to get around the regime's censorship of broadcast media. Students used it to plan their moves and gauge international support in building up to the massive nationwide demonstrations that finally led to the collapse of the Suharto regime. In the final days, several students occupying the parliament building were using laptop computers to 'send out news online while the Army tightly guarded the perimeter'.[1]

The global enthusiasm about the Internet's capacity to democratise communication and therefore political systems had infused Indonesia's reception of the technology from the start. Indonesia remains one of the least-networked countries in South-East Asia, though estimates of numbers of subscribers at the end of 1997 ranged from 50000 to 100000. Whatever the numbers, the Internet was embraced warmly by both the technophilic developmentalists in the New Order government personified by the new President, B.J. Habibie (who as Minister for Technology was central in developing the Internet in Indonesia), and by the middle-class opposition to the Suharto government. Of course the Internet, like any other technology, lends itself to a varied, even contradictory, range of possibilities. In this chapter we look at the reception and use of the Internet in Indonesia in the context of the struggle for political liberalisation.

As we have noted earlier, the national identity of media products is difficult to establish in an era of increasing mobility and disappearing lines between original productions and copies, translations or adaptations of foreign material. In regard to the Internet, what constitutes 'Indonesian' becomes even more problematic, as so much of the cybertraffic defies attempts to contextualise its spatial or national source or target. Our definition of 'Indonesian cyberspace' is thus arbitrary, dependent on assumptions about the physical location of the contributors to a website or mailing list. We describe the expansion and regulation of the Internet within the sovereign territory of the Indonesian nation. However, we cannot exclude from our analysis of Indonesian political activity on the Internet, sites that were global in their address and located outside the reach of the Indonesian state. Both aspects are central to any understanding of the place of the Internet in Indonesian politics.

Information Superhighway Reaches Indonesia

Like its South-East Asian neighbours,[2] by the early 1990s the Indonesian government had embraced the information superhighway as part of its developmental dream. Much of the groundwork for the superhighway in Indonesia was laid by what one industry executive dubbed 'Habibie's kids', the generation of foreign- and locally trained technologists who benefited from the policies championed, and largesse bestowed, by the former Minister for Research and Technology (1978–98), B.J. Habibie who, not surprisingly, was the first Indonesian Minister to have a homepage on the Internet.[3]

In 1986 the National Research Council (*Dewan Riset Nasional*), under Habibie, recommended the development of science and technology information services. In 1989 this crystallised (under the BPPT, the Agency for the Assessment and Application of Technology) into the design for the information network, IPTEKnet. University campuses were among the first to experiment with Internet links, in the mid 1980s. Prestigious universities, like Bandung Institute of Technology (ITB), Surabaya Institute of Technology (ITS), Gadjah Mada (UGM) and the University of Indonesia (UI), collaborated from 1986 in the establishment of an inter-university network, UniNet, funded by the Department of Education and Culture. In April 1993, the IPTEKnet Planning Committee commenced trials of a Micro-IPTEKnet prototype, involving six government instrumentalities and several major universities and research institutes.

Many of the computer engineers were the beneficiaries of Habibie's 'grand vision' of a high-tech Indonesia, leapfrogging into the twenty-first century. In the 1980s they staffed universities such as ITB and research centres (like BPPT and LAPAN, the Indonesian Aeronautics and Space Institute, both chaired by Habibie), promoting the concept of, and subsequently trialling, the Internet. In the mid 1990s the same people established the first commercial Internet companies, like RADNET. The boom in demand for Internet access began in late 1995 and peaked in the first half of 1996. At the same time, the speed and efficiency of the technology was improving exponentially.[4]

By the end of 1995 there were an estimated 15000 Internet users in Indonesia, being serviced by five commercial Internet Service Providers (ISPs) in addition to IPTEKnet. Over the following six months the figures mushroomed. By May 1996, twenty-two ISPs were listed with the Directorate-General of Tourism, Post and Telecommunications.[5] By September two more had permits to operate, but only about fifteen were actually running. Towards the end of 1996 there were an estimated 40000 subscribers, about 25000 of them using commercial providers.[6] The numbers of ISPs and their subscribers continued to rise, but much more slowly than the highly optimistic industry projections of 1996.[7]

However, given the common practice of sharing passwords and accounts, the number of people with access to the Internet was in effect much larger than the number of accounts. The Internet also had a presence on the media and in politics well beyond the actual number of connections (a microscopic proportion of the total population). Government, business and radicals were all talking about it. Major daily newspapers, such as *Kompas*, *Media Indonesia* and *Republika* devoted regular sections or columns to the Internet and associated computer technologies. Businesses were assured that the Internet had 'changed the para-

meters of marketing. For half the cost of a full-page advertisement in a national newspaper, you can have your own World
Wide Web (WWW) server and address an audience of millions'.[8]
The Internet was touted as offering on-line employment services, information on the latest medical advances, travel book-
ings, Indonesian rock music, education and cultural data—a
window on the world.[9] E-mail addresses were being included on
the business cards of company directors and political activists.
There were even television game-shows in which people participated from home via computer and modem.

There appear to be no verifiable or even widely accepted statistics on who uses the Internet. The Department of Tourism,
Post and Telecommunications estimated in 1995/96 that the
information technology market in Indonesia was worth more
than Rp.100 billion (approximately $US43.5 million), about 40
per cent of it in the banking and finance industries.[10] Geographically, the largest concentration of users was in Jakarta, where
commercial ISPs dominated, followed by Bandung, where universities (primarily ITB) provided the service.[11] An unsourced set
of 1996 figures which appeared both on the *apakabar* mailing list
(the largest Indonesia-related mailing list) and in *InfoKomputer*
(then Indonesia's foremost computer magazine) was as follows:
commercial enterprises (national and multinational, and including the World Wide Web versions of terrestrial publications) 42.8
per cent, research institutes 5.8 per cent, universities 29.5 per
cent, government departments and instrumentalities 20.9 per
cent and non-government community organisations (NGOs) 1
per cent.[12]

In the mid 1990s public-access Internet put the latest information technology in the hands of people outside such institutions,
people who did not own computers or even have telephone connections. Since the mid 1980s government-owned and private
wartel (telecommunication kiosks, offering public telephone and
fax facilities), had mushroomed in the Indonesian urban landscape.
By the early 1990s there were 25000 public phones and 800 *wartel*
around the country.[13] Faxes sent from *wartel* were often a relatively
safe mode of semi-public political communication.[14] PT Pos
Indonesia, the postal service corporatised in June 1995, had used
the Internet internally since 1988. Around 1993 it began planning

for *Warpostron* (e-mail kiosks) to be established at post offices, par-allelling existing arrangements for long-distance fax and telephone facilities. By early 1998 the postal service's Wasantara Internet facilities were available in seventy cities. Public-access Internet not only opened the fastest available mode of communication to large sections of the literate urban population, but this communication was less susceptible to surveillance than public fax and phones.

The information superhighway in Yogya

In Yogyakarta, three public Internet access points were opened in September 1996, two in the higher-education heartland of this old university town. Throughout the month bunting was hung on bamboo poles every 50 m. down Colombo and Gejayan Streets, from the campuses of Atma Jaya and Sanata Dharma uni-versities, past the IKIP (teachers' college), and along the southern face of prestigious Gadjah Mada University (UGM). For over a week a bustling crowd of young people and a thick bunch of parked motorcycles and the odd bicycle outside a small *warung* (kiosk) drew attention to the information superhighway's brand new pitstop—the Maga *warnet* (*warung internet*), or Internet cafe. When it opened on 17 September, offering free access for the inaugural week, its seven booths were in constant use throughout the opening hours, 9 a.m. to 10 p.m. Less than a kilometre away, on Jalan Simandjuntak on the western edge of the UGM campus, about 300 m, from the university's own Internet computer centre GAMA-net, another Internet cafe, Pujayo.C@fe.Net opened on 9 September. Its eight computer terminals were visible through the glass walls, occupying about a third of the downstairs floor-space of Pujayo's popular eatery and karaoke lounge.

With much less fanfare, on 12 September a third public-access Internet point began operations. Wasantara-net, the national ISP established by the government postal service, started up its *warung pos internet* (Internet post shop) with three computers tucked away in a ground floor corner of the Central Post Office. Wasan-tara had only begun offering dial-in services for business and individual clients in Yogya in February 1996 and by September had built up a clientele of about 700, levelling off at about sixty or seventy new subscribers monthly.[15] The *warnet* was a logical extension of Wasantara's services.

Even compared with Jakarta (where dial-in Internet access had been available for private customers since May 1995), the multiplication of public-access Internet points in Yogya seemed rapid. In Jakarta only a couple of Internet cafes had been established by the end of 1996.[16] Surabaya, with a much larger population than Yogya, had only one Internet cafe at that time—the CCF Cybercafe, in the French Cultural Centre, which opened in mid July 1996.[17] But Yogya's high ratio of tertiary students per head of population (second only to Jakarta)[18] and a concentration of higher education institutions at the northern end of the city proved ideal for the expansion of pay-by-the-hour Internet. Rates started at about Rp.100 (approximately US5c) per minute, about twice the cost of local timed phone-calls but vastly cheaper than long-distance calls, and were affordable to many university students. According to staff at the three public-access Internet points, most Indonesian users were young (under thirty) and male.

By mid 1998, the monetary crisis had reduced the number of paid-up Internet subscribers with personal accounts. In Yogya, Wasantara ISP had a third fewer subscribers in 1998 than in 1996. But in the same two years the number of Internet kiosks in the city had risen from three to about a dozen. It is difficult to know whether the financial crisis has actually reduced the total number of Indonesians with access to the Internet.

From the kiosks' point of view, servicing pay-by-the-hour customers often took precedence over fear of a government crackdown, in part perhaps because there was, as yet, no clear government policy or practice, but partly also because a certain conviction about the anarchic and individualist character of the Internet permeated the discourse about the technology. On the local Internet *warung*, the hand of government regulation rested lightly. Permits to open the Yogya Internet cafes were no more difficult to obtain than those required to open computer-rental businesses, which surround the campuses. Staff at the Yogya public-access Internet points claimed that there was no checking or blocking of clients' access to any site. Even the Wasantara *warnet,* which because of its association with the government's postal service might have been security-conscious, kept no record of client identity.[19]

Politics on the Internet

Compared with the USA, and even compared to some of its Asian neighbours such as Singapore, concern about pornography on the Internet has been muted in Indonesia. The Yogya *warnet* suggested that demand for pornographic sites was low. The kiosk staff believed that interest in political information was strongest, followed by academic research, and they chose not to intervene or block clients' access to any site—pornographic or political. However, Jakarta's Internet cafe Cyber Corner posted notices forbidding access to pornographic sites.

From the point of view of the Suharto government, by far the most problematic aspect of Internet usage was its capacity to distribute uncensored political information. The news-magazine *Tempo* (banned in June 1994) went on-line as *Tempo Interaktif* in March 1996. Subscribers' registration details in the initial six months (March–August) suggested that just over 10 per cent of Indonesia's 40000 networked population in that period were logging into *Tempo Interaktif*.[20] Our own experience in the aftermath of the 27 July 1996 civil unrest showed that, in Yogya at least, surfing the Net had become, like listening to shortwave foreign news broadcasts and distributing underground bulletins, a symbolic act of resistance and an important source of contraband information.

One of the major irritants for the Army and the Department of Information was the enormous success of a e-mail discussion list 'Indonesia-l', popularly called *apakabar*, moderated by John MacDougall in Maryland, USA. In 1994–95 *apakabar* came to be regarded by many activists in the NGO community as a valuable means of disseminating material and a crucial source of uncensored domestic and international news. As one writer from a University of Indonesia address put it, the list had become 'an extraordinary mechanism by which to state our opinions and our thoughts freely and openly'.[21] Due to MacDougall's efforts to ensure the anonymity of participants on *apakabar*, it was impossible to determine precisely how many people had access to the mailing lists. Around the end of 1995, MacDougall estimated the number of identifiable recipients of *apakabar* material at about 13000, most of them Indonesians living in Indonesia, followed by Indonesians living or studying abroad.[22] This estimate was made prior to the boom in interest generated by the 27 July 1996 incident and subsequent references to *apakabar* in the Indonesian press.

In late 1995 several articles in the mainstream national print media drew attention to *apakabar*, especially the speed with which politically sensitive news was posted. The weekly *Gatra* wrote, for instance, that news of the arrest and release of some prominent activists was on *apakabar* within hours, but could not make the local papers until the following morning.[23] There were many more references to *apakabar* in the Indonesian print media in the wake of the 27 July incident, effectively advertising the list.[24] *Republika*, for instance, noted the 'dozens of pieces on the riots…published by John Mac Dougall [sic] on his apakabar@clark.net' and quoted from them the views of radical organisations such as the pro-democracy alliance, PIJAR, about the 27 July affair.[25]

Within hours of the 27 July attack on the PDI headquarters, *apakabar* was running a detailed chronology of the unfolding events. The PDI itself posted on *apakabar* a poignant appeal from <pdi.megawati@indonesia.raya> urging 'brothers and sisters throughout the country' to circulate details of the attack as widely as possible, by e-mailing, or printing it out 'because at the moment all sources of information (newspapers, TV etc.) have been pressured not to broadcast what really happened'.[26] Comparing coverage of the 27 July incident on the *apakabar* with two Indonesian and two Australian daily newspapers, Sharon Tickle concluded that *apakabar* 'outperformed the four print publications' with regard to both the 'timeliness' and 'accuracy' of its reports.[27]

When the Internet cafes opened in Yogyakarta six weeks after the 27 July riots in Jakarta, there were many eager to scan the Internet for information presumed to be unavailable in the national media. Pujayo's estimated that about 40 per cent of Indonesian clients sought out *apakabar* and consulted it regularly. In those early weeks both privately owned Internet cafes in Yogya offered information to help customers connect to *apakabar*.

The technological difficulty of censoring the flow of messages on the Internet is well-known. Those who used the Internet to distribute critical political information were confident that if a link were cut by the government, information could be rapidly redirected around the severed node. If the government closed down a domestic site or news-posting group, another would spring up at a different location. One example of the Internet's capacity to challenge the curfews and cordons set by the New Order was the continued presence there of the Democratic People's Party (*Partai Rakyat Demokratik*, PRD), a small, pro-labour, student-based party accused by the authorities of planning the 27 July riots. Despite the authorities' crackdown on the PRD after 27 July, the arrest of the party leadership and the harassment and intimidation of the rank-and-file, the party continued posting on the Internet and on *apakabar* from an ISP outside Indonesia, maintaining its political presence nationally and internationally and thumbing its nose at the government. The military's spokesman on social and political affairs, Lieutenant-General Syarwan Hamid, reportedly acknowledged this presence in a meeting with the major Jakarta NGOs and professional and religious organisations some weeks after the 27 July affair. He commented that the PRD's considerable power is 'evident in its activity on the Internet. Their writings are published at least twice a week. If they are prepared to show themselves on the Internet, it means they are strong. If they were not strong they would not be visible'.[28] Virtual political presence was thus being equated with real politics by both sides: the Internet's invincibility protected the virtual radicals and marked the limits of the New Order's power.

Policy on the Internet

The pace of change in global communication technologies in the 1990s caught many national and international regulatory bodies, including the New Order government, unprepared. The Internet also posed a definitional problem in the context of the Indonesian government's departmental divisions: was it a broadcast medium, which would be primarily under the Department of Information, or was it an extension of the postal service to be placed under the Department of Tourism, Post and Telecommunications? The Internet, like radio and television, became the joint responsibility of the two departments. But, as discussed in earlier chapters, institutional histories of the two older electronic media put the primary responsibility for regulation in the hands of the Department of Information. In the case of the Internet, the departmental arrangements remained unclear.

Policy differences between the departments reflected the tensions within the Indonesian bureaucracy since the mid 1980s about how to respond to ideas and technologies of globalisation. In the last decade of Suharto's rule, the Army and other security departments sought barricades against global influences, while the economic ministries saw many aspects of globalisation as new openings for growth and development. The Department of Information, one of the powerful ministries of the New Order, responsible for censorship and propaganda, was in the former category. The Department of Tourism, Post and Telecommunications, a new portfolio created in 1983 whose primary function was international services and infrastructural development, was in the latter category. Caught between two positions, the Indonesian government, like many others in the region, was simultaneously enabling an expansion of computer networking capacity and trying to control the informational content on the Internet. In the early 1990s the Department of Tourism, Post and Telecommunications enthusiatically embraced information technologies and their economic potentials. The Departments of Information and of Defence and Security remained primarily concerned with regulation, monitoring and control of the information flows made possible by new technologies.

Provision of Internet services depended on PT Telekomunikasi Indonesia (Telkom), the national telephone network, and PT Indosat, the state's international telecommunications carrier, both under the authority of the Department of Tourism, Post and Telecommunications and among the earliest government enterprises to be partially privatised.[29] In a 1996 table of the country's largest and best-performing publicly listed companies (known as the *SWA100*), Indosat ranked fourth and Telkom fifty-first.[30] In early 1996 Telekom joined with PT Pos Indonesia and STT Telkom (Telecommunications Technology College) to establish Wasantara.net to offer Internet services in the high-volume provinces and then throughout the country, with local nodes in every provincial capital and other major cities. Through the mid 1990s, the Department of Tourism, Post and Telecommunications oversaw massive infrastructural developments, notably exponential increases in the number and variety of telephone services.

The 1997 *Indonesia Country Commercial Guide* (prepared by the US Embassy in Jakarta for US businesses) listed telecommunications as among Indonesia's 'principal growth sectors' and ranked computer systems and telecommunications equipment respectively first and tenth under the category of 'best prospects' for US exports in the 'non-agricultural sector'.[31] The global telecommunications revolution transformed the Department of Tourism, Post and Telecommunications from a much-criticised government service provider into a significant economic ministry managing the cutting-edge of global technology. The Internet itself was a relatively small part of this burgeoning empire, but one that grew with the whole digital telecommunications sector.

For the armed forces (ABRI) and the Department of Defence and Security (HANKAM), the only significance of the Internet seemed to be its potential political use. There was so much criticism of the New Order on *apakabar* that one wag claimed that 'Internet' actually stood for '*Indonesia terkenal negatif terus*' (Indonesia is always infamous)![32] Being unable to block out or censor its output, the military attempted counter-propaganda on the Internet. In October 1995 ABRI announced the establishment of a special Internet unit, to go on-line as 'HANKAM/ABRInet'.[33] Its stated aim was to correct inaccuracies in international information about Indonesia. Many believed that ABRInet's real target was not foreigners who 'got it wrong', but locally gathered information that was correct but contravened government interpretations, and was circulating on mailing lists such as *apakabar*,[34] KDP-net, SiaR and other virtual news-pools that emerged in 1996. The ABRInet site never managed to gain credibility or popularity. But it was widely assumed by political activists that much of the pro-government material placed on popular bulletin-boards or mailing lists came from ABRI's Internet unit. One columnist described it as 'ABRI's "Information War" in Cyberspace'.[35]

The Department of Information, which had formal responsibility for Internet content, was even slower to react. The Department, used to dealing with broadcast media such as radio and tele-vision, seemed to have difficulty coming to grips with a medium whose broadcast capacity exceeded all other media (since any message can be sent instantly throughout the world) but which could simultaneously narrowcast to a single individual. For instance, the *Kompas* homepage can be accessed by anyone with a com-puter, modem and phone-line anywhere in the world but a mail-ing list such as *KdPnet* is targeted to a select range of individual addresses in a dozen countries.

The Broadcast Bill gave some indication of the confusion over the Internet. When the Information Department's draft of the Bill came before parliament in May 1996 the Internet was not even mentioned. The Bill had been drafted to regulate the older electronic media, radio and television. During lengthy debates in the House Committee, which continued until December, mem-bers attempted to write the Internet into the existing control structures that operated for radio and television. The term 'Inter-net' was not mentioned. It was collapsed under *'jasa layanan infor-masi'* (informational services). Most provisions of the Act, restricting broadcast area, language of broadcast, proportion of foreign material broadcast and so on, were entirely incompatible with the way the Internet works. It was also not clear whether the *'lembaga penyiaran'* (broadcast organisations) which, according to the Bill, were to be principally responsible for broadcast con-tent, referred to the ISPs which carried the Internet information, or to the individuals or institutions that maintained homepages or moderated mailing lists. As far as the Internet was concerned, the Bill was probably unenforceable.

Department of Information officials participated in ASEAN (Association of South-East Asian Nations) discussions in Singa-pore in September 1996 regarding Internet control but, although expressing support for the principle of strict control agreed in such forums, the Indonesian Department of Information never had the legal or technological means to enforce direct monitor-ing of Internet usage or official restrictions on particular sites, such as had been undertaken by the Singapore government.[36]

As with the other media, much of the Internet monitoring and censoring was done covertly and outside the visible government institutions. In the weeks after the 27 July incident, suspicions were rife that Internet messages both within Indonesia and to the outside world were being monitored and interfered with. The English-language *Jakarta Post* printed a number of letters complaining about various forms of interference with the Internet around this period. That three servers, IdOLA, IPTEKnet and Wasantara-net, were 'down' for various periods in early August was attributed by some to 'letterbombs', massive amounts of messages sent deliberately to overload and thus crash a server. On 4 August IPTEKnet sources confirmed that its troubles may indeed have been the result of such a letterbomb.[37] Then, and later in the weeks building up to Suharto's resignation, any interruptions to Internet traffic in and out of Indonesia raised the spectre of intervention by the security apparatus striving to stifle information.

ISPs were reluctant to confirm whether they had been asked explicitly or were expected implicitly to block public access to particular sites or types of information. The industry has the technology to monitor the traffic on their lane of the superhighway. ISPs could monitor which sites their clients connect to and in most cases what messages (except encrypted ones) flow via e-mail addresses. It is possible, for example, to sit in the computer room of an ISP and watch on-screen the log of traffic through the ISP, second by second. While the technical capacity for such monitoring exists, the effort involved is exceptionally high and ISP technicians we spoke to were adamant that spying was not their concern. However, as with many newspapers and television stations, there were rumours that informants and security intelligence staff were employed within ISPs to monitor information and report to the Department of Information.

Chapter X of the Broadcast Act, finally approved by the President in October 1997, appeared to be an attempt to legalise such modes of surveillance. Titled 'Investigation', the section stated 'Apart from the police...particular civilian employees of departments whose work and responsibility involves broadcast, are given special authority as investigators under Act No. 8, 1981 of the Criminal Code (*Hukum Acara Pidana*)'.[38] A civilian investigator's duties included 'receiving reports or complaints from individuals regarding criminal acts in the area of broadcasting' and questioning and fingerprinting suspects. The section was retained despite the strenuous objections of PDI representatives, who sought to restrict criminal investigations to the police service.

As shown in earlier chapters, censorship in the Indonesian media, particularly from the early 1980s, had been effective due rather to self-censorship within media industries than to consistent government action. But self-censorship depended on the threat of punishment. With the Internet the target for such punishment was hard to define: who was to blame for a critical, anti-government message? The author? The ISP through which the message was transported? The reader who downloaded the message from a website? Moreover, in a new industry, whose global *raison d'être* was unhampered flow of information, ISPs located in Indonesia needed to be internationally competitive in ensuring client confidentiality and access to information. Otherwise, for the price of a brief international phone-call, Indonesian consumers might prefer to use ISPs located outside Indonesian territory. Many Internet users, including some of the largest semi-underground mailing lists as well as legal newspapers and magazine websites, used ISPs located abroad.[39] Suharto's last Information Minister, Alwi Dahlan, was only stating the obvious when he told the foreign press, just weeks before the President's fall, that 'I do not see how you could regulate the Internet'.[40]

Local Politics, Global Information

In the last few years of the Suharto regime, as dissent against the New Order grew, Indonesian citizens could and did speak without constraint, in Indonesian and in English, on websites and mailing lists located on ISPs in various parts of the world. But the relation between freedom of speech on the Internet and democracy at the level of parliament and the streets of Indonesia is neither obvious nor direct. In this last section we look at Internet accounts of 1996 riots in a small town in Java. We will show that the Internet was available, well before the collapse of the Suharto regime, as a medium in which to build up a story, an interpretation of the events, that was qualitatively different from that of the older national media, such as television or newspapers.

On 10 October 1996 the curious trial of a Muslim, accused of insulting Islam, in the East Java provincial town of Situbondo brought down a verdict deemed insufficient by the thousands of faithful in attendance. Their anger spilled into the streets and was directed at the minority Christian community.

Indonesian national dailies carried the news on the morning of 12 October after the press had been briefed by the Secretary of State, Moerdiono. The leading daily, *Kompas,* published a report of the briefing on its front page, followed by its own coverage of the riots in Situbondo. In terms of material information about the incident *Kompas* reported that 2000–3000 people from Situbondo and neighbouring towns had run amok after the court gave what they considered an inadequate sentence against blasphemy. As for the damage, 'cars and several buildings were burnt, including the district court…Later the crowd attacked and burnt other buildings in Situbondo and surrounding townships, including schools, churches and a Chinese temple'.[41]

In apparent attention to detail the article identified all but one of the eight vehicles the crowd had burnt, but gave no detail of schools or churches that had been destroyed. Neither did it name, other than Situbondo, towns affected by the rioting. Through the following week, *Kompas* carried news or editorial pieces referring to the Situbondo affair almost daily. But all the stories emanated from Jakarta, and gave the views of ministers and social commentators about ways of preserving national and social harmony. Even its coverage of the investigatory visit to the area by the National Human Rights Commission (*Komnas HAM*) did not generate any further detail about the incidents in East Java.

On the Internet, however, an enormous amount of local detail was emerging. Within a day of the riots an umbrella organisation, the Surabaya Christian Communication Forum (FKKS), which covered a diverse range of Christian organisations, institutions and foundations in Surabaya and East Java,[42] had circulated a statement addressed to the world Christian community via a US-based Internet homepage, FICA-net. The statement was picked up the following day by *apakabar.* In subsequent weeks, the FKKS placed several statements and declarations regarding the Situbondo incident on the Internet.

The FICA-net reports gave graphic details of the riots, which started in Situbondo around 10 a.m. and by afternoon had extended to the neighbouring towns of Besuki (20 km away), Penarukan, Asem Bagus (30 km away) and Wonorejo. The rioters had desecrated or destroyed twenty-four churches, a Buddhist temple, four Christian schools, and a Christian orphanage. The buildings and their location were given in the report. Five people had died: a Christian minister and his family, including a six-year-old child. A chronology placed on the FICA-net on 16 October contained an hour-by-hour account of the incidents, even the slogans chanted by rioters.

On 17 October, the FKKS addressed a letter to 'the Christian Community around the world' asking for their prayers and financial support. Having appeared immediately on FICA-net, with the note 'After receiving this letter, please circulate it to other colleagues in your area', it was posted on *apakabar* on 22 October. Details were updated in subsequent months. The site contained photographs of the incident, a detailed chronology, a list of newspaper articles in English and Indonesian, messages of concern placed on FICA-net, information about 'prayer action', 'observations from project Open Book' (which included eyewitness accounts from the area) and details for those who wished to send donations to the victims.

The Internet also acted as a forum for arguments and debates. 'Jelantik Padmono' listed details of the Situbondo riots on another Christian mailing list, paroki-net, on 11 October, which appeared the next day on *apakabar*, and sparked spirited responses from individuals identifying themselves as Muslims. 'Gagak Rimang' (13 October 1996) questioned the emphasis on church-burning in Internet reports of the incidents and sought explanation of the local issue that had triggered the incident: 'What is the problem between Soleh [the man charged with defamation] and Kyai Arsyad [the highly regarded local Kyai deemed to have been defamed]'? 'Muaz' put postings both on *apakabar* (13 October) and on <is-lam@isnet.org> mailing list (14 October) (which appeared the following day on *apakabar*) criticising the emotionalism of the FICA-net reports. He also explained the rioters' actions in terms of the anger felt by the local population at the insult to a revered figure. Beyond the obviously partisan accounts of FKKS, the Internet thus became a place to query and test what happened and why, in and around Situbondo.

There were occasions when FKKS was mentioned in the national press,[43] but only in passing as an interested party, without mentioning the detailed documentation it had compiled or the numerous public statements it had released.[44] As an FKKS spokesperson explained:

For several reasons, almost all of the information which the FKKS placed on Internet was not published in the ordinary mass media (press, TV, radio). None of our publications, including the Chronology of Events, Statements of Concern, and other reports ever appeared in the mass media, although we sent copies of the manuscripts by fax to the media. The FKKS is known by the world Christian community precisely through the Internet. They can get frank [*lugas*] news reports from FKKS publications on Internet about the damage which occurred to churches recently, which was not reported in detail in the conventional mass media.

Sometimes Indonesians in Indonesia who can only get access to TV, radio or newspapers do not get complete information about the destruction which occurs, for example, the number and name of churches which fall victim, or the *modus operandi* of the destruction. For example, the destruction of ten churches in Surabaya on 9 June 1996 was not given any mention in the domestic mass media; evidence of very effective press control in Indonesia.[45]

Our point is not that these local details are any more true or valid than the news covered by the formal news media. It is that the 'local'—local detail, local voices, local accounts and opinions—simply disappeared from the formal media, replaced by generalised, standardised views from the capital. On the Internet, however, local knowledge bypassed the national media and went global.

Conclusion

It was not so much the content of political discourse on the Internet that seemed important in the final months of Suharto's rule, but the sense that absolutely anything could be said with impunity. The very freedom of the Internet became a constant reminder of the absence of openness and freedom in the other media. Universities' Internet facilities, intended for academic purposes, were equally suited to coordinating student political action around the country. The same infrastructures which the New Order government promoted to serve big business could be utilised with equal ease by small, disparate groups to disseminate their views and information. Similarly, the human skill-base produced by the Habibie-driven technology training policies of the New Order produced the technicians who staffed both high-tech offices in the skyscrapers of Jakarta and the stuffy backrooms of community action groups around the country. Smart university graduates set up ISPs like RADNET and cyberpublications such as *Tempo Interaktif*. The speed of expansion of the Indonesian stretch of the information superhighway, the amount and disorder of its traffic, seemed to make policing it almost impossible. Seen thus, the Internet successfully breached the censorship and restrictions on freedom of expression imposed by the New Order government.

Our argument is not that the Internet and its ability to transgress the national boundaries were a cause of the decline in Suharto's power, but that those transgressive capacities were harnessed with great effect by opposition forces generated by the long repressive reign. The technology could have been used for vastly different purposes. But in the crisis-ridden Indonesian economy, gold and platinum 'corporate Net' lines advertised by the ISPs[46] seemed far less important than the wired *warnet* and their motorcycle-riding student clients, who marched in the streets in the days before Suharto's resignation. In spite of public-access e-mail, the Internet is not, and will not in the foreseeable future, be available to the large majority of Indonesians, not only because of economic constraints but also because its usage depends on a degree of linguistic and technological literacy. In that sense, the political function of the Internet has been defined by the growing middle-classes and their discontent, both spawned by the New Order. To put it differently, the definition of the Internet in Indonesia as a political medium has been determined not by the technology *per se* but by the political agency of a section of Indonesian society.

Notes

1   Sentot E. Baskoro, 'Peranan Internet dalam Reformasi Indonesia', *Infokomputer*, July 1998, located at http://www.infokomputer.com/analisa/100798-1.shtml (sighted on 19 December 1998).

2   See Garry Rodan, *Information Technology and Political Control in Singapore*, Working Paper No. 26, Japan Policy Research Institute,

Cardiff, USA, November 1996, for Singapore; and Krishna Sen, 'Australia, Asia and the Media' (pp. 44–9) in Gavin Jones (ed.), *Australia in its Asian Context,* Occasional Paper No. 1, Academy of the Social Sciences in Australia, Canberra, 1996.

3   On 3 January 1997, Habibie launched his homepage <http://habibie.ristek.go.id>, and within three weeks about 1200 log-ons had been recorded (according to INDONESIA-L, 21 January 1997, sourced to *Tempo Interaktif*, 'Ketika Habibie Mejeng di Internet' on http://www.tempo.co.id/mingguan/47/f_nas1.htm).

4   In 1994 the connection speed from Indonesia via IPTEKnet, the sole provider, was only 64 Kbps (kilobytes per second). In 1995 this had increased tenfold to 640 Kbps, with a similar increase in providers. By October 1996, it exceeded 7 Mbps (megabytes per second). Onno W. Purbo, 'Ceramah Ilmiah: Komunikasi Internet dan Dunia Pendidikan' (pp. 43–7) in *Duta Wacana menyongsong Budaya Teknologi*, Dies Natalis ke34, Duta Wacana Christian University, Yogyakarta, 31 October 1996.

5   A list of twenty-two commercial ISPs, sourced to the Directorate-General of Tourism, Post and Telecommunications, appeared on <indonesia-l@igc.apc.org>, 16 May 1996.

6   'Bisnis Internet Service Provider: Harus kreatif', *InfoKomputer*, September 1996, pp. 132–4.

7   By May 1997, the government had issued permits to forty-one ISPs, of which thirty-two appeared to be operational. One source estimated total Internet subscribers at a maximum of 83 000 (estimate from figures in Rahmat M. Samik-Ibrahim, 'Indonesia-102: The Internet Service Providers', http://www.tjt.or.id/rms46/imho-eisp.html, with number of permits given in Indonesian Internet Service Provider Association (APJII), 'D. Profile', on http://www/apjii.or.id', both sighted 17 May 1997). The figure of 85 000 subscribers was still being given in April 1998 (see 'Penyelenggara Internet Bentuk Konsortium', *Kompas Online*, 9 April 1998), which suggests a dramatic slowing of growth in the light of the economic crisis.

8   Advertisement for Fujitsu Internet Web Servers, *Kompas*, 10 July 1996, p. 17.

9   See, for example, 'Sartono Tawarkan Cari Pekerjaan Lewat Internet', *Kompas*, 26 September 1996, p. 3; 'Memanfaatkan Jaringan

INTERNET', *Media Indonesia*, 3 September 1996, p. 14; 'Kanker di Internet', *Media Indonesia*, 1 September 1996, p. 18; 'Indonesian artists leap onto Internet', *Jakarta Post*, 28 June 1996, p. 2; 'Data Pendidikan Indonesia Dapat Diakses di Internet', *Kompas*, 11 November 1996, p. 20.

10 'HP World '96: Joop Ave: Kebutuhan Instalasi Jaringan Komputer di Indonesia masih tinggi', *InfoKomputer*, September 1996, p. 119.

11 Onno W. Purbo, 'Bisnis di Internet Menggiurkan', *InfoKomputer*, Special Internet Edition, n.d. (September 1996), pp. 42–7, particularly p. 43.

12 The source of the estimated user percentages is not given, but they also appear in Purbo, 'Bisnis di Internet Menggiurkan'. Purbo, one of Indonesia's leading researchers and writers about the Internet, is from the highly regarded Computer Network Research Group in the Inter-University Center on Micro-electronics, at the Bandung Institute of Technology.

13 Naswil Idris & Marwah Daud Ibrahim, 'Communication scene of Indonesia' (pp. 59–86) in Anura Goonasekera & Duncan Holaday (eds.), *Asian Communication Handbook,* Asian Mass Communication Research and Information Center, AMIC, Singapore, 1993. Statistics from p. 63.

14 For instance, the first detailed account of the 27 July 1996 attack on the headquarters of the Indonesian Democracy Party (PDI) in Jakarta reached the UGM campus by fax. The disturbances had started sometime before dawn. By 11 a.m. a three-page fax from the Jakarta Legal Aid Institute (LBH) had reached various student groups and NGOs in Yogya.

15 Interview with Sariyono Setyabudi, unit head of Wasantara Yogyakarta, 5 December 1996, who believed that nationally Wasantara had about 2000 subscribers.

16 During a November 1996 visit to Jakarta, we were able to locate and visit only one Internet cafe, the Cyber Corner in the Twilite Cafe, Kemang. We were told that at least one other existed, but were not able to clarify precisely where. There were two articles on cyber-cafes in a special Internet edition of *InfoKomputer* magazine (undated, but on sale in September 1996) but except for the statement that 'One cybercafe soon to be built in Jakarta is the K@FE.INTERNET' (p. 58), there was no mention of any existing

in Indonesia. Nor were any listed in the international cybercafe guide, http://www.easynet.co.uk/pages/cafe/ccafe.htm (when checked 17 January 1997). However, in November 1996, two TGA Internet Cafes opened, both located in Toko Gunung Agung bookshops (at the Taman Anggrek Mall, central Jakarta and the Mega Mall, Pluit, north Jakarta). The ventures were collaborations between the bookshops, IndoInternet and PT Skill, a computer and information technology company. Details from <skillnet@skill.co.id>, February 1997.

17 Details of the CCF Cybercafe which, like the TGA cafes in Jakarta, was sponsored by IndoInternet, are given on the homepage http://www/surabaya.indo.net.id/euro.htm (sighted 31 January 1997).

18 'About higher education', on the Indonesian Department of Education and Culture's homepage, http://www.pdk.go.id/New/3rd.htm (sighted 22 February 1997).

19 We found that there was far greater concern about the political content of books we were air-freighting out of Yogya than we experienced in our almost daily usage of Wasantara's services.

20 Figures provided by Saiful B. Ridwan, Information Technology Manager, *Tempo Interaktif*, 14 November 1996, in a two-page typescript, titled 'Tempo Interaktif'.

21 Posting dated 1 February 1997, from Manneke Budiman, <manneke@makara.cso.ui.ac.id>. (Original: Saya seorang pengikut setia forum yang istimewa ini dan saya senang bahwa kita punya sebuah sarana yang luarbiasa untuk menyatakan pendapat dan pikiran dengan bebas dan terbuka.)

22 Information provided by John MacDougall via e-mail, 19 January 1997.

23 'Ini Milik MacDougall', *Gatra*, 2 December 1995 on <apakabar@clark.net> (sighted 28 November 1995).

24 'Indonesia-L alias *apakabar*. Paduan fenomena politik dan Internet', *Republika Online*, 26 September 1996.

25 *Republika*, 29 July 1996, posted via KdP on <apakabar@clark.net> (sighted 30 July 1996).

26 Posting headed 'To: Internet users of Indonesia; Subject:Kronologi penyerbuan 27 Juli', on <apakabar@clark.net> (sighted 29 July 1996).

27   Sharon Tickle, 'Assessing the "real story" behind political events in Indonesia: Email discussion list Indonesia-L's news coverage of the 27 July 1996 Jakarta riots', unpublished MA thesis, School of Media and Journalism, Queensland University of Technology, 1997, p. 95. The comparison was with *Suara Merdeka, Kompas*, the *Australian* and the *Courier-Mail.*

28   Siar, 'Kasospol ABRI Kumpulkan 83 Ormas dan Orpol Untuk Menggolkan Keadaan SOB' on <Indonesia-L@userhome.com> (sighted 23 February 1997).

29   See Jay Solomon, 'A private affair: Indonesia's 1997 state sell-offs may only benefit the few', *Far Eastern Economic Review*, 30 January 1997, posted on <indonesia-p@igc.apc.org> (sighted 5 February 1997).

30   '100 Perusahaan Terbaik 1996', *SWAsembada*, 22 August–11 September 1996, pp. 16–19.

31   *Indonesia Country Commercial Guide, Financial Year 1997*, prepared by US Embassy, Jakarta, for the Trade Coordinating Committee, US Government, posted on <apakabar@clark.net>, 20 February 1997 and available on <http://www.usia.gov/abtusia/posts/ID1/wwwhcg97.html>.

32   From 'Humorous Abbreviations Dictionary', listed on INDONESIA-L (sighted 20 January 1997).

33   'Perangi Info Sampah ABRI Masuk Internet' *Republika*, 20 October 1995, and posted that day on <apakabar@clark.net>; and 'Gosip Politik, Berdagang, Sampai Artis Telanjang', *Gatra*, 2 December 1995, posted on <apakabar@clark.net> on 28 November 1995. As noted on <apakabar@clark.net> (19 January1996), an identical military homepage, HANKAM/ABRInet, can be found at both <www.abri.mil.id> and <www.hankam.go.id>.

34   While MacDougall continued the service known as *apakabar* as a free website 'Indonesia-l' (at http://www.indopubs.com/archives> or http://www.uni-stuttgart.de:81/indonesia/news/index.html), from May 1997 he introduced new commercial e-mailed services, such as the news service 'Indonesia-p', which were directly sent only to paid subscribers.

35   Atantya H. Mulyanto, 'Cyberspace: ABRI dan "Perang Informasi"', *Republika Online*, 17 October 1996 (posted on INDONESIA-L).

36 'ASEAN setuju memblokir Internet', *Kompas*, 7 September 1996, p. 3; David Watts, 'Net users' free speech curbed', *West Australian*, 21 January 1997, p. 22; and Rodan, *Information Technology and Political Control in Singapore*.

37 RM Roy Suryo, 'Awas Bom Surat di Internet', *Media Indonesia*, 22 August 1996, p. 21.

38 Undang Undang Penyiaran, Bab X, Pasal 62 (Broadcast Act, Chapter X, Clause 62).

39 For example, SiaR News Service uses an Australian server, http://apchr.murdoch.edu.au/minihub/siarlist (sighted 20 September 1998).

40 Dr Alwi Dahlan quoted in 'Information "key to restoring Indonesia's credibility"', *Straits Times*, on http://www.asia1.com.sg/straitstimes/pages/stsea4.html (sighted 1 May 1998).

41 'Pemerintah Sesalkan Kerusuhan Situbondo', *Kompas*, 12 October 1996, pp. 1, 15.

42 FKKS included the following organisations: PGI (Persekutuan Gereja-gereja di Indonesia), PII (Persekutuan Injili Indonesia), DPI (Dewan Pantekosta Indonesia), GGBI, BAMAG (Badan Musyawarah Antar Gereja), PIKI (Persatuan Intelegensia Kristen Indonesia), PARKINDO (Partisipasi Kristen Indonesia), GMKI (Gerakan Mahasiswa kristen Indonesia), GAMKI (Gerakan Angkatan Muda Kristen Indonesia), Perkantas (Persekutuan Kristen Antar Universitas), LPMI (Lembaga Pelayanan Mahasiswa Indonesia), Yayasan Persekutuan PA Lahai Roi, GPPS (Gereja Pantekosta Pusat Surabaya) and GBIS.

43 For example, 'FKKS Jatim Layangkan Pernyataan Keprihatinan ke Komnas HAM', *Suara Pembaruan*, 23 October 1996 <www.SuaraPembaruan.com/News/1996/10/231096/Headline/fkks/fkks.html> posted on Indonesia-P, 24 October 1996.

44 For example, a keyword search of the Indonesia-l/*apakabar* database (for 'situbondo' and 'fkks') produced twenty-six documents, of which only five were newspaper reports and only one (cited in note 43) referred in any detail to the material produced by the FKKS. Most of the *apakabar* documents were those originating from the FKKS itself. (Gopher://gopher.igc.apc.org:2990/0REG-INDONESIA/r.856328776.11277.27, conducted 19 February 1997.)

45 Personal e-mail correspondence with an FKKS contact person, confidential, dated 20 February 1996.

46 See advertisement for Sistelindo (p. 13) and information on INDOSATnet outlined in 'Didukung Citra, SDM dan Peralatan Canggih' (p. 76) in *InfoKomputer*, special issue on the Internet (September 1996).

END OF AN ERA?

We finished writing this book at a time of great excitement about the political demise of the thirty-year Suharto regime. There is little doubt that that excitement has coloured our reading and permeated our analysis of the media. When we documented the crumbling of censorship and the expansion of the media market in ways that governments everywhere find hard to control, we seem to have confirmed a certain liberal capitalist faith in the connections between a free, privately owned media and liberal democratic politics. Now, more than a year after Suharto's resignation, as racial and religious tensions appear on Internet sites and in pop-song lyrics and burst into physical violence across so many provinces, optimistic projections about cultural freedoms and democracy clearly need to be tempered. On the other hand, Indonesia now has its first democratically elected government since 1955. At any rate, there can be no simple connections between the erosion of government censorship, the opening up of the media and the establishment of a pluralist democracy as understood in the West.

Nor is there a straightforward way to measure the impact of the media on the current political transformations. At the end of the twentieth century in Indonesia, as in the rest of the Asia-Pacific region, citizens' social and political interactions are 'mediated', that is deeply imbued with media images and messages. Even in undemocratic political systems such as New Order Indonesia, media are among the building-blocks of power and contests over it. Films about Suharto created the myth of his historical role; satellite television brought images of political conflict from around the world; censorship of newspapers kept stories of corruption from becoming information; Internet technology challenged the New Order's ability to determine information. The point is not that the Suharto dictatorship or its demise were caused by television or radio or the Internet or imported rock music, but that this history is impossible to imagine without the media. It is in this broad sense that we have tried to understand the struggle over media institutions and media content in New Order Indonesia and its aftermath.

The New Order was characterised by political repression and economic expansion. This produced a set of contradictions for the culture industries. Economic growth expanded media markets and invited diversification of cultural products for the larger range of consumers. But political repression restricted the range of domestic productions within a very narrow set of prescriptions. Not only was it cheaper and financially safer to publish translations of tried and tested foreign works and to broadcast imported television programs, it was also politically safer to circulate imports than to take responsibility for creating new domestic cultural texts. There was always the danger that a new piece of work would not be acceptable to some section of government, that it would not fit the state-sponsored definition of 'national culture'.

If national identity is 'as much about exclusion as about inclusion',[1] then our reading of Indonesian media policy suggests that the New Order's vision of national culture was about excluding regional cultures, local specificities and local allegiances. In the New Order's curious battle against the 'local', global imports and foreign images were lesser threats than local languages and images that might show up cracks and contradictions, even just differences, in the national body-politic. The Suharto government's critique of Western cultural imperialism was not only muted in comparison to Sukarno's radical nationalism, it was muted even in comparison to some of the more strident positions taken by other South-East Asian leaders. Over three decades New Order media policy and new globalising communication technologies increasingly integrated Indonesia into global cultural markets. The jury is still out on some of the questions about globalisation with which we started this book. However, the amount of foreign linguistic and visual material circulating in Indonesia was undeniably greater at the end of the New Order than at the beginning, and we have documented the ways in which foreign icons permeated domestically produced films, popular music, popular fiction and so on.

Prior to the financial crisis, the expansion of domestic production was undermining the state's capacity to circumscribe variety and allowing local specificities to surface even in film and television, the two most-censored media. The popularity of Betawi programs, and images of unrest contradicting official 'news', were early signs that cracks were widening even on television, whose unified national discourse had most successfully emasculated the 'local'—its images, languages and events. Self-consciously hybrid cultural texts combined parochial and global symbolism, sometimes to express overt political critique but more often to show the mood of class- and generation-based discontent against the New Order. Such texts domesticated the foreign, nationalised the regional, and began to challenge the very definitions on which the state's media and culture policies had been ordered. These texts were evidence of the erosion of the New Order's political and ideological legitimacy.

It is difficult to generalise a mode of articulation of culture and politics across the range of media that we have dealt with in this book. Particular media technologies enable or circumscribe particular kinds of communication. We have argued, for instance, that radio was the best vector for regional cultural and political discourse. Television was at the epicentre of national ideological control. The Internet both breached the New Order's national information border controls and brought local issues into national and international focus. We do not, however, argue for some variant of technological determinism. In each case the technology could have been put to different use. Indeed, in other national and historical situations the same medium has developed in different ways. In India, for instance, radio has remained under state control. In China, domestic television has become regionally diversified. In many national contexts the Internet has been used more for virtual sex than for virtual politics. Each chapter has aimed to show that the characteristics of a medium's function depend on the social and historical context in which the medium is introduced and embedded.

The institutional and textual features described in this account of the culture industries will not change overnight. The legacy of the Suharto rule will continue, even in the most unpredictable of times, to limit and enable particular directions of change. The curtain has not yet been pulled on the New Order. The agenda of the post-Suharto governments in media policy to date has been legalising changes that were looming in the closing years of the New Order. Many of the changes, particularly removing the restrictions on licensing of print media and later of television, had long been demanded by the business community. Even the closure of the New Order's seemingly all powerful and much maligned Department of Information is not a revolutionary act but an acknowledgement that its functions had become illegitimate and indeed impossible to carry out.

Postscript

'Reformasi' is in some ways a continuation of the New Order. Nevertheless, the policy tables have been turned. The New Order, we have said, was characterised by economic expansion and political restrictions. 'Reformasi' to date has been the reverse—marked by an erosion of political restrictions and a contraction of the economy. The politics and economics of 'Reformasi' are again pulling the media in opposite directions. Political change is driving towards opening the media markets. Publication permits are no longer required. Cable television has been legalised. There is little doubt that foreign investment in some guise will soon be permitted in domestic media industries. The political imperatives of post-Suharto politics are also opening channels for cultural plurality which had been suppressed under Jakarta's central control. Policy is in place to decentralise the television industry by establishing provincial channels.

On the other hand, shrinking disposable incomes mean shrinking media markets and, ultimately, fewer media outlets. In the face of reduced advertising revenue since mid 1997, television profits have fallen drastically. Stations have cut broadcast hours and have reverted to using cheap imports. The plummeting rupiah has caused the prices of imported materials to rise enormously. For book publishers, imported raw materials like paper and ink have so increased their costs that even major firms like Grafitipers and Pustaka Sinar Harapan have closed completely or substantially wound back their operations. Daily newspapers, dependent on imported newsprint, have increased their cover-prices and reduced the number of pages. Some have even reduced their frequency of publication, and thus ceased being dailies. New dailies and magazines are disappearing almost as fast as they are acquiring business permits.

The crisis has curbed the growth of the Internet in Indonesia. Prices of imported computer equipment have risen as the rupiah has fallen. PT Telkom increased the tariff for timed local telephone-calls by 56 per cent between December 1997 and February 1999, with a knock-on effect on the cost of Internet use for subscribers.[2] The percentage of lapsed accounts has grown, but more subscribers have joined to keep overall subscriber numbers rising, though at a vastly slower rate than predicted prior to the downturn.[3] Corporate usage has also continued to increase, presumably at the expense of other modes of communication.[4]

The financial crisis has not affected all sections of the culture market uniformly. Domestic live entertainment is reportedly booming. Nightspots and entertainment venues, unable to afford high-profile international acts, are increasingly using local performers. There is an explosion of cultural activities outside the large media institutions. Whether the crisis will change the balance between media-mediated cultural activity and the more participatory forms of performance is yet to be seen. The mood of the moment is best reflected in the latter. Too much is happening in too many places too far away to be adequately reflected in a financially stricken media industry still centralised in Jakarta and not used to considering distant provinces or ordinary citizens as key political and cultural players.

It is too early to predict what kind of Indonesia will emerge from the ashes of the Asian economic crisis and the national political turmoil. But the story of a unified Indonesia told from a single point of view, disenfranchising all alternative accounts, which much of the media formerly sold to the population, is no longer an option. Tinkering with media institutions and market mechanisms will not in themselves create a new legitimate sense of nationhood to take Indonesia into the twenty-first century.

The media will not save the nation from disintegrating. But in its pores, new and necessarily contradictory visions of national culture will need to be inscribed.

Notes

1   P. Schlesinger, 'On national identity', *Social Science Information*, 26:2, 1987, p. 235, cited in David Morley, 'Electronic communities and domestic rituals: Cultural consumption and the production of European cultural identities' (p. 68) in Michael Skovmand & Kim Christian Schroder (eds), *Media Cultures: Reappraising Transnational Media*, Routledge, London and New York, 1992.

2   A timed unit (*pulsa*) for a local call increased from Rp.115 to Rp.125 (1 January 1998), then to Rp.145 (1 April 1998) then to Rp.180 (1 February 1999).

3   'Para ISP Makin Terengah-Engah', *InfoKomputer Online*, June 1998, on wysiwyg://148/http://www.infokomputer.com/0698/bisnis/bisnis.shtml (sighted on 27 January 1999).

4   Observation of Feronica Laksana, Marketing Manager, PT Rahajasa Media Internet, cited in 'Para ISP Makin Terengah-Engah'.

BIBLIOGRAPHY

English-language Sources

Abeyasekere, Susan, *Jakarta: A History*, OUP, Oxford and New York, 1987.

Adam, Ahmat B., *The Vernacular Press and the Emergence of Modern Indonesian Consciousness (1855–1913)*, South-East Asia Program, Cornell University, Ithaca, 1995.

Aditjondro, George Junus, *Bali, Jakarta's Colony: Social and Ecological Impacts of Jakarta-based Conglomerates in Bali's Tourism Industry*, Working Paper No. 58, Asia Research Centre, Murdoch University, 1995.

Anderson, Benedict R. O'G., *Java in a Time of Revolution*, Cornell University Press, Ithaca, 1972.

Anderson, Benedict R. O'G., *Language and Power: Exploring Political Cultures in Indonesia*, Cornell University Press, Ithaca and London, 1990.

Anderson, Benedict, *Imagined Communities: Reflections on the Origin and Spread of Nationalism*, rev. edn, Verso, London and New York, 1991.

Anderson, Benedict, 'Rewinding "back to the future": the left and constitutional democracy' (pp. 128–42) in David Bourchier & John Legge (eds), *Democracy in Indonesia: 1950s and 1990s*, Centre of South-East Asian Studies, Monash University, Melbourne, 1994.

Ang, Ien, *Watching Dallas: Soap Opera and the Melodramatic Imagination*, Methuen, London and New York, 1985.

Ang, Ien, *Living Room Wars: Rethinking Media Audiences for a Postmodern World*, Routledge, London and New York, 1996.

Appadurai, Arjun, 'Disjuncture and difference in the global cultural economy', *Public Culture*, 2, 1990, pp. 1–24.

Article XIX, *Muted Voices: Censorship and the Broadcast Media in Indonesia*, Article XIX, London, 1996.

Article XIX, *Indonesia: Freedom of Expression and the 1997 Elections*, Article XIX/Forum-Asia, London, 1997.

ASIRI, *We were Playing Music even before the Borobudur Temple was Built*, ASIRI, Jakarta, 1995.

Aspinall, Edward, Herb Feith & Gerry van Klinken (eds), *The Last Days of President Suharto*, Monash Asia Institute, Melbourne, 1999.

Atkins, William, *Satellite Television and State Power in South-East Asia: New Issues in Discourse and Control,* Centre for Asian Communication, Media and Cultural Studies, Edith Cowan University, Perth, 1995.

Axford, Barrie, *The Global System: Economics, Politics and Culture,* Polity Press, Cambridge, 1995.

Bahtin, Mikhail (trans. Helene Iswolsky), *Rabelais and his World*, Indiana University Press, Bloomington, 1984.

Baulch, Emma, 'Punk, rastas and headbangers: Bali's Generation X', *Inside Indonesia*, 48, October–December, 1996a, pp. 23–.

Baulch, Emma, 'Bandung Underground II: a subcultural smorgasboard', *HM*, Pacific Publications, Sydney, December, 1996b, pp. 32–3.

Bhabha, Homi (ed.), *Nation and Narration*, Routledge, London and New York, 1990.

Bourchier, David & John Legge (eds), *Democracy in Indonesia: 1950s and 1990s*, Centre of South-East Asian Studies, Monash University, Melbourne, 1994.

Brandes, J.L.A., *Pararaton (Ken Arok) of Het Boek der Koninger van tumapel en van Majapahit,* Martinus Nijhoff, The Hague, 1920.

Broughton, Simon et al. (eds), *World Music: The Rough Guide*, Rough Guides, London, 1994.

Buell, Frederick, *National Culture and the New Global System*, Johns Hopkins University Press, Baltimore and London.

Chambert-Loir, Henri (trans. James T. Collins), 'Those who speak prokem', *Indonesia*, 37, April 1984, pp. 105–17.

Company Profile of Televisi Pendidikan Indonesia, PT Cipta Televisi Pendidikan Indonesia, Jakarta, c. 1992.

Cribb, Robert, 'Problems in the historiography of the killings in Indonesia', in Robert Cribb (ed.), *The Indonesian Killings, 1965–1966: Studies from Java and Bali*, Centre of South-East Asian Studies, Monash University, Melbourne, 1990.

Cribb, Robert, *Historical Dictionary of Indonesia,* Scarecrow Press, Metuchen and London, 1992.

Cribb, Robert & Colin Brown, *Modern Indonesia: A History since 1945*, Longman, London and New York, 1995.

Crouch, Harold, *The Army and Politics in Indonesia*, Cornell University Press, Ithaca, 1978.

Department of Information, *Indonesia 1992: An Official Handbook*, Indonesian Department of Information, Jakarta, 1992.

Department of Information, *Indonesia 1998: An Official Handbook*, Jakarta, c. 1998.

Dhakidae, Daniel, 'The state, the rise of capital and the fall of political journalism: Political economy of the Indonesian news industry', unpublished PhD thesis, Cornell University, Ithaca, 1991.

Eddy, Matthew, 'Music tastes and their expression: University students in Yogyakarta, 1997', unpublished BA (Hons) thesis, Monash University, Melbourne, 1997.

Ellis, J., *Visible Fictions: Cinema, Television, Video*, Routledge & Kegan Paul, New York and London, 1982.

Euromonitor, *International Marketing Data and Statistics 1997*, Euromonitor, London and Chicago, 1997.

Featherstone, Mike, Scott Lash & Roland Robertson (eds), *Global Modernities*, Sage, London, 1995.

Feith, Herbert & Lance Castles (eds), *Indonesian Political Thinking 1945–1965*, Cornell University Press, Ithaca, 1970.

Foedermayr, Franz and Burlas, Ladislav (eds), *Ethnologische, Historische und Systematische Musikwissenschaft: Oskar Elschek zum 65 Geburtstag*, Slowakian Academy of Sciences (ASCO Art and Science), Bratislava, 1998.

Forrester, Geoff & R.J. May (eds), *The Fall of Soeharto*, Crawford House Publishing, Bathurst, 1998.

Foulcher, Keith, *Social Commitment in Literature and the Arts: The Indonesian 'Institute of People's Culture' 1950–1965*, Monash Papers on South-East Asia, No. 15, Centre of South-East Asian Studies, Monash University, Melbourne, 1986.

Frederick, William H., 'Rhoma Irama and the Dangdut style: Aspects of contemporary Indonesian popular culture', *Indonesia*, 34, October 1982, pp. 103–30.

Frith, Simon (ed.), *World Music, Politics and Social Change*, Manchester University Press, Manchester, 1989.

Geertz, Hildred, 'Indonesian cultures and communities' (pp. 24–96) in Ruth T. McVey (ed.), *Indonesia*, South-East Asia Studies, Yale University and HRAF Press, New Haven, 1963.

Goonasekera, Anura & Duncan Holaday (eds), *Asian Communication Handbook*, Asian Mass Communication Research and Information Centre, Singapore, 1993.

Hadiz, Vedi, *Popular Music and Youth Culture,* lecture, Murdoch University, 27 April 1992.

Hall, Stuart, 'Coding and decoding in the television discourse' in Stuart Hall et al. (eds), *Culture, Media, Language*, Hutchinson, London, 1980.

Harsono, Andreas, 'A star is banned', *Inside Indonesia*, 21, 1989, pp. 14–15.

Hartley, John, *The Politics of Pictures: The Creation of the Public in the Age of Popular Media*, Routledge, London and New York, 1992.

Haslach, R.D., *Netherlands World Broadcasting*, Laurence Miller Media, Pennsylvania, 1983.

Hatch, Martin, 'Popular music in Indonesia' in Simon Frith (ed.), *World Music, Politics and Social Change*, Manchester University Press, Manchester, 1989.

Hatley, Barbara, 'Cultural expressions' in Hal Hill (ed.), *Indonesia's New Order: The Dynamics of Socio-economic Transformation*, Allen & Unwin, Sydney, 1994.

Hefner, Robert W., 'Print Islam: Mass media and ideological rivalries among Indonesian Muslims', *Indonesia*, 64, October 1997, pp. 77–103.

Hendratmoko, Heru (ed.), *Journalist Slain: The Case of Fuad Muhammad Syafruddin*, Alliance of Independent Journalists, Asian Forum for Human Rights and Development and Institute for the Studies on Free Flow of Information, Jakarta, 1997 (translation by Shinta Larasati, of *Terbunuhnya Udin*, Aliansi Jurnalis Independen and Institut Studi Arus Informasi, Jakarta, 1997).

Heryanto, Ariel, 'Discourse and state-terrorism: A case study of political trials in new order indonesia [sic] 1989–1990', unpublished PhD thesis, Department of Anthropology, Monash University, Melbourne, 1993.

Hill, David T., *Who's Left? Indonesian Literature in the Early Eighties*, Working Paper, Centre of South-East Asian Studies, Monash University, Melbourne, 1984.

Hill, David T., '"The two leading institutions": Taman Ismail Marzuki and *Horison*' in V.M. Hooker (ed.), *Culture and Society in New Order Indonesia*, OUP, Kuala Lumpur, 1993.

Hill, David T., *The Press in New Order Indonesia*, UWA Press/ARCOSPEC, Perth, 1994.

Hill, David T. (ed.), *Beyond the Horizon: Short Stories from Contemporary Indonesia*, Monash Asia Institute, Melbourne, 1998.

Hill, Hal (ed.), *Indonesia's New Order: The Dynamics of Socio-economic Transformation*, Allen & Unwin, Sydney, 1994.

Hill, Hal, 'The Indonesian economy: The strange and sudden death of a tiger' (pp. 93–103) in Geoff Forrester & R.J. May (eds), *The Fall of Soeharto*, Crawford House Publishing, Bathurst, 1998.

Hodge, Errol, *Radio Wars: Truth, Propaganda and the Struggle for Radio Australia*, CUP, Cambridge, 1995.

Hooker, V.M. (ed.), *Culture and Society in New Order Indonesia*, OUP, Kuala Lumpur, 1993.

Huizinga, J., 'Klank die wegsterft', *De Gids*, January 1928, cited in J. Kunst, *Music in Java: Its History, Its Theory and Its Technique*, 3rd edn, E.L. Heins (ed.), Martinus Nijhoff, The Hague, Vol. 1, 1973.

Idris, Naswil & Marwah Daud Ibrahim, 'Communication scene of Indonesia' in Anura Goonasekera & Duncan Holaday (eds), *Asian Communication Handbook,* Asian Mass Communication Research and Information Centre, Singapore, 1993.

Iskan, Dahlan, *Prospects for Socio-political Change Stemming from the Development of the Mass Media in Indonesia,* paper presented at the Paradigms for the Future Conference, Asia Research Centre, Murdoch University, July 1993.

Jackson, Karl D. & Lucian W. Pye (eds), *Political Power and Communications in Indonesia*, University of California Press, Berkeley, 1978.

Kartomi, Margaret J., 'From Kroncong to Dangdut: the development of the popular music of Indonesia', in Franz Foedermayr and Ladislav Burlas (eds), *Ethnologische, Historische und Systematische Musikwissenschaft: Oskar Elschek zum 65 Geburtstag*, Slowakian Academy of Sciences (ASCO Art and Science), Bratislava, 1998, pp. 145–66.

Katjasungkana, Nug, 'Slank's music: A portrayal of current-day youth culture', typescript dated Sunday, 7 April 1991, photocopy provided by Bimbim Sidharta, 22 May 1997.

Katzenstein, Peter J. & Takashi Shiraishi (eds), *Network Power: Japan and Asia*, Cornell University Press, Ithaca and London, 1997.

Kimman, E.J.J., *Indonesian Publishing: Economic Organisations in a Langganan Society*, Hollandia, Baarn, 1981.

Kitley, Philip, 'Tahun Bertambah Zaman Berubah: Television and its audiences in Indonesia', *Review of Indonesian and Malaysian Affairs (RIMA)*, 26, 1992, pp. 71–109.

Kitley, Philip, 'Television, nation and culture in Indonesia', unpublished PhD thesis, Murdoch University, 1997.

Koichi, Iwabuchi, 'Return to Asia: Japan in the global audio-visual market', *Sojourn*, 9:2, October 1994, pp. 226–45.

Kunst, Jaap, *Music in Java: Its History, Its Theory and Its Technique*, 3rd edn, E.L. Heins (ed.), Martinus Nijhoff, The Hague, Vol. 1, 1973.

Kurasawa, Aiko, 'Propaganda media on Java under the Japanese 1942–1945', *Indonesia*, 44, October 1987, pp. 59–116.

Legge, J.D., *Sukarno: A Political Biography*, Penguin, Harmondsworth, 1972.

Lent, John A. (ed.), *Asian Popular Culture*, Westview Press, Boulder, 1995.

Liddle, R. William, *Leadership and Culture in Indonesian Politics*, Allen & Unwin, Sydney, 1996.

Liebes, T. & E. Katz, *The Export of Meaning: Cross-cultural Readings of Dallas*, OUP, New York, 1990.

Lindsay, Jennifer, 'Making waves: Private radio and local identities in Indonesia', *Indonesia*, 64, October 1997, pp. 105–23.

Lindsey, T., 'Captain Marvel meets Prince Rama: "Pop" and the Ramayana in Javanese culture', *Prisma*, 43, March 1987, pp. 38–52.

Lockard, Craig A., '"Hey, we equatorial people": Popular music and contemporary society in Malaysia' in John A. Lent (ed.), *Asian Popular Culture*, Westview Press, Boulder, 1995.

Mackie, Jamie & Andrew MacIntyre, 'Politics' (pp. 1–53) in Hal Hill (ed.), *Indonesia's New Order: The Dynamics of Socio-economic Transformation*, Allen & Unwin, Sydney, 1994.

Magenda, Burhan, *Ethnicity and State-building in Indonesia: The Cultural Bases of the New Order*, paper presented to the Colloquium on Ethnicity and Nations: Process of Inter-Ethnic Relations in Latin America, South East Asia and the Pacific, Houston, October, 1983.

Maier, H.M.J., 'From heteroglossia to polyglossia: The creation of Malay and Dutch in the Indies', *Indonesia,* 56, October 1993, pp. 37–65.

Malik, Adam, *In the Service of the Republic*, Gunung Agung, Singapore, 1993.

McDaniel, Drew O., *Broadcasting in the Malay World: Radio, Television, and Video in Brunei, Indonesia, Malaysia, and Singapore*, Ablex, Norwood, 1994.

McHoul, Alec & Tom O'Regan, 'Towards a paralogics of textual technologies', *Southern Review*, 25:1, 1992, pp. 5–26.

McQuail, Denis, *Mass Communication Theory: An Introduction*, 3rd edn, Sage, London, 1994.

Miller, G., 'Current issues facing the Indonesian book publishing industry', *South-East Asian Research Material Group Newsletter*, 36, June 1989, pp. 7–16.

Miller, Toby & Alec McHoul, *Popular Culture and Everyday Life*, Sage, London, 1998.

Morfit, Michael, 'Pancasila: The Indonesian state ideology according to the New Order Government', *Asian Survey*, XXI:8, August 1981, pp. 838–51.

Morley, David, 'Electronic communities and domestic rituals: Cultural consumption and the production of European cultural identities' in Michael Skovmand & Kim Christian Schroder (eds), *Media Cultures: Reappraising Transnational Media*, Routledge, London and New York, 1992.

Notosusanto, Nugroho & Ismail Saleh, *The Coup Attempt of the 'September 30th Movement' in Indonesia*, Pembimbing Masa, Jakarta, 1968.

Oey, Hong Lee, *Indonesian Government and Press during Guided Democracy*, Centre for South-East Asian Studies, University of Hull/Inter Documentation Co., Zug, 1971.

Palmier, Leslie, 'Mass media exposure of Indonesian graduate officials', *Indonesia*, 44, October 1987, pp. 117–28.

Pioquinto, Ceres, 'Dangdut at Sekaten: Female representations in live performance', *Review of Indonesian and Malaysian Affairs (RIMA)*, 29:1, 2, Winter/Summer 1995, pp. 59–89.

Piper, Suzan & Sawung Jabo, 'Indonesian music from the 50s to the 80s', *Prisma*, 43, March 1987, pp. 24–37.

Poeze, Harry, 'Tan Malaka strijder voor Indonesie's vrijheid: levensloop van 1897 tot 1945', PhD thesis, M. Nijhoff, Gravenhage, 1976.

Pro-Democracy Movement Clobbered, Human Rights Watch/Asia and Robert F. Kennedy Memorial for Human Rights, New York and Washington, October 1996.

Quinn, G., 'The case of the invisible literature: Power, scholarship and contemporary Javanese writing', *Indonesia*, 35, April 1983, pp. 1–36.

Ramage, Douglas E., *Politics in Indonesia: Democracy, Islam and the Ideology of Tolerance*, Routledge, London and New York, 1995.

Robertson, Roland, 'Glocalization: Time–space and homogeneity–heterogeneity' in Mike Featherstone, Scott Lash & Roland Robertson (eds), *Global Modernities*, Sage, London, 1995.

Robison, Richard, *Indonesia: The Rise of Capital*, Allen & Unwin, Sydney, 1986.

Rodan, Garry, *Information Technology and Political Control in Singapore*, Working Paper No. 26, Japan Policy Research Institute, Cardiff, USA, 1996.

Schlesinger, P., 'On national identity', *Social Science Information*, 26:2, 1987, quoted in David Morley, 'Electronic communities and domestic rituals: Cultural consumption and the production of European cultural identities' in Michael Skovmand & Kim Christian Schroder (eds), *Media Cultures: Reappraising Transnational Media*, Routledge, London and New York, 1992.

Sen, Krishna, 'Hidden from history: Aspects of Indonesian cinema 1955–65', *Review of Indonesian and Malaysian Affairs*, 19:2, 1985, pp. 1–50.

Sen, Krishna, 'Si Boy looked at Johnny', *Continuum*, 4:1, 1991, pp. 136–51.

Sen, Krishna, *Indonesian Cinema: Framing the New Order*, Zed Books, London and New Jersey, 1994.

Sen, Krishna, 'Australia, Asia and the media' in Gavin Jones (ed.), *Australia in its Asian Context*, Occasional Paper No. 1, Academy of the Social Sciences in Australia, Canberra, 1996.

Shiraishi, Saya S., 'Japan's soft power: Doraemon goes overseas' (pp. 234–72) in Peter J. Katzenstein & Takashi Shiraishi (eds), *Network Power: Japan and Asia*, Cornell University Press, Ithaca and London, 1997.

Siegel, James T., *Solo in the New Order: Language and Hierarchy in an Indonesian City*, Princeton University Press, Princeton, 1986.

Sinclair, John, Elizabeth Jacka & Stuart Cunningham (eds), *New Patterns in Global Television: Peripheral Vision*, OUP, Oxford, 1996.

Skovmand, Michael & Kim Christian Schroder (eds), *Media Cultures: Reappraising Transnational Media*, Routledge, London and New York, 1992.

Smith, Edward C., 'A history of newspaper suppression in Indonesia 1949–1965', PhD dissertation, University of Iowa, 1969.

Statistical Year Book 1993, United Nations, New York, 1995.

Stallybrass, Peter & Allon White, *The Politics and Poetics of Transgression*, Methuen, London, 1986.

Straubhaar, Joseph, 'Beyond media imperialism: Asymmetrical interdependence and cultural proximity', *Critical Studies in Mass Communications*, 8:1, 1991, pp. 39–59.

Subakti, Baty & Ernst Katoppo (eds), *Media Scene 1991–1992 Indonesia*, PPPI, Jakarta, 1992.

Subakti, Baty & Ernst Katoppo (eds), *Media Scene 1995–1996 Indonesia*, PPPI, Jakarta, 1996.

Sukarno, *Political Manifesto Republic of Indonesia of 17 August 1959*, Department of Information, Republic of Indonesia, special issue No. 53, Jakarta, 1959.

Susanto, Astrid, 'The mass communications system in Indonesia' in Karl D. Jackson & Lucian W. Pye (eds), *Political Power and Communications in Indonesia*, University of California Press, Berkeley, 1978.

Sutton, R. Anderson, 'Commercial cassette recordings of traditional music in Java: Implications for performers and scholars', *World of Music*, 27:3, 1985, pp. 23–43.

Teeuw, A., *Modern Indonesian Literature*, 2 vols, Martinus Nijhoff, The Hague, 1967–79.

Tickell, Paul Graham, 'Good books, bad books, banned books: Literature, politics and the pre-war Indonesian novel', unpublished MA thesis, Monash University, Melbourne, 1982.

Tickle, Sharon, 'Assessing the "real story" behind political events in Indonesia: E-mail discussion list Indonesia-l's news coverage of the 27 July 1996 Jakarta riots', unpublished MA thesis, School of Media and Journalism, Queensland University of Technology, 1997.

Toer, Pramoedya Ananta (trans. Max Lane) *Footsteps*, Penguin, Melbourne, 1990.

Toer, Pramoedya Ananta (trans. Max Lane), *Awakenings* (combining *This Earth of Mankind* and *Child of All Nations*), Penguin, Melbourne, 1991.

Toer, Pramoedya Ananta (trans. Max Lane), *House of Glass*, Penguin, Melbourne, 1992.

Tomlinson, John, *Cultural Imperialism*, Johns Hopkins University Press, Baltimore and London, 1991.

Tracy, Michael, 'Popular culture and the economics of global television', *Intermedia*, 16:2, 1988, pp. 9–25.

US Information Service, 'A brief guide to the Indonesian media', 2 vols, USIS, Jakarta, 1992.

Wiji Thukul, 'Warning' in James Balowski, Helen Jarvis, Max Lane & Vanessa Tanaja (trans.), *The Struggle for Democracy in Indonesia: Action in Solidarity with Indonesia and East Timor*, ASIET, Sydney, 1996.

Wild, Colin, 'Indonesia: A nation and its broadcasters' *Indonesia Circle*, 43, June 1987, pp. 15–40.

Wild, Colin, 'Radio midwife: Some thoughts on the role of broadcasting during the Indonesian struggle for independence', *Indonesia Circle*, 55, June 1991, pp. 34–42.

Wolff, Janet, *The Social Production of Art*, Macmillan, London, 1981.

Yampolsky, Philip, *Lokananta: A Discography of the National Recording Company of Indonesia 1957–1985*, Center for South-East Asian Studies, University of Wisconsin, Madison, 1987.

Yampolsky, Philip, 'Hati yang luka: An Indonesian hit', *Indonesia*, 47, 1989, pp. 1–17.

Yoshihara, Kunio, *The Rise of Ersatz Capitalism in South-East Asia*, OUP, Singapore and New York, 1988.

Zainu'ddin, Ailsa, *A Short History of Indonesia*, Cassell, Stanmore, 1968.

Zoetmulder P.J. (with S.O. Robson), *Old Javanese–English Dictionary*, Martinus Nijhoff, The Hague, 1982.

Indonesian–language Sources

Adhi, Aloysius Pitono, 'Gagasan "Pembangunan" dalam TVRI: Analisa Discourse atas Program Siaran TVRI', Honours (S1) thesis, Department of Communication, University of Indonesia, 1993.

Atmakusumah, *Kebebasan Pers dan Arus Informasi di Indonesia*, Lembaga Studi Pembangunan, Jakarta, 1981.

Biro Pusat Statistik, *Statistik Indonesia 1991*, BPS, Jakarta, 1992.

Biro Pusat Statistik, *Statistik Indonesia 1995*, BPS, Jakarta, 1995.

Budiman, Arief, 'Wiji Thukul: Penyair Kampung' (pp. vii–xvi) in Wiji Thukul, *Mencari tanah lapang,* Manus Amici, Amsterdam, 1994.

Budiman, Arief, 'Kata Pengatar: Udin: Dari wartawan ke inteligensia' in Heru Hendratmoko (ed.), *Terbunuhnya Udin,* Aliansi Jurnalis Independen and Institut Studi Arus Informasi, Jakarta, 1997.

Bujono, B., P. Setia & T. Hadad (eds), *Mengapa Kami Menggugat*, Yayasan Alumni TEMPO, Jakarta, 1995.

Cholis, Noor, 'Tentang Komik: Yang Menggemaskan, Yang Cerdas', *Kalam*, 7, 1996, pp. 41–51.

Data Kewartawanan IPPPN Tahun 1995, Proyek Pembinaan Pers, Departemen Penerangan, Jakarta, 1995/96.

Data Tiras Peredaran IPPPN Tahun 1995, Proyek Pembinaan Pers, Departemen Penerangan, Jakarta, 1995/96.

Departemen Pendidikan dan Kebudayaan RI, *Kamus Besar Bahasa Indonesia*, 2nd edn, Balai Pustaka, Jakarta, 1989.

Departemen Penerangan RI, *Pedoman Pembinaan Pers, Grafika dan Penerbitan Pemerintah*, Deppen, Jakarta, 1982.

Departemen Penerangan Republik Indonesia, *Data Dan Fakta 1993/1994 Program Tahun 1 Pelita VI*, Direktorat Jenderal Radio, Televisi, Film, Jakarta, 1994.

Dhakidae, Daniel, 'Kesusastraan, Kekuasaan, dan Kebudayaan Suatu Bangsa', *Kalam*, 6, 1995, pp. 74–102.

Ensiklopedi Musik, 2 vols, PT Cipta Adi Pustaka, Jakarta, 1992.

Faruk, *Pengantar Sosiologi Sastra: Dari Strukturalisme Genetik Sampai Post Modernisme*, Pustaka Pelajar, Yogyakarta, 1994.

Faruk, *Perlawanan Tak Kunjung Usai: Sastra Politik Dekonstruksi* jar, Yogyakarta, 1995.

Gayatri, Gati, *Apresiasi Masyarakat Terhadap Siaran TVRI*, paper presented at the Seminar Membangun Citra Aara Seni dan Budaya Media Televisi, Yogyakarta, 21–22 August 1996.

Gerakan Pro Demokrasi Digebuk: tentang Peristiwa 27 Juli 1996 (translated from *The Pro-Democracy Movement Clobbered*, Human Rights Watch/ Asia & Robert F. Kennedy Memorial for Human Rights, New York and Washington, October 1996).

Hamid, Syamsul Rijal & Estu Rahayu (eds), *Daftar Buku 1996*, Ikatan Penerbit Indonesia (IKAPI), Jakarta, 1996.

Hanazaki, Yasuo (trans. Danang Kukuh Wardoyo & Tim Cipinang), *Pers Terjebak*, Institut Studi Arus Informasi, Jakarta, 1998.

Harahap, Abdul Rivai, 'Rhoma Irama (1): Surat Terbuka', *Forum Keadilan*, 14:5, 21 October 1996, p. 11.

Haryanto, Ign(atius) (ed.), *Laporan Akhir Tahun: Pers Indonesia Terus di-Pres*, Aliansi Jurnalis Independen and Lembaga Studi Pers dan Pembangunan, Jakarta, 1997.

Hendratmoko, Heru (ed.), *Terbunuhnya Udin*, Aliansi Jurnalis Independen and Institut Studi Arus Informasi, Jakarta, 1997 (translated by Shinta Larasati as *Journalist Slain: The Case of Fuad Muhammad Syafruddin*, Alliance of Independent Journalists, Asian Forum for Human Rights and Development and Institute for the Studies on Free Flow of Information, Jakarta, 1997).

Heryanto, Ariel, 'Masihkah Politik Jadi Panglima? Politik Kesusasteraan Indonesia Mutakhir', *Prisma*, 8, 1988, pp. 3–16.

Hilman, *Lupus: Interview with the Nyamuk!*, Gramedia Pustaka Utama, Jakarta, 1995.

Intani, Retno (ed.), *Sarasehan Nasional Pertelevisian*, papers presented at Seminar on the Thirty-Sixth Anniversary of TVRI, Aditya Media, Yogyakarta, 1998.

Junaedhie, Kurniawan, *Ensiklopedi Pers Indonesia*, Gramedia Pustaka Utama, Jakarta, 1991.

Katalog Komik 1995–1996, EMK, Jakarta, 1996.

Kristianto, J.B, *Katalog Film Indonesia 1926–1995*, PT Grafiasri Mukti, Jakarta, 1995.

Kusumasari, Susanti, 'Pola Bantuan Manajemen KKG kepada Pers Daerah', unpublished Sarjana thesis, Jurusan Ilmu Komunikasi, Fakultas Ilmu Sosial dan Ilmu Politik, Universitas Gadjah Mada, Yogyakarta,

us: Banjir Bacaan Untung Siapa?', *Prisma*, May 1987,

Laporan Pengembangan Siaran Nasional TVRI 1980–1981, Pusat Penelitian Dan Pengembangan Media Massa, Jakarta, 1980/81.

Lesmana, Tjipta, *20 Tahun Kompas: Profil Pers Indonesia Dewasa Ini*, Erwin-Rika Press, Jakarta, 1985.

Marga, T., *Karmila*, Gramedia, Jakarta, 1973.

Massardi, Noorca M., Mega Simarmata & Salomo Simanungkalit (eds), *Udin, Darah Wartawan*, Penerbit Mizan and Pustaka Republika, Bandung, 1997.

Media Kerja Budaya Editorial Committee, 'Televisi: Mesin Kebudayaan', *Media Kerja Budaya*, Vol. 2, 1995.

Moedjanto, G., B. Rahmanto & J. Sudarminta (eds), *Tantangan Kemanusi-aan Universal: Antologi filsafat, budaya sejarah-politik & sastra: Kenangan 70 Tahun Dick Hartoko*, Kanisius, Yogyakarta, 1992.

'Musisi Underground dan industri tergantung telinga', *HAI*, XX:29, 1996, pp. 4–8.

Nugraha, Yudhistira Ardi, *Arjuna Mencari Cinta*, Cypress, Jakarta, 1977.

Perkembangan Jumlah Penerbit Anggota IKAPI dan non-anggota IKAPI Tahun 1995, Pusat Informasi Kompas, dated 17 May 1996.

'Pertanggungan Jawab Penilaian Oleh Dewan Juri FFI 1980 Semarang', *Bulletin KFT*, 3:VIII.

Pradopo, Rachmat Djoko, *Beberapa Teori Teori Sastra, Metode Kritik, Dan Penerapannya*, Pustaka Pelajar, Yogyakarta, 1995.

PRSSNI *Petunjuk Radio Siaran Swasta Nasional '95*, Pengurus Pusat PRSSNI, Jakarta, 1995.

Pudjianto, Koes, *TVRI Sebagai Inisiator Pengembangan Industri Pertelevisian Nasional,* paper presented at the Seminar Membangun Citra Acara Seni dan Budaya Media Televisi, Yogyakarta, 21–22 August 1996.

Purbo, Onno W., 'Ceramah Ilmiah: Komunikasi Internet dan Dunia Pen-didikan' in *Duta Wacana menyongsong Budaya Teknologi*, Dies Natalis ke34, Duta Wacana Christian University, Yogyakarta, 1996.

Puri, T.A., 'Penggunaan Antena Parabola Di Kalangan Pemirsa Televisi Di Jakarta', Honours (S1) Thesis, University of Indonesia, 1988.

Rahardja, Prathama & Henri Chambert-Loir (eds), *Kamus Bahasa Prokem*, Pustaka Utama Grafiti, Jakarta, 1988.

Raillon, François, *Politik dan Ideologi Mahasiswa Indonesia: Pembentukan dan Konsolidasi Orde Baru 1966–1974*, LP3ES, Jakarta, 1985.

Refleksi Kebudayaan, Panitia Dialog Terbuka Refleksi Kebudayaan, Jakarta, 1996.

'Riwayat Ringkas Persatuan Radio Siaran Swasta Nasional Indonesia (PRSSNI)' in PRSSNI, *Petunjuk Radio Siaran Swasta Nasional '95*, Pengurus Pusat PRSSNI, Jakarta, 1995.

Salamun (ed.), *Dampak Masuknya Media Komunikasi terhadap Kehidupan Sosial Budaya Masyarakat Pedesaan Daerah Istimewa Yogyakarta*, Departemen Pendidikan dan Kebudayaan, Direktorat Jenderal Kebudayaan, Directorat Sejarah dan Nilai Tradisional, Proyek Penelitian, Pengkajian dan Pembinaan Nilai-nilai Budaya, Jakarta, 1992/93.

Sastrosatomo, Soebadio, *Era Baru Pemimpin Baru: Badio menolak rekayasa rezim Orde Baru*, Pusat Dokumentasi Politik 'Guntur 49', Jakarta, 1997.

Sekretariat Pengurus Pusat PRSSNI, *Kumpulan Peraturan tentang Radio Siaran Swasta di Indonesia: Tahun 1970 s/d 1992*, PRSSNI, Jakarta, 1992.

Simatupang, Lono L., '"Dangdut is very...very...very Indonesia": The search of cultural nationalism in Indonesian modern popular music', *Bulletin Antropologi*, XI:20, 1996, pp. 55–74.

Siregar, Ashadi, *Kampus Biru*, Gramedia, Jakarta, 1974.

Siregar, Ashadi, *Kugapai Cintamu*, Gramedia, Jakarta, 1974.

Siregar, Ashadi, *Terminal Cinta Terakhir*, Gramedia, Jakarta, 1976.

Soe Hok Gie 1990, *Di bawah lentera merah: riwayat sarekat Islam Semarang 1917–1920*, Franz Fanon Foundation, Jakarta.

Stanley (ed.), *Bayang-bayang PKI*, Institut Studi Arus Informasi, Jakarta, 1995.

Sukarno, *Penemuan Kembali Revolusi Kita (The Rediscovery of our Revolution): Manifesto Politik Bung Karno pada 17 Agustus 1959*, Penerbitan Chusus Pemuda, Jakarta, 1959.

Surianto, Teddy et al. (comps), *Kompas-Gramedia Group Indonesia*, Kompas-Gramedia Group, Jakarta, 1995.

Suryadi, Linus A.G., *Pengakuan Pariyem: Dunia Batin Seorang Wanita Jawa*, Penerbit Sinar Harapan, Jakarta, 1981.

Susanto, Budi, 'Dangdut Sekatenan: Penguasa, "Agama" dan musik rakyat di Yogyakarta' in G. Moedjanto, B. Rahmanto & J. Sudarminta (eds), *Tantangan Kemanusiaan Universal: Antologi filsafat, budaya sejarah-politik & sastra: Kenangan 70 Tahun Dick Hartoko*, Kanisius, Yogyakarta, 1992.

Toer, Pramoedya Ananta, *Bumi Manusia*, Hasta Mitra, Jakarta, 1980.

Toer, Pramoedya Ananta, *Nyanyi Sunyi Seorang Bisu*, Lentera, Jakarta, 1995.

Tony, Made, 'Bius Sosial di balik goyang dangdut', *Basis*, 3–4:45, May–June 1996, pp. 42–51.

Toriyama, Akita, *Dragon Ball*, Book 1, Indonesian version, EMK, Jakarta, 1996 (Japanese version, Bird Studio, Tokyo, 1985).

Wahyudi, J.B., *Televisi Republik Indonesia dan Televisi Siaran*, Mitra Citra Mulia, Jakarta, 1989.

Wiji Thukul, *mencari tanah lapang*, Manus Amici, Amsterdam, 1994.

Internet Sources

Dailies and periodicals

Asiaweek, <http://pathfinder.com/@@mjlASQYA*ZOGNy7s/Asiaweek/
Bali Post, <http://dps.mega.net.id/news/balipost/
Billboard, <http://sbweb2.med.iacnet.com/infotrac/session524/806/
  3621992/5?xrn_1>
Far Eastern Economic Review,
  <http://feer.com/Restricted/july_18/media_ju18.html>
Gatra, <http://www.gatra.com/III/41/med-41.html>
Jawa Pos, <http://www.jawapos.co.id/21desember/dep21d1.htm>
Suara Pembaruan Online, <http://www.SuaraPembaruan.com/News/
SWA Online, August, <http://www.swa.co.id/
Tempo Interaktif, <http://www.tempo.co.id/
Tempo, <http://www.tempo.co.id/mingguan/

Homepages

Armed Forces of the Republic of Indonesia, <www.abri.mil.id>;
  <www.hankam.go.id>
CCF Cybercafe, <http://www/surabaya.indo.net.id/euro.htm>
Elpamas, <http://www.lookup.com/homepages/74753/alb2.htm>
Gramedia, <http://bermuda.pacific.net.it/~gramedia>
Habibie, B.J., <http://habibie.ristek.go.id>
Indonesian Department of Education and Culture,
  <http://www.pdk.go.id/New/ 3rd.htm>
International cybercafe guide,
  <http://www.easynet.co.uk/pages/cafe/ccafe.htm>
Koil, <http://www.melsa.net.id/~karatan>
Live Aid, <http://www.herald.co.uk/local_info/live_aid.html>
Music site, <http://www.batavianet.com>
Pane, Irma, *Haruskah* IPB-Disc Productions,
  <http://users.aol.com/hbraam/musicians.htm>
Pramoedya site,
  <http://www.access.digex.net/~bardsley/prampage.html>
Ragadi, <http://members.aol.com/ragadi/home.html>
Rahardjo, Budi, <http://www.ee.umanitoba.ca/~rahard/music.html>
Syahreza, <http://www.hway.net/syahreza/main.shtml>
UNESCO,
  <http://www.unesco.org/general/eng/stats/asia.wt0901.e.96.html>

<gopher://gopher.igc.apc.org:2998/OREG-INDONESIA/
<http://www.klasik.co.id/network.html>
<http://www.usia.gov/abtusia/posts/
XPOS, <http://apchr.murdoch.edu.au/minihub/xp>

Mailing lists
<alt.culture.indonesia>
<apakabar@clark.net>
<indonesia-l@igc.apc.org>
<indonesia-l@userhome.com>
<indonesia-p@igc.apc.org>
<indonesia-p@indopubs.com>
<kdpnet@usa.net>
<manneke@makara.cso.ui.ac.id>
<nusa-musik@nusanet.com>
<SiaR@mole.gn.apc.org>
<skillnet@skill.co.id>
<soc.culture.indonesia'>

Filmography

Catatan Si Boy, Nasri Cheppy (dir.), PT Bola Dunia Film, Jakarta, 1987.

Catatan Si Boy II, Nasri Cheppy (dir.), PT Bola Dunia Film, Jakarta, 1988.

Catatan Si Boy III, Nasri Cheppy (dir.), PT Bola Dunia Film, Jakarta, 1989.

Catatan Si Boy IV, Nasri Cheppy (dir.), PT Parkit Film, Jakarta, 1990.

Catatan Si Boy V, Nasri Cheppy (dir.), PT Bola Dunia Film, Jakarta, 1991.

Catatan Si Doi, Atok Suharto (dir.), PT Andalas Kencana Film, Jakarta, 1988.

Cinta Dalam Sepotong Roti (Love in a Slice of Bread), Garin Nugroho (dir.), PT Prasidi Teta Film and PT Mutiara Eranusa Film, Jakarta, 1990.

Harimau Campa, D. Djajakusuma (dir.), Perfini, Jakarta, 1953.

Mandau Dan Asmara, S. Marcus (dir.), PT Panah Mas Film, Jakarta, 1977.

Para Perintis Kemerdekaan, Asrul Sani (dir.), PT Taty & Sons Jaya Film, Jakarta, 1977.

Pengkhianatan G30S/PKI, Arifin C. Noer (dir.), Pusat Produksi Film Negara, Jakarta, 1982.

Perawan Desa, Frank Rorimpandey (dir.), PT Safari Sinar Sakti Film, Jakarta, 1978.

Saur Sepuh (Satria Madangkara), Imam Tantowi (dir.), PT Kanta Indah Film, Jakarta, 1988.

Saur Sepuh II (Pesanggrahan Keramat), Imam Tantowi (dir.), PT Kanta Indah Film, Jakarta, 1988.

Saur Sepuh III (Kembang Gunung Luwu), Imam Tantowi (dir.), PT Kanta Indah Film, Jakarta, 1989.

Serangan Fajar, Arifin C. Noer (dir.), Pusat Produksi Film Negara, Jakarta, 1981.

Surat Untuk Bidadari, Garin Nugroho (dir.), PT Mutiara Eranusa Film, Televisi Pendidikan Indonesia and Pusat Produksi Film Negara, Jakarta, 1992.

Newspapers and Magazines

Antara

Australian, Indonesia supplement

Bali Post

D&R

DeTIK

Editor

Far Eastern Economic Review

Independen

InfoKomputer

Jakarta Post

Kompas

Media Indonesia

Media Indonesia Minggu

Merdeka

SWAsembada

Vista TV

Warta Ekonomi

West Australian

INDEX

Note that all personal names are listed in this index under the final part of
the name, even where the more commonly used form of the name
(adopted in the text of this book) may be another part. For example,
'Pramoedya Ananta Toer' is generally referred to as 'Pramoedya', but is
indexed here under 'Toer'.

6142